Sarah Elizabeth Talbot.

1942.

COMPLETE HOME KNITTING

ILLUSTRATED

Easy to understand instructions for making garments for the Family. How to combine knitting with fabric. How to make new clothes from old

BY

MARGARET MURRAY
AND JANE KOSTER

Over 200 illustrations

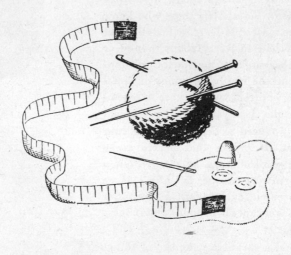

ODHAMS PRESS LIMITED, LONG ACRE, LONDON, W.C.2

FOREWORD

T HE phrase "well dressed" has taken on a new meaning. It means being simply and economically, yet charmingly dressed in spite of restrictions. Fortunately those who know how to make the most of little, score heavily over those who never had to worry about money or planning wardrobes carefully. You must think hard before you expend the family's coupons or you'll find gaps in their wardrobes. Clothes are so expensive, you must make them yourself when you can.

This book is produced to help you solve your clothes problems. It proves that nearly every garment in the wardrobe can be made from a minimum of yarn with two needles and look as though it had been cut out of fabric by a master tailor. *And* yarn is cheaper in coupons and money.

Finally in the "New Garments from Old" section you'll find a surprising number of things you can do—including combining knitting and fabric—to give your old clothes a new lease of life.

CONTENTS

PAGE

FROM BEGINNING TO END IN
KNITTING AND CROCHET . . 5

WOMEN'S GARMENTS

TAILORED SHIRT IN TWO- OR THREE-
PLY 37
LONG AND SHORT SPORTS JERSEY . 41
TWO-COLOUR SPORTS JERSEY . . 47
CARDIGAN IN MOSS STITCH . . 53
LARGER SIZE CARDIGAN . . . 57
VEST AND PANTIE SET . . . 61
LACY VEST AND PANTIE SET . . 63
LACE RIB CAMI-KNICKERS . . . 67
OPEN RIB STOCKINGS . . . 71
ANKLE SOCKS 73
CARDIGAN 75
JUMPER (LARGER SIZE) . . . 80
CLASSIC JUMPER 82
CHECKED CLASSIC JUMPER . . 85
TWISTED YOKE JUMPER . . . 89
BLACK LACE JUMPER . . . 91
AFTERNOON JUMPER IN RAYON OR
BOUCLÉ 95
GLOVES IN BOUCLÉ 99
GAUNTLET GLOVES 101
MITTENS 104
OPEN WORK GLOVES IN COTTON OR
WOOL 105
CABLE RIB CAP 108
SUIT FOR THE MATRON . . . 111
WHITE COLLAR FROCK . . . 117
FANCY RIB JUMPER (LARGE SIZE) . 123
QUILTED BEDJACKET . . . 127
QUILTED HOOD 129
BEDROOM SLIPPERS . . . 130

MEN'S GARMENTS

CLASSIC CARDIGAN . . . 131
RIBBED LUMBER JACKET . . . 135
SLEEVELESS PULLOVER . . . 137
SLEEVED RIBBED PULLOVER . . 139
STRAIGHT NECK PULLOVER . . 143
SLEEVELESS PULLOVER . . . 144
SOCKS WITH CLOCKS . . . 146
CROCHET BÉRET 148
SPORTS SCARF 150
PLAIN RIBBED GLOVES . . . 151
RIBBED WAISTCOAT . . . 153
TAILORED SPORTS SHIRT . . 157

PAGE

HELMET WITH EAR FLAPS . . . 160
POLO-NECK CLASSIC . . . 162
NEW STITCHES TO CHOOSE FROM . 167

CHILDREN'S GARMENTS

FIRST-SIZE RIBBED BABY VESTS . . 171
PILCH 174
CARRYING SHAWL 175
JERSEY AND KNICKER SUIT . . 176
FROCK AND MATINEE COAT . . 181
COAT AND LEGGINGS SUIT . . 186
VEST FOR A TWO TO FOUR YEARS' OLD . 191
SUN-SUIT AND SHORTS FOR UNDER SIX
YEARS' OLD 192
LACE OR PLAIN SOCKS FOR THE EIGHT
TO TEN YEARS' OLD . . . 198
THREE QUARTER SOCKS FOR TEN TO
TWELVE YEARS' OLD . . . 199
WRIST OR GAUNTLET GLOVES . . 203
BOY'S PLAIN VEST 205
BEST JUMPER FOR A TWELVE-YEAR-OLD 207
ROUND-NECKED JERSEY . . . 210
TAILORED CARDIGAN FOR A TWELVE
TO FOURTEEN YEARS' OLD . . 213
PICK UP THESE STITCHES . . . 216
BOY'S LUMBER JACKET . . . 221
BOY'S SCHOOL JERSEY . . . 224
POLO-NECKED PULLOVER . . . 225

NEW GARMENTS FROM OLD

RE-KNITTING WOOL 229
DEALING WITH FELTED GARMENTS . 230
ODDS AND ENDS 230
RE-KNITTING UNPICKED YARN . . 231
RIBBED JUMPER WITH CONTRASTING
PANELS 232
SPORTS JERSEY FROM OLD CARDIGAN . 235
COMBINING KNITTING AND FABRIC 237
CHILD'S FABRIC AND KNITTED FROCK (1) 237
CHILD'S FABRIC AND KNITTED FROCK (2) 241
WOMAN'S FABRIC AND KNITTED FROCK
(1) 243
MAN'S SHIRT IN TERRY TOWELLING . 248
WOMAN'S FABRIC AND KNITTED FROCK
(2) 251
ENLARGING FABRIC GARMENTS WITH
KNITTING 254
RE-FOOTING AND RE-HEELING SOCKS
AND STOCKINGS 256
WHAT TO DO WITH WORN GLOVES . 256

"*Bring your wool over like this, dear.*" *Knitting, so much a modern accomplishment, is one of the most ancient of handicrafts, and every generation could have supplied this picture as mothers passed the art down to their daughters.*

IN KNITTING & CROCHET

WHEN you are thinking of knitting or crocheting a garment your first thought is of the materials that you will use, and to begin with you should know something about them, and the best kinds to use.

Materials

Yarns.—Yarn may be defined as threads which have been specially spun for knitting or weaving into garments. The thread may be hand or machine spun and may consist of wool, cotton, rayon, silk, hair, flax, hemp, metal, and so on. For knitted garments woollen yarns are, on the whole, most satisfactory in wear, but there are several other yarns which are almost equally good and which you may use with confidence especially at a time of wool shortage when it may be difficult to procure the best quality woollen yarn.

Choose your yarn carefully, keeping in mind the type of garment you wish to make. Soft, fine, loosely twisted yarns are best for underwear, babies' clothes and so on, any garments, in fact, which you know are to be worn next to the skin; tough hard-wearing yarns are best for sports garments, children's outdoor garments, etc. There are on the market many

interesting fancy and bouclé yarns which are suitable for fashion garments; cotton yarns are good for blouses and accessories such as gilets, jabots, collars and cuffs, but remember never to use cotton yarns for garments that hang, because these yarns have very little elasticity and fall out of shape. Rayon yarns are best when spun into a crêpe yarn which is warm, light and washes well. It can be used for most children's and women's garments, for it is hard wearing and very serviceable. Pure silk makes luxurious underwear, stockings, blouses or jumpers for "dress" occasions and it washes and wears well, in fact, quite as well as wool. Pure silk combined with wool is really the best for any garments to be worn next to the skin and is often recommended by the authorities for babies' vests, preferably even to pure wool.

Unless you are buying home-spuns always try to buy branded yarns. Every ounce of branded yarn is guaranteed to produce the same length of knitting, and the colours are fast. If you do not use a branded yarn or choose a different brand from the one suggested in the instructions you propose to use, you should be particularly careful to test the tension at which the yarn knits up before you start. Although the yarn may be marked 3-ply or 4-ply it often knits up into a fabric which is as thick as that produced by quick or double knitting yarns. You should remember this, particularly when wool is short, because shoddy wool is often spun to produce a heavy yarn.

When buying fancy yarns such as crêpe or bouclé, it is best to buy exactly what is mentioned in the instructions unless you feel yourself competent to deal with the alterations that have to be made if there is any considerable variation in the thickness of the yarn. Even in the case of an ordinary 3-ply or 4-ply yarn it is often found that one well-known brand will vary in thickness from another. The difference in good yarns, however, is slight and can usually be adjusted by changing the size of the needles to produce the tension stated in the instructions (*see* TENSION). One last tip: whatever the yarn you are buying always buy enough to complete your garment, not only because it might be difficult to buy more wool of the same kind, but because dyes are apt to vary slightly and you may find it impossible to match the exact shade.

If you see a garment that is of a shape that you like, remember that its whole character can be altered by knitting it in a different yarn. For example, a perfectly plain bolero knitted in Angora wool will make a most delightful evening coat, and a plain classic round-necked jumper knitted in a bouclé yarn will make a really lovely afternoon blouse. If you are using a fancy yarn, you will find always that a plain stitch is the most satisfactory.

The following is an explanation of a few of the better known and easily obtainable yarns, with suggestions for their use.

Alloa Yarn or Wheeling.—This is a thick woollen yarn usually made in 3-ply and sold in 2-oz. skeins. It is chiefly made in Alloa, and when of good quality is very serviceable and makes excellent outdoor garments, such as socks, gloves and so on. The more often this particular yarn is washed, the softer it becomes.

Baby Wool.—A term used to describe an enormous variety of yarns of all prices and qualities. It is loosely spun and produces a soft fleecy thread. The good quality yarns of lambs' wool are very soft and elastic. It should be used for babies' and children's clothes, and underwear.

Crêpe Yarn.—This is a close, tight, corded yarn, which is hard wearing, and knits up into very good-looking fabric. It may be used for all fashion garments.

Mixture Yarns.—There are a number of good quality yarns which are mixed for a definite purpose, as opposed to yarns which are spun in pure silk or wool; for example, a wool and cotton or a wool and silk yarn. These are specially good for making into under garments and are a blessing to the many people who cannot bear the irritation of pure wool next to their skin. You should take special care with the tension of these mixture yarns as they lack the elasticity of pure wool. As a general rule, the ribbing should be worked on really fine needles, and in fact, the whole garment will be found more satisfactory if worked more closely than it would be if a pure wool yarn were used.

Oily Yarn.—This yarn is specially prepared to be water resisting, and is used for fishermen's jerseys, sea-boot stockings, and so on. It is natural in colour and is usually sold in $\frac{1}{2}$-lb. balls.

Vest Wool.—This is a term applied to a multitude of yarns of all qualities. Generally speaking, however, it is made of wool guaranteed to be already shrunk so that it will not shrink further in washing.

Needles.—Needles can be obtained in steel, wood, bone, plastic materials and a combination of steel and plastic material. The ideal needle is light and smooth, with points that taper gradually and are not too sharp. You should always discard a needle which has become the slightest bit rough as it will pull the wool and fluff it.

Sizes of needles range from 000 to 24, the higher the number the smaller the needle. You should buy two pairs of needles, one pair long and the other short, in the following sizes: 4, 5, 6, 7, 8, 9, 10, 11, 12, 13 and 14, and sets of four needles, with points at both ends for socks, gloves, neck ribbing, in sizes 10, 11, 12, 13, 14 and 15. This should cover your requirements for all garments you are likely to knit.

Most needles are numbered, but if they are not, the size can easily be discovered by means of a needle gauge. These are

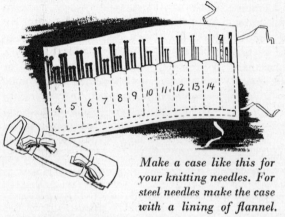

Make a case like this for your knitting needles. For steel needles make the case with a lining of flannel.

made in plastic, steel, or cardboard. The most reliable is the old-fashioned steel bell-shaped model. Never think that it is sufficient to measure an unmarked needle against a marked one. A gauge should always be used to ensure that you have the right size.

You should keep your needles in a needle case of the kind shown here. Keep your steel needles in a separate case lined with flannel. The material absorbs the moisture in the atmosphere and prevents the needles from rusting.

The following are some of the more usual types of needles and their uses.

Steel Needles.—These are not very satisfactory in large sizes, as they are heavy and very tiring to use. They are generally used for socks and stockings, and can be

bought in sizes 10 to 24, although the smaller sizes, 16 to 24, which are required for lace making, are very difficult to obtain. Steel needles should never be used when working with a yarn that is a mixture of wool and rayon as they will turn it black; nor are they to be recommended for white or pastel shades because they tend to discolour the yarn.

The best way of keeping them from rusting is as described above, in a case lined with flannel. Even the finest emery paper used to rub off rust will roughen the surface and cause the yarn to fluff.

Wooden Needles.—These are made in large sizes, and, as they are very light, they are used for bedjackets or shawls, where it is necessary to use a really large needle to produce a light open fabric. The sizes are not standard and vary considerably with the different brands. They are apt to splinter; when buying them, choose smooth and gradually tapering needles.

Plastic Needles. — These needles are excellent for all general purposes, for they are light, resilient, smooth and cheap. When buying them see that they taper gradually and that the points are not too sharp. They are rather apt to become bent in use, but can easily be straightened by standing them in a jug of hot water for a few minutes, then taking them out, and leaving them to harden between the pages of a book.

Painted Aluminium Needles.—These are very light, but are not very satisfactory in use because they are apt to bend, and the paint is inclined to chip off.

Plastic-covered Steel Needles.—These are the best needles on the market for all purposes. They are rather more expensive than other needles, but the extra expense is justified by the good service they give, and the even work they help to produce.

Circular Needles.—These needles consist of a length of flexible wire, usually steel, with 4-in. or 5-in. needle points at both ends. They are used for large tubular garments such as vests, seamless jerseys and skirts, and in fact all such garments involving a large number of stitches.

Crochet Hooks.—These are made of bone, steel or composition materials. When you are choosing a crochet hook, the great point to remember is to see that the hook is quite smooth and that it has a sharp enough point to go through the stitch easily.

The sizes of hooks vary considerably according to the brand of manufacture. Some workers prefer to alter the tension of the garment they wish to make so that they can use a favourite hook, rather than use the number and brand of hook stated in the instructions.

Quantities

THE quantity of wool needed for making various garments depends very largely upon the quality of the yarn used. Good quality yarn, including branded yarns, although more expensive to buy will be found to be cheaper in the long run. They are lighter in weight than the poorer quality yarns, and therefore have more rounds to the ounce and go materially further. In the case of two separate ounces of wool of the same ply it was found, when the length of wool in each ounce was measured, that the

	2-ply	3-ply	4-ply
Short-sleeved jumper, 34-in. to 36-in. bust	4 oz.	6 oz.	8 oz.
Long-sleeved jumper, 34-in. to 36-in. bust	5 oz.	7 oz.	10 oz.
Cardigan (as above) .	—	—	—
Men's socks, average size	3 oz.	4 oz.	5 oz.
Golf stockings . .	—	6 oz.	8 oz.
Pullover, sleeveless .	—	6 oz.	8 oz.
Pullover, with sleeves	—	9 oz.	12 oz.
Cardigan (as above) .	—	—	—

cheaper yarn was one-third shorter than the more expensive one.

The quantities in column one are based on good quality yarns, and in times of wool shortage, when good quality branded wools are difficult to obtain it should not be regarded as infallible, but should be used only as a working basis for calculations when you are buying yarns.

Winding and Joining Wool

Winding Wool.—The elasticity of pure wool is one of its chief characteristics. It is this which makes it more suitable than most other yarns for knitted garments, but this great virtue of wool can be ruined by incorrect winding. The great point to remember is that the wool should not be stretched. It should be wound into a soft ball, by winding the wool loosely over two fingers for about thirty turns, slipping the coils off the fingers and holding them in the hand, and

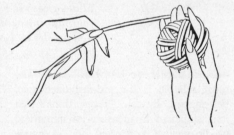

The illustration shows the right method of winding wool. The wool should be wound round the fingers holding the ball.

winding another thirty turns over them and the two fingers. Continue in this way until the skein is fully wound.

Joining Wool.—It is best never to join wool in the middle of a row by any method, and especially never to knot the two ends together except at the end of a row. However carefully knotting is done it produces an uneven look in the fabric and the knot is apt to wear through on to the outside after some wear. There are several satisfactory ways of joining that are practically invisible and will stand up to wear and tear.

1. **Splicing.**—This is the ideal way of joining the two ends of wool, and when well done it is quite invisible. Fray out the ends for a few inches, cut off half the thickness from each end and twist the remaining two halves together, making a yarn of the same thickness as the original.

2. **Knotting.**—This is quite a good method of joining if the wool is knotted at the beginning of a row. When the work is completed untie the knot and either use the ends for sewing the garment together or darn them in neatly.

3. **Knitting Double.**—This is not a method that is greatly to be recommended; it gives rather a clumsy effect when finished. But if you wish to join wool in this way, place the two ends together for a few inches and knit with the double yarn that results.

4. **Weaving.**—While working the first few stitches with the new thread weave the old end in at the back of the work by the Fair Isle method (*see* "FAIR ISLE" KNITTING).

Abbreviations

THE following abbreviations are those in general use, though a few of them apply particularly to the terms used in this book.

* = asterisk. In knitting instructions this is used as a sign of repetition, and indicates that the instructions written after a * or between two **s have to be repeated either to the end of the row, or the number of times stated. For example, * k. 1, p. 1, rep. from * 3 times, means that you have to repeat the k. 1, p. 1 3 times after having done it once; that is you do it 4 times in all.

beg. = beginning.

k. = knit (*see* BASIC STITCHES—KNIT STITCH).

p. = purl (*see* BASIC STITCHES — PURL STITCH).

st. = stitch.

sts. = stitches.

sl. = slip. Instead of knitting or purling the next stitch on the left-hand needle it is simply transferred to the right-hand needle without being knitted. It is a term often used in instructions for fancy patterns, and, in addition, unless otherwise stated the stitch should always be slipped purlwise (*see* "p.w." below).

g.st. = garter stitch (*see* BASIC STITCHES —GARTER STITCH).

st.st. = stocking stitch (*see* BASIC STITCHES—STOCKING STITCH).

inc. = increase or increasing.

dec. = decrease or decreasing.

p.w. = purlwise; that is by inserting the point of the right-hand needle into the front of the stitch, as if to purl.

k.w. = knitwise; inserting the point of the right-hand needle into the front of the stitch and out at the back as if to knit.

p.s.s.o. = pass slipped stitch over. A term used in instructions for lace patterns and sometimes for decreasings. To do this slip one stitch on to the right-hand needle and knit the next stitch and pass it on to the right-hand needle in the usual way. Now lift the slipped stitch over the knitted stitch and over the point of the needle. Sometimes the slipped stitch has to be passed over more than one stitch and in this case the instructions would read: "p.s.s.o. the k. 2." If more than one slipped stitch has to be passed over, the instructions would read "p.s.sts.o."

m. = make. This may be done in three different ways depending on whether the preceding and following stitches are knit or purl stitches:—

(*a*) **Between 2 Knit Stitches.**—Bring the wool forward between the needles and take it back over the needle to knit the next stitch.

(b) **Between 2 Purl Stitches.**—Take the wool back over the needle then forward between the needles after purling the first stitch.

(c) **Between a Purl and a Knit Stitch.**—After purling the first stitch, take the wool over the needle to knit the next stitch instead of between the needles. Any of these methods may be used when the instructions say "m. 1" according to the position of the stitch to be made.

w.fd., = wool forward (*see* (*a*) above).

w.r.n. = wool round needle (*see* (*b*) above).

w.o.n. = wool over needle (*see* (*c*) above).

w.b. = wool back.

t.b.l. = through back of loop or loops.

rep. = repeat.

tog. = together.

ins. = inches.

patt. = pattern.

ch. = chain (*see* BASIC STITCHES — CROCHET).

s.c. = single crochet (*see* BASIC STITCHES —CROCHET).

d.c. = double crochet (*see* BASIC STITCHES —CROCHET).

tr. = treble (*see* BASIC STITCHES — CROCHET).

l.tr. = long treble (*see* BASIC STITCHES— CROCHET).

Casting On

CASTING ON is the process of making the first row of loops of yarn on the needle, and is the basis on which the rest of the knitting is to be worked.

There are several ways of casting on these stitches:—

Thumb Method. — This is generally accepted as being the most satisfactory as it produces a firm but elastic edge that is not noticeably different from the rest of the fabric. It is done with one needle and can be worked either single or double:—

(*a*) **Single Thumb Method.**—Make a loop near the end of the wool and place it on the needle. Now wind the wool round the thumb, insert the needle upwards through the loop on the thumb and slip it off on to the needle. Repeat for the number of stitches required.

(*b*) **Double Thumb Method.**—Leave a long end of wool, about a yard is sufficient for the average garment, make a loop in it and place loop on the needle. Pass the short end of wool round the thumb, as shown in the illustration, and with the ball end knit into it in the ordinary way thus making another stitch on the needle. Repeat for the number of stitches required.

Casting on by the double thumb method. Make a loop by winding the wool round the needle and the thumb as shown above, and knit into the loop.

Casting On with Two Needles. — The edge produced by casting on by this method is apt to be rather untidy and loopy unless in the first row of knitting you knit into the back of your cast-on stitches, a slow and laborious business for most people, and one which is almost bound to produce a slightly inelastic edge. It is, however, quite satisfactory for thick yarns, and for edges that will not be subjected to a great deal of stretching.

Make a loop near the end of the wool and place it on the left-hand needle. Place right-hand needle in the loop, slipping it under the needle, as for knitting (*see* BASIC STITCHES, KNIT STITCH), pass the wool between the needles and draw a second loop through and place it on the left-hand needle. Repeat this process until the required number of stitches has been cast on to the needles.

Cable Cast On.—This method produces a very strong edge, and is particularly suitable for heavy garments; it is not quite so elastic as the edge produced by the thumb method, but it is more decorative. Begin in the same way as for casting on with two needles, and having made a loop and one stitch, make the third stitch and the following

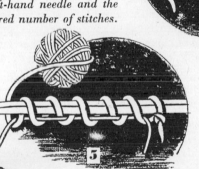

Casting on with two needles. **1.** *Make a loop, slip it on to the left-hand needle, then insert the right-hand needle and bring the wool round between the two needles.* **2.** *With the right-hand needle draw through a second loop.* **3.** *The second loop is passed from the right-hand needle to the left-hand needle and the process is repeated for required number of stitches.*

5. *Invisible edge cast on. Here you see the odd length of yarn used as the basic thread, and the knitting yarn wound over the two needles held very firmly together.*

4. Cable cast on. Here the right-hand needle is inserted between the cast-on loops and the newly made loop is about to be drawn through.

stitches by putting the right-hand needle between the loops, drawing the wool through and placing the loop thus made on the left-hand needle.

Invisible Edge Cast On.—This is an unusual method of casting on, but is very useful for scarves and shawls which have to be finished with a fringe. Take a long length of yarn, preferably of a different colour from the wool used for knitting, and use it as a basic thread. Make a loop near the end of the knitting wool, and place it on the two needles held together in the right hand, keeping the basic thread

6. *Casting on with four needles. Four needles are used for socks, stockings, gloves, seamless vests, neck bands, etc.*

under the two needles. Now * bring the knitting wool forward under the needles and the basic thread, pass it over the needles and bring it round towards the front again, this time passing it between the needles and the basic thread, so that the basic thread is behind the knitting wool. Now pass it under the thread and back over the needle. Repeat from * until the required number of stitches has been cast on.

Take one needle out and continue in the ordinary way, knitting into the front of the stitches in the first row. When the knitting is completed the basic thread should be pulled out leaving a row of loops into which a fringe can be worked, or which can be picked up for knitting a lace border. The illustration will show you exactly how to wind the yarn round the needles and the position of the basic thread (page 11).

Casting On on Four Needles. — Any of the methods described above may be used, but it should be remembered that the tops of socks and stockings and edges of gloves require a particularly elastic edge.

It is quite a good idea when using 2-ply wool or superfine wool to cast on with double wool, using any of the methods given above. Double wool will give a stronger edge than could otherwise be given in such fine wool and one which will not break so easily. At the same time it will be quite elastic.

Basic Stitches in Knitting

THERE are really only two stitches to be learnt in knitting—a knit or plain stitch, and a purl stitch. From these any number of patterns can be worked out. Besides giving instruction for the working of these two stitches, this section also gives instructions for working combinations of them, which are so commonly used that they also may be called basic stitches.

Knit Stitch.—Having cast on the number of stitches required, hold the needle containing the stitches in the left hand, with the point about $\frac{1}{2}$ in. above the thumb and the first finger. Hold the other needle in the right hand, and insert the point in the first stitch from left to right, putting it in the front of the stitch and through to the back. Pass the wool which, when doing this stitch, is always at the back of the work, between the points of the two needles and draw a loop through.

1. *Knit or plain stitch. The first stage is to insert the right-hand needle through the first loop on the left-hand needle.*

3. *Knit or plain stitch. Pull left-hand needle under right-hand needle at the same time drawing a loop through with it.*

2. *Knit or plain stitch. The next stage is to bring the wool from the back of right-hand needle and over.*

4. *Knit or plain stitch. Finally, slip stitch off left-hand needle, leaving new loop on right-hand needle.*

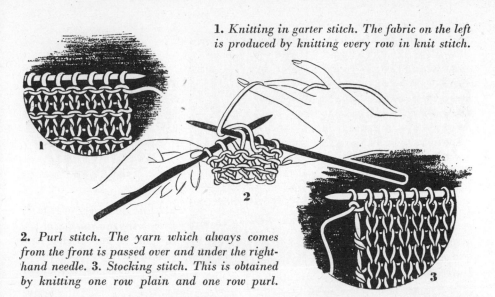

1. *Knitting in garter stitch. The fabric on the left is produced by knitting every row in knit stitch.*

2. *Purl stitch. The yarn which always comes from the front is passed over and under the right-hand needle.* **3.** *Stocking stitch. This is obtained by knitting one row plain and one row purl.*

Keep this loop on the right-hand needle and let the old loop slip off the left-hand needle. Continue in this way to the end of the row, and begin a new row by transferring the needleful of stitches to the left hand.

Purl Stitch.—Hold the needle containing the cast-on stitches in the same way as for the knit stitch, but keep the wool to the front of the work. Insert the right-hand needle into the front of the first stitch from right to left, keeping it in front of the work. Then pass the wool round the point of the needle and draw a loop through, keeping it on the right-hand needle and letting the old loop slip off the left-hand needle as for knit stitch.

These are the two basic stitches which it is necessary to learn in order to be able to knit. The following are some combinations of them which are in general use.

Garter Stitch. — This is sometimes referred to as "plain knitting" and is the fabric produced when every row is worked in knit stitch. It results in a series of ridges and is rather heavy. It must not be confused with "plain smooth fabric" which is stocking stitch (*see* below).

Stocking Stitch is sometimes called "stocking web" or "plain smooth fabric." It consists of alternate rows of knit stitch and purl stitch, thus bringing all the ridges to one side of the fabric. The ridged side is usually regarded as the wrong side of the work, but it can be used with great effect, however, as the right side of the work and is useful to show up a pattern as it forms a very good background. Stocking stitch is the most commonly used stitch, and is more economical than garter stitch in time and material.

Moss Stitch. — A reversible stitch, showing simple knit and purl stitches, alternating horizontally and vertically. It is most easily worked on an uneven number of stitches by working every row k. 1, p. 1 to end, ending with k. 1. If it has to be worked on an even number of stitches, the first row will begin k. 1, p. 1, and the second p. 1, k. 1.

Rib Stitches. — These consist of a combination of knit and purl stitches which form vertical lines and have the effect of contracting the width of the work, while keeping the basic size, and at the same time making the fabric very elastic. On account of this it is used for close-fitting garments such as vests, and for the

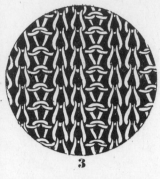

1. *Moss stitch. This fabric is obtained by alternating plain and purl stitches horizontally and vertically.* **2.** *Cable stitch. Cable pattern is produced by*

2

twisting a number of stitches by altering the knitting order. **3.** *Knit 2, purl 2 rib. This type of fabric is used for contracting at necks, wrists, etc.*

fitted parts of garments such as the welts of jumpers, the wrist and neck bands of jerseys, and so on. For such purposes a simple rib of k. 1, p. 1 or k. 2, p. 2 is generally found to be the most successful.

The amount of contraction produced by a rib depends largely upon the proportion of the knit to the purl stitches. When the rib consists of an even number of knit and purl stitches the contraction will be greatest, and will be reduced as the difference becomes wider. For example a rib of k. 6, p. 1 will have very little effect on the width.

Once the principles of plain knitting have been grasped, an endless variety of garments can be knitted from plain, simple instructions for classic garments like jumpers and cardigans, simply by varying the stitch and by substituting a fancy pattern for a plain stitch, or inserting bands of a fancy stitch. A point to remember when substituting a pattern is to see that the number of stitches recommended in the original are applicable to the fancy pattern, and can be adjusted accordingly. A stitch or two more or less will not make a great deal of difference to the size of the garment, but large patterns should generally be avoided except in

garments especially designed for them, as they are difficult to fit into armhole and neck shapings. Elaborate stitches are generally more effective when used as bands of decoration across yokes, as front panels, etc., and when combined with a plain stitch to act as a background.

Cable Stitches.—Although these cable patterns sometimes look very elaborate, they are, in fact, extremely simple to do and are very effective for men's pullovers and for women's heavy sports garments.

To produce a cable pattern you must twist a number of stitches by altering the order in which they are knitted. The usual method is to leave the first half of the group to be twisted on a spare needle, either at the back or front of the work, according to the instructions and the direction of the twist, and knit the second half, afterwards returning to the stitches left on the spare needle and knitting them. The spare needle should be short and have points at both ends.

It must be remembered that cables hold the fabric firmly and will not allow much stretching, so it is as well to allow a few extra stitches when introducing a cable into a garment that was not designed for it.

Double Knitting.—This produces a very

firm double fabric which will not curl and is suitable for belts, tops of skirts and so on. Cast on in the ordinary way, then, in the first row, * w.fd., sl. 1st st. p.w., w.b., k. the next st. and rep. from * to end of row. Rep. this row for the length required, always knitting the sl.st. of the previous row.

Basic Stitches in Crochet

Chain.—Make a slip knot and place it on the hook, now holding the hook in the right hand and the thread between the thumb and the first finger, held taut by the second and third fingers and looped under the little finger, pass the hook under the thread and pull the loop through.

Continue in this way until a sufficient length of chain has been made.

Single Crochet.—Make a chain, then insert the hook into a stitch in this foundation, pass the hook under the thread, draw the thread through the foundation and through the loop on the hook. This stitch is chiefly used for passing from one part of work to another and is practically invisible in the pattern.

Double Crochet.—Insert the hook into the foundation, pass the hook under the thread and pull the loop through the foundation, pass the hook under the thread again and draw the loop through both loops on the hook.

Treble.—Pass the hook under the thread and then into the foundation; pass it

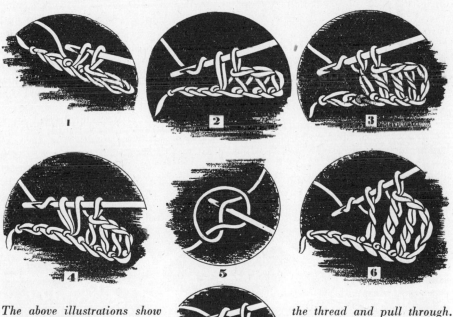

The above illustrations show the method of making basic stitches in crochet. 5 shows the first step in making a chain. Make a slip knot and place it on the hook, which should be held in the right hand. The thread is held between the thumb and finger of the left hand. Pass the hook under

the thread and pull through. Continue for the length of chain required as shown in 7. 1 shows single crochet used chiefly for passing from one part of the work to another. 2 shows double crochet. 3 shows making a treble. 4 shows making a short treble and 6 making a long treble.

under the thread again, and draw a loop through—there are now three loops on the hook—pass the hook under the thread and draw through the first two loops on the hook, pass the hook under the thread and draw through remaining two loops.

Short Treble.—Work as for ordinary treble, but when there are three loops on the hook, draw the thread through all three at once.

Long Treble.—Pass the hook under the thread twice and into the foundation, pass the hook under the thread and draw through; there are now four loops on the hook. Pass the hook under the thread, draw through two loops, pass the hook under the thread and draw through two more loops, pass the hook under the thread and draw through remaining loops.

Casting Off

CASTING OFF is the process of removing the stitches from the needle when the garment has been completed, or when some particular part of it has been completed, and at the same time interlocking the stitches so that they will not unravel. Unless instructions specify that casting off is to be either loose or tight it should be the same tension as rest of garment.

When casting off children's garments or other garments which have to be pulled over the head, it is a good idea to use a needle two sizes larger than the needles used for the rest of the garment.

Always cast off in an appropriate stitch; for instance, in purl on the purl side of the work, in plain knitting on the knit side and in a combination of the two for ribs. This is most important when casting off a rib, as casting off in all knit or purl would make the edge tight.

When working a fancy pattern which has an increased number of stitches on some rows, either avoid casting off on these rows, or decrease the extra stitches by knitting or purling them together during the casting off.

When the instructions allow the casting off to be done on either the knit or purl side of the work, it is often advisable to cast off in purl on the purl side, as the edge thus produced will have less tendency to roll than if cast off on the knit side, also it will be less visible on the right side of the work.

There are several methods of casting off.

Simple Casting Off.—Knit or purl the first two stitches, then, with the left-hand needle, lift the first stitch over the second. Knit or purl the next stitch and repeat the

1. *Double casting off, first method. The second stitch is knitted; the old loop is to be knitted and cast off when the first stitch is cast off.*

2. *Simple casting off. Above you see the first stitch being slipped over the second stitch and off the right-hand needle altogether.*

3. *Double casting off, second method. The thread between the stitches is picked up, knitted and then cast off. This gives much greater elasticity.*

process. Continue in this way all along the row, and until one loop remains. Break off the wool and draw the end through the loop and darn it into the fabric.

Double Casting Off. This can be done in two ways, and is used to spread out the cast-off edge of a garment and give it greater elasticity.

(a) Knit the first stitch and knit the second stitch, but do not slip the loop of the second stitch off the left-hand needle. Cast off the first stitch in the usual way, then knit into the loop of the second stitch, which remains on the left-hand needle, and cast off the second stitch. Continue in this way, knitting into the stitch and then into the loop, and finish off as in simple casting off.

(b) This method is more elastic although less neat than the first method, and is done by picking up, knitting, and casting off the loop between the stitches as well as the stitch on the needle. Finish off in the usual way.

Invisible Edge Cast Off.—This is used in the same way as the invisible edge cast on for the ends of scarves or shawls. When the garment is completed, run a thread through the last row of stitches and remove the needle.

Crochet Casting Off.—This method probably dates back to the time when knitting needles were made with hooked ends. It is a very useful method for all

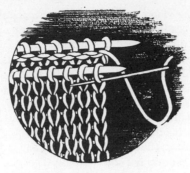

Grafting. The needles are shown in the correct position, and the needle threaded.

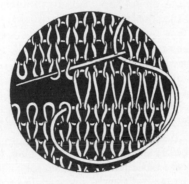

The correct method of grafting stitches which have been slipped off the needles is shown.

garments, particularly when casting off in a yarn which has less elasticity than wool, because it is easier to gauge the tension of the edge than when casting off by other methods.

Use a medium-sized crochet hook and, holding the work in the left hand, insert the hook through the first and second stitch and draw the second stitch through the first, letting the first stitch go. Continue in this way, securing the last stitch by darning in the end of the wool.

Casting Off Two Sets of Stitches Together.— To cast off two sets of stitches together as for shoulders, knicker gussets, sock toes, etc., hold the two needles with the right sides of the work facing and knit together the first stitch from each needle, then knit together the second stitch from each needle; there are now two stitches on the right-hand needle. Cast one off in the usual way and continue knitting two stitches together each time.

Grafting.—This is another method of casting off the stitches from two needles, but in this case the stitches are joined, and you avoid leaving a ridge.

The pieces to be joined should be placed together, with the wrong sides facing, and with the stitches equally divided between the two needles. Thread a length of wool through a wool needle for the grafting. Pass the wool needle purlwise through the first stitch on the front needle, but leave the stitch on the needle; pass the wool needle knitwise through the first stitch on the back needle, but leave that stitch on the needle also. * Pass the wool knitwise through the first stitch on the front needle and slip the stitch off the needle; pass the wool purlwise through the first stitch on the front needle and slip the stitch off the needle; pass the wool purlwise through the second stitch on the front needle, but do not slip off; pass the wool purlwise through the first stitch on the back needle and slip off; pass the wool knitwise through the second stitch on the back needle but do not slip off. Repeat from * till all the stitches are worked off.

The illustration shows the correct position of the needles and the wool needle in position to be passed purlwise through the first stitch of the front needle.

A perfectly satisfactory method of grafting and one which is preferred by a great many knitters, is to slip all the stitches off both needles before the grafting is begun; but in this case the stitches must be pressed at once to prevent them from running.

For the method of grafting when the stitches are slipped off the needle in this way see the illustration on page 17.

These instructions are for grafting in stocking stitch on the knit side.

Tension

THIS term in knitting means the number of stitches across and the number of rows down required to make one square inch of knitted fabric.

To make a success of hand knitting a knowledge of the principles of tension and its application is absolutely essential. Always knit a tension sample, using the wool and needles specified in the instructions before beginning the garment. A sample about two inches square is usually sufficient to enable you to measure the tension accurately, but if you are using a large, elaborate pattern it is worth while working a larger sample. The importance of knitting this sample cannot be too heavily stressed, especially in times of wool shortage, when it is necessary, not only to use to the best advantage any good wool you are able to obtain, but to be able to substitute a yarn which is not specified in the instructions you propose to use. The whole success of the garment will depend on working it to a correct tension.

The following table gives the average tension in stocking stitch worked in good quality wools.

Size Needles	2-ply	3-ply	4-ply
12	9 sts.	8½ sts.	8 sts. to 1 in.
11	8½ sts.	8 sts.	7½ sts. to 1 in.
10	8 sts.	7½ sts.	7 sts. to 1 in.
9	7½ sts.	7 sts.	6½ sts. to 1 in.
8	7 sts.	6½ sts.	6 sts. to 1 in.
7	6½ sts.	6 sts.	5½ sts. to 1 in.

This should, however, be used only as a guide for plain stocking stitch, as ribs and certain fancy patterns tend to draw in and so produce more stitches to the inch, or spread and produce fewer to the inch. Average knitters will find their sample is correct, but if your stocking stitch is tighter, that is if you get more stitches to the inch, or looser, that is if you get fewer stitches to the inch than the average, adjust it by using larger needles in the first case and smaller in the second. You will see from the table that a difference of one size in needles makes a difference of about half a stitch per inch, so that if your garment is to be 36 ins. when finished, worked at a tension of 7 stitches to 1 in., and you only get 6 stitches to 1 in., it will measure 42 ins. This is just one example to show how vitally important the whole question of tension is.

It is very difficult to lay down definite rules for rows tension, since this is apt to vary with the individual knitter, some knitters producing a long stitch and others a short round stitch. It is quite common for a knitter to achieve average stitch tension and inaccurate row tension. Once the discrepancy has been found, it can be allowed for whenever instructions state a number of rows instead of a measurement.

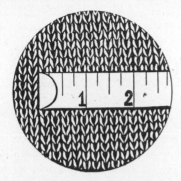

Measuring the tension of stitches.

A point to remember is that a difference of one size in needles will make a difference of about half a row per inch in length.

When measuring tension great care should be taken not to overlook half rows or half stitches, as these will make an enormous difference over the whole width or length of a garment.

There is no need to abandon a design you like because the instructions are for a garment that will not fit you. Once you have grasped the principles of tension, the garment can be adjusted to your size in the making either by altering the tension, or by actually adding or subtracting the extra number of stitches and keeping the original tension.

The simplest method is usually to alter the tension, but this can only be done if the difference in size is not too great, otherwise the fabric produced will be either too open or too close.

If a garment is to be made smaller than the original it is necessary to work at a tighter tension, that is to produce more stitches to the inch. To find the measurements of the garment if needles one size smaller are used, divide the number of stitches at the widest part by the stated tension, plus half a stitch; for example if the original tension is 7 stitches to 1 in., divide the stitches by $7\frac{1}{2}$. The result multiplied by 2 (to include front and back) will give the bust measurement resulting from using the smaller needles.

On the other hand, if the garment has to be made larger than the original, the process has to be reversed, and instead of dividing by $7\frac{1}{2}$ you would divide by $6\frac{1}{2}$.

When altering the width of a garment it is usually necessary to alter the length as well. This will largely depend on the form in which the instructions are given, as some instructions are based on measurements and some on numbers of rows. For simple garments the instructions are generally based on measurements, and it is a simple matter to substitute your own measurements for those given. In such cases the only place where the rows ten-

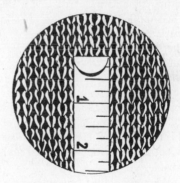

Measuring the tension of rows.

sion comes into the calculations will be in the neck shaping, and it will usually be found that this will adjust itself in proportion with the alteration made in the width tension.

A point that must be considered when altering tension is the amount of "straight" allowed after the side and sleeve shapings have been completed, and before the armholes and tops of the sleeves are begun. Sometimes very little "straight" is allowed, and it is just as well to calculate beforehand the difference in length that the new tension will make, and decide whether in the case of a looser tension the shapings must be more closely spaced so that the required number of stitches is reached in fewer rows. For example, if you cast on 108 stitches for a jumper and increase at both ends of every 6th row after completing the welt, until there are 130 stitches on the needle, you will have worked 66 rows, at the stated tension. This length will be shorter if the new tension is tighter, and longer if the tension is looser, and this might seriously affect the required length of the garment.

Another point that must not be lost sight of is that the armhole must always be adjusted to take the extra width of the sleeve when a looser tension is used. Half the extra width of the sleeve must be added to the front and back of the armhole before the neck shaping is begun, not forgetting that some of the extra depth will be supplied by the looser tension in the neck shaping.

Altering the size of garments by adding or subtracting stitches does not properly belong to tension, as in that case it is assumed that the garment is worked to the original tension. But it may be useful to add here a few points.

This method of altering the size should only be used in the following circumstances:—

(a) When the adjustment in size is very slight so that any alteration in the tension of even half a stitch per inch would make too big a difference.

(b) When the adjustment to be made is large and alteration of the tension would produce a fabric too close or too open.

(c) When the exact texture of a fabric is of real importance.

(d) When the original garment is in a plain stitch or fairly simple pattern. If this method is applied to garments knitted in elaborate patterns, containing say 20 stitches, it will be found necessary in most cases to add a complete pattern when making adjustments, and the difference in size will be enormous. In addition the distribution of the extra pattern in the neck and armhole shapings might present difficulties, as such garments are usually designed especially for these large patterns.

Edges

IF A knitted garment is to look neat and have a tailored appearance it must have neat edges. It is far better to ensure a neat edge while you are knitting, although a garment can, to a certain extent, be neatened in the sewing up. A very important point in making a cardigan is to see that the edges of the fronts are neat and unstretched.

For edges that have to be sewn together the best way is to knit the first and last stitches of every row, quite irrespective of the pattern. To do this it is often necessary to add two extra stitches, but it will give edges with a series of knobs along them, which are easy to match when sewing them together.

For edges which will show, such as the fronts of a cardigan, etc., it is usually best to slip the first stitch knitwise, and knit the last stitch on every row. If working a rib of k. 1, p. 1, slip the first stitch and knit the second stitch, thus ending the row with k. 1. This will give you a neat, firm edge.

There are, of course, several ways of neatening the edges of a knitted garment and of decorating it with an edging worked when the garment has been completed. For these, *see* under MAKING UP.

Hems

HEMS on knitted garments are made as follows:—

(a) To make a 2-in. hem knit for 4 ins., fold the work in half and with right side of work facing knit 1 stitch from the needle and pick up and knit 1 stitch from the cast-on edge, knitting these 2 stitches together all along the row. To keep the hem flat, it is most important to see that all the cast-on stitches are picked up, otherwise the hem will twist.

(b) To make a knitted picot hem 1 in. deep, knit for 1 in., then work a row of holes by k. 1, m. 1, k. 2 tog., work another inch plain, then fold work in half and proceed as described above.

The illustration above shows the work doubled and the right-hand needle inserted into the cast-on edge to form a hem.

In some cases it is better not to have a turned-up hem on the bottom of a knitted garment as the weight of the double fabric may drag it out of shape and cause it to drop. If a hem effect is desired it can be achieved by working a band of contrasting stitch, say moss stitch or garter stitch, for the required depth. This will give just enough additional weight to make a skirt hang properly.

Turning

THE turning method of shaping is used where extra depth is required at certain points only and not across the whole width of the fabric. It is frequently used to lengthen the backs of the knickers in the centre without lengthening the side edges, which must be kept the same length as those of the front. This extra length in the centre is obtained by working a short distance past the centre, turning and working back an equal distance past the centre on the other side. Then turn and work past the centre of the work again, but this time working in a few more stitches.

Continue in this way until all the stitches have been worked in, and proceed with the garment, working right across all the stitches.

It is difficult to turn in the ordinary way without leaving small holes in the fabric, but these holes can be avoided in the following way.

On a knit row, before turning, bring the wool forward, slip the first unworked stitch on the left-hand needle on to the right-hand needle, take the wool to the back again, then replace the stitch on to the left-hand needle. When you are turning on a purl row, use the same method but take the wool to the back first and bring it forward the second time.

Decreasing

ALL knitted garments require a certain amount of shaping; for example, most jumpers need shaping at the sides above the waist, at the armholes and also at the neck.

To make this shaping, the knitting has to be increased (or "widened") or decreased (or "narrowed") at certain places. The position of these increasings and decreasings will be found in the instructions, but here are a few notes on the various ways of decreasing by reducing the number of stitches.

By knitting or purling 2 stitches together and thus reducing them to 1 stitch. This is the method which is generally used when the decreasing has to be sudden, for instance at the waist of a frock. If you have 100 stitches on the needle and want to reduce them to 50 in

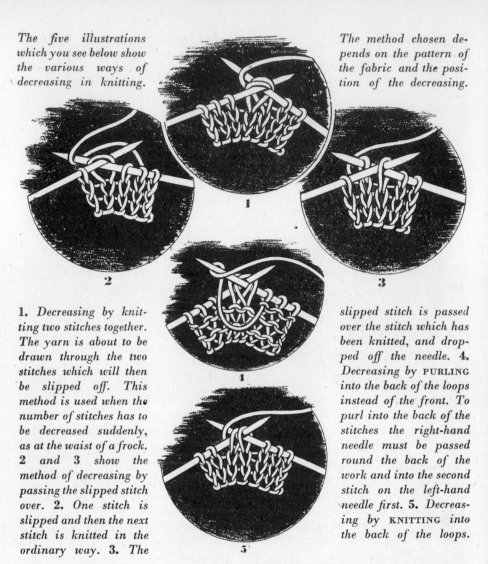

The five illustrations which you see below show the various ways of decreasing in knitting.

The method chosen depends on the pattern of the fabric and the position of the decreasing.

1. *Decreasing by knitting two stitches together. The yarn is about to be drawn through the two stitches which will then be slipped off. This method is used when the number of stitches has to be decreased suddenly, as at the waist of a frock.* **2** *and* **3** *show the method of decreasing by passing the slipped stitch over.* **2.** *One stitch is slipped and then the next stitch is knitted in the ordinary way.* **3.** *The* slipped stitch is passed over the stitch which has been knitted, and dropped off the needle. **4.** Decreasing by PURLING into the back of the loops instead of the front. To purl into the back of the stitches the right-hand needle must be passed round the back of the work and into the second stitch on the left-hand needle first. **5.** Decreasing by KNITTING into the back of the loops.

1 row for the bodice, the best way is to knit 2 together all across the row.

If knitting a fancy pattern or decreasing at a point which will show when the garment is finished, it must be remembered that this method of knitting 2 stitches together will produce a stitch with a slope from left to right.

By slipping the first stitch, knitting the next stitch and passing the slipped stitch over the knitted stitch. This will produce a stitch which slopes from right

to left and should be combined with the first method when knitting garments in which it is necessary for the decreasings to converge, as in flared skirts. To match the purl decreasing of purling two stitches together, a variation of this method is used. Purl the first stitch and put it back on the left-hand needle; slip the next stitch over it and then return the purled stitch to the right-hand needle.

By knitting or purling 2 stitches together into the back of the loops instead of into the front. This is a variation of the method (a) and is generally used in fancy patterns. To purl into the back of the stitches, the right-hand needle must be passed round the back of the work and into the second stitch on the left-hand needle first.

Increasing

THERE are several ways of increasing the number of stitches in a garment to produce the necessary shaping.

By knitting or purling twice into the same stitch. This method produces an irregular effect, and although it is the method most commonly used, it should be employed only where such increasings will not show, for instance, at the side edges of a jumper, where they will be sewn into the seam. It is a very useful method, however, when it is necessary to count the increasings, as it can easily be seen.

By knitting or purling into a loop between the stitches of the previous row. If you pick up the loop with the needle and twist it by knitting into the back of it,

it will close up the hole which would otherwise be made, and which would spoil the evenness of the work.

By knitting or purling into a stitch on the previous row, and not into the loop between the stitches. This method can be used in the middle of a garment as it is almost invisible.

By making a stitch by any of the methods described in ABBREVIATIONS (M. = MAKE). This can be used only where it is desired to make a definite hole.

Buttonholes

BUTTONHOLES are of great importance in the final appearance of a knitted garment, which can easily be spoilt if these are untidy or badly made.

There are two methods of making buttonholes in the garment during the knitting :—

Horizontal Buttonholes. These are the most usual buttonholes, and are used where the strain is from side to side, as in a front fastening.

To make a buttonhole of this kind, work to the desired position, cast off the required number of stitches according to the size of the buttonhole and work to the end of the row. On the following row cast on the same number of stitches and work to the end of the row.

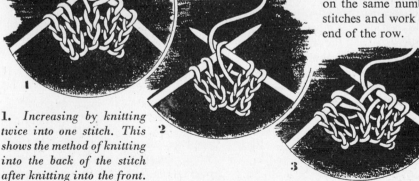

1. *Increasing by knitting twice into one stitch. This shows the method of knitting into the back of the stitch after knitting into the front.*

2. *Making a stitch by picking up and twisting loop between stitches before knitting it. This method leaves no hole in fabric.*

3. *Making a stitch by knitting into the stitch in the row below as well as the stitch itself—neat and fairly invisible.*

1. *A horizontal buttonhole. Cast off the required number of stitches, work to end of row, cast on same number on return row above cast-off stitches.*

2. *Vertical buttonhole. Divide the stitches and work on one section for required length. Work other side to match. Finally work right across all the stitches.*

3. *Cut buttonholes. Run a thread round the proposed hole before cutting, as shown, and then buttonhole stitch round the hole in the usual way.*

Buttonholes made in this way are apt to stretch, so that only a few stitches should be cast off. It is a good idea to buttonhole stitch round the hole to neaten it, when making up the garment.

A very small buttonhole can be made by m. 1, k. 2 tog., in the required position, and will be found very suitable for babies' clothes, etc.

Vertical Buttonholes. These are not so common, but are used when the strain is up and down, as in knickers, pocket flaps, etc. They are very simple to make.

Divide the stitches at the required position and work on one section for the length of the buttonhole; then work on the other section to correspond, finally work right across all the stitches.

There are several methods of making buttonholes on a garment when the knitting has been completed.

Cut Buttonholes.—These must be done with great care and on a close, firmly knitted fabric. Run a thread round the proposed hole before cutting and then buttonhole stitch round the hole in the usual way.

Crochet Loops.—Chain loops, made by attaching lengths of chain to a garment, are very effective on children's garments and for a small front opening, but should not be used to fasten the front of a cardigan or on heavy fabrics.

Buttonhole-stitch Loops. — These can be quite effective and are made by buttonholing in the usual way over double threads of yarn.

Space Buttonholes.—Quite good and neat buttonholes can be made if a space is left when sewing on a band to a front.

Pockets

INSET pockets are usually more practical for knitted garments than patch pockets. Sometimes, of course, it is more useful to have patch pockets because they can be made separately and sewn into position when the garment is finished.

To make a straight inset pocket, knit the lining of the pocket the width and depth required and leave on a spare needle. When the position of the pocket is reached in knitting the garment, cast off the number of stitches in the pocket lining, and on the following row work across the stitches of the lining in place of the cast-off stitches.

To complete the pocket the border may either be knitted separately and sewn on afterwards to the cast-off edge, or the cast-off stitches may be picked up and knitted up for the depth required. A third method is to make the border in one with the pocket by leaving the stitches for the pocket top on a stitch holder instead of casting them off, and then knitting on them for the border. If you prefer your pocket to have no border, a row or two of double crochet will neaten it.

To make sloping inset pockets is rather more difficult, but they can be very effective, especially if they are finished with a border of a contrasting colour or stitch.

Make the pocket lining (in the same way as above) the required depth, to the lowest point of the slope and leave stitches on a spare needle. Work the garment as far as the lowest point of the slope for the pocket slit to begin, and divide the stitches at this point. Work on the stitches on the pocket side, decreasing one stitch either on every row or on every alternate row, according to the sharpness of the slope required, until the horizontal measurement of the decreased section is equal to width of the pocket lining, that is, until

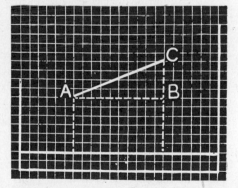

Diagram of sloping inset pocket. Vertical dotted lines indicate edges of pocket lining. Dotted line A-B where pocket lining stitches are inserted. Point C where all stitches are assembled on one needle.

the number of stitches worked off in the decreasings is equal to the number of stitches cast on for the pocket lining. Leave these stitches for the present. Return to the other stitches left on the needle when the work was divided for the slope and work across the stitches for the lining in the same way as for the straight inset pocket, with the difference that the row will end at one edge of the pocket lining. Work on these stitches until the number of rows corresponds with the number of decreasing rows in the sloped edge of the pocket. Then work right across all the stitches and continue with the garment in the usual way.

When sewing pocket linings into position see that the edges follow a straight line of stitches.

Collars

THERE are several ways of making collars for knitted garments. The size and shape of a collar depend on the design of the garment. Generally, however, it will be found that a narrow collar is neat and effective, while a wider one is inclined to be dowdy.

Straight collars, that is, without any shaping, are the simplest to make, but are not usually as satisfactory as shaped ones. If, however, you prefer a straight one, all you require is a strip of garter stitch knitted lengthwise. This can be eased in slightly when being sewn on to the garment, so that the outside edge spreads and gives the collar a certain amount of shape. A straight strip of ribbing knitted widthwise—that is, by casting on enough stitches for the full length of the collar and knitting for the required depth—will have a certain amount of shape because you have the advantage of the full elasticity of the rib on the outside edge. The cast-on edge should always be used for the outside in this case as it gives more stretch than the cast-off edge. More shape can be given to a collar of this type by changing to smaller needles when about half the collar has been worked.

Collars with a definite curve may be made by knitting them widthwise casting on more stitches than are required for the neck edge and decreasing the extra stitches at intervals all along one or more rows, beginning the decreasing rows when about half the collar has been worked and spacing them evenly.

A very satisfactory collar can be made by the turning method. Cast on a sufficient number of stitches for the width of the collar, and turn within $\frac{1}{2}$ in. to 1 in. of the end of the row at intervals of about 6, 8 or 10 rows, until the shortest edge is the same length as the neck edge of the garment.

When sewing collars to garments, fold the collar in half and mark the point with a pin; then do the same to the neck edge. Beginning at the centre back oversew the two edges together on the right side of the work, so that when the collar is turned over it will cover the seam.

Flares

FLARES are most commonly used in skirts, and are made by converging lines of decreasings from the hem to the waist, usually separated by straight panels.

To make a flared skirt with a straight centre panel and two straight side panels, a little simple calculation is all that is necessary. Work out the number of stitches according to the tension of the knitting that will have to be cast on for the lower edge of the skirt, and the number of stitches that will be required to give the necessary width at the waistline. Subtract the number of stitches at the waist from the number of cast-on stitches and divide the result by two. This number is the number of stitches that you will have in each of the flared panels at their widest point, and each of these flares will be completed at the waistline.

As all the stitches in the flares will have been decreased by the time the waist is reached, the number of waist stitches is the number of stitches in the straight panels; divide this number by two which will give you the number of stitches in the centre panel, and by dividing this number by two again you will find the

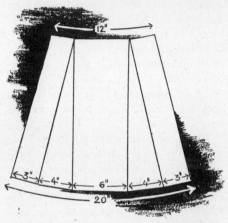

Diagram of flares for a skirt. The diagram shows how the flares are divided by straight panels and the lines of decreasing.

number of stitches in the straight side panels, which should be half the width of the centre panel.

For example, if the cast-on edge of the skirt has 168 stitches, which are reduced to 84 stitches by the time the waistline is reached, the number of stitches in the widest part of each flare will be 168 minus 84 which leaves 84; divided by 2 gives 42. Now divide the waist stitches (84) by 2 which gives you the number of stitches in the centre panel as 42; now divide 42 by 2 and you have the number of stitches for the side panels, namely 21.

The flares are made by decreasing four times, at the edge of each flared panel, all across a row at definite intervals up the skirt. The actual decreasings are made by knitting two stitches together on the left-hand edge and sl. 1, k. 1, p.s.s.o. on the right-hand edge (*see* DECREASINGS).

The intervals between the decreasing rows must be determined by finding the rows tension, and so deciding on the number of rows that will be required to complete the skirt by multiplying the number of inches in the skirt by the number of rows in 1 in. of knitting (*see* TENSION). When working out the flared portion of a skirt always subtract the straight bands at the waist or hem from the total length and disregard them in the calculation. For example, a skirt 12 ins. long, worked at a tension of 9 rows to 1 in. will have 108 rows. Divide the number of stitches in both flares (say 84) by 4 (21), this gives you the number of decreasing rows that have to be worked; divide this number into the total number of rows (21 into 108) and you will have the number of rows in each group (4 plain rows and 1 decreasing row repeated throughout).

If it is not possible to have equal intervals between the decreasing rows throughout the skirt, they should be farther apart at the bottom and closer towards the top.

A skirt can, of course, be knitted from waist to hem, and in this case the same principle would apply, but the method would be reversed and the extra stitches obtained by increasing instead of decreasing.

Belts

KNITTED belts can be very satisfactory and decorative on knitted or cloth garments, particularly if worked in double knitting (*see* BASIC STITCHES), which is firm and will not curl or stretch too much. If ordinary knitting is used the belt should be backed with ribbon to prevent it from stretching and becoming shapeless, and a stitch such as moss stitch or garter stitch, which will not curl, is the best stitch to use. A very satisfactory belt can be made of double crochet. You will find that this will neither curl nor stretch.

Picking up Stitches

THIS is usually the best method of adding bands to necks, fronts and sleeves of garments and gives more elasticity to the edge than if the pieces were sewn on afterwards.

Hold the work in the left hand and insert the needle into the edge of the work as if using a crochet hook. Pass the wool round the point of the needle, as for knitting and draw a loop through. Repeat this process for the number of stitches required.

Unless the instructions state otherwise, always pick up stitches with the right side of the work facing. It is sometimes difficult to pick up the exact number of stitches stated in the instructions, and the best way usually is to pick up as many as possible, so as to produce an even band and then decrease or increase, as the case may be, in the first row of knitting. Generally, it will be found that a few stitches more or less will make very little difference.

Picking up stitches. Inserting the needle through the loop at the cast-off edge and putting the wool round the needle.

Bands

IT is usually advisable to knit all bands which have to be sewn on to the finished garment on finer needles than those used for the rest of the garment, so that you produce a firmer fabric. The bands should always be made slightly shorter than the edge to which they have to be sewn, and stretched out to the required length as they are stitched.

The stitches used for bands must be those that will not curl, such as even ribs of k. 1, p. 1 or k. 2, p. 2, moss stitch or garter stitch. A very satisfactory band can be made by knitting in stocking stitch double the width required and folding it in half before sewing it to the garment.

Fair Isle Knitting

THIS is the name given to knitting in which colours form the pattern; it is derived from Fair Isle in the Shetlands, where so many of the traditional designs originated.

There are two ways of carrying the wools across the back of the work.

The appearance of the back of the work when using the stranding method in Fair Isle knitting.

The appearance of the back of work in the weaving method in Fair Isle knitting.

Stranding. — Hold the work in the usual way, with the basic colour — for instance, natural—in the right hand as for ordinary knitting. Hold another colour —for instance, red—in the left hand, over the middle finger away from the work. Knit the natural stitches in the usual way passing over the red wool held out at the back by the left hand, and thus stranding

it. To knit a red stitch, pass the natural wool to the left hand and hold it there in the same position, pass the point of the right-hand needle into the next stitch as if for knitting, then over and under the red wool from right to left, pulling the red wool through the loop.

The points to watch when using this method are that the wool that is being stranded does not become too taut and so pucker the work, and that the change from one colour to another is neat, without altering the tension of the stitches.

Weaving. — When the wool has to be carried across a large number of stitches the weaving method should be used. Hold the colour to be woven in the left hand, as described above, and knit with the basic colour, but at every alternate stitch pass the point of the right-hand needle through the stitch, then, under the colour that is being woven, pass the basic colour over the point of the needle and draw a loop through, allowing the other colour to drop off.

To purl in this style of work, work in a similar way, first under and then over the wool that is being woven.

Continental Knitting

THIS is merely an alternate way of knitting, as the appearance of a garment knitted in this way is exactly the same as that of one knitted in the English manner. There is one point about it, however, and that is that once the principle has been grasped, it is much quicker than the English way, and from that point of view appeals to a great many people.

To Cast On. Single Casting On.— Holding both needles in the right hand, begin with a loop round the left thumb, as shown in the illustration for English casting on. Insert both needles into the loop and take off the required number of stitches in the ordinary way.

Using both needles for casting on in

Single casting on. The needles are held in the right hand, and the loop is made with the thumb of the left hand.

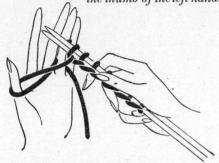

this way makes a looser edge which is easier to knit into and which is unlikely to break in wear.

When you have cast on enough stitches take out one needle for the actual knitting.

Double Casting On. — Using both needles as above begin with a loop, leaving one end of yarn according to the number of stitches required, in the same way as you would do for the English double casting on by the thumb method. Now loop the ball end over the first finger and the other end over the thumb. Control the flow of the yarn by holding both threads in the palm of the left hand with the third and little fingers. Then make a loop by taking the needles in front and under the first thread of the thumb loop, then over

Making a knit stitch, continental style. The illustration shows the needle inserted through loop ready to hook round yarn.

the first finger loop, drawing a loop through the thumb loop.

This sounds a complicated process, but it will be found quite simple to work.

Knit Stitch. — Holding the needle with the cast-on stitches in the left hand and with the yarn twisted over the first finger and controlled in the palm of the hand, put the point of the right-hand needle through the first loop and hook it round the yarn which is held taut by the first finger. Draw the loop through and continue in this way to the end of the row. The action is rather like reversed crochet stitch.

Purl Stitch. — Hold the work as for the

Purl stitch. From the back of the work the right-hand needle is inserted through the loop. The yarn is kept in front of the work all the time.

knit stitch; then put the right-hand needle through the loop from the back of the work, keeping the yarn in front. Now hook the needle round the yarn and pull a loop through. The main difficulty that knitters will experience when experimenting with this method of knitting is keeping the tension even; but that should come with practice.

Once you have learned how to do continental knitting you will probably prefer it to the English way, for, as was said at the beginning of this section, it is much quicker to do, also it tends to produce a somewhat more even fabric.

Making Up

A KNITTED garment can be made or marred by the way it is pressed, sewn together and finished off. That is something which cannot be too strongly stressed.

First of all, pin out all the pieces on to an ironing board to the correct size and shape and press lightly with a warm iron over a damp cloth. It is most important to press and not iron, that is, to lift the iron from one place to another, not slide it along the surface. Unless the garment has to be shrunk, the iron should not be too hot or the cloth very damp, as it will spoil the yarn; for all rayon yarns use a cool iron—that's an important point to remember. Do not press any ribbing unless it forms the hem of a garment or has to be pressed out deliberately. If the garment has been well knitted, it should require very little pressing.

The garment is now ready to be sewn together, and there are various ways of making the seams.

1. Edge-to-Edge Seams.—This is a very good method, but can only be used when the edges are neat and even. With the

Making up. The illustration shows how the bodice and sleeve stripes should be matched when making up a garment knitted in a pattern of this description.

right sides of the pieces to be joined facing, place them flat, edge to edge. With the yarn used for knitting the garment, join them by taking a stitch through the edge of first one side and then the other, keeping the pieces flat all the time.

When well done, this join is practically invisible and is very useful for joining the pieces of babies' garments, when ridges are undesirable, or for reversible pullovers, etc.

2. Oversewn Seam.—With the wrong sides outside, place the two pieces to be joined together, edge to edge, holding them in the left hand. Use the same yarn as the garment is knitted in, and oversew the seam pulling the yarn fairly tight and matching row for row as far as possible.

3. Back-stitch Seam.—This is the most satisfactory method of sewing uneven edges together because it is sewn about one-eighth of an inch from the edge so that the unevenness does not show on the right side. Place the two pieces of knitting together as for an oversewn seam, and back stitch, afterwards pressing the seam open.

4. Machine-stitched Seams.—This method is only suitable for garments that do not have to be pulled on over the head, or subjected to any other great strain. Machine-stitched seams are completely inelastic, and will break if they are stretched. The method is, however, ideal for all tailored garments. Work in the same way as for hand back-stitched seams.

It is usually found more satisfactory to use the back-stitch seam for armholes and shoulder seams because these edges are often a little uneven due to the shapings. For garments that are likely to have a lot of strain put on them it is a good idea to tape these seams, or finish them with bias binding.

When you are sewing sleeves into the armholes, the centre of the top of the sleeve should be sewn to the shoulder seam, except in the case of a garment in which the front armhole is longer than the back. In this case the centre of the top of the sleeve should be sewn to the point where the shoulder seam would be if the armholes were of equal length. Any fullness in the sleeves should be brought well

Fringe edging. A loop is drawn through the edge of the knitting with a crochet hook. The ends are drawn through the loop as shown above, and then tightened.

to the top and gathered or pleated evenly before being sewn in.

When making up a striped jumper, whether the stripes are in the pattern or in colour, always be careful to match them round the armholes as well as up the side seams.

Darts.—It is often necessary to make darts in knitted garments to ensure a perfect fit, particularly if the garment is of the tailored type. These darts need not be made in the knitting, but may be machined in the knitted fabric as if it were ordinary material, before the garment is made up. If the garment is knitted in very thick yarn or if the darts are very deep, it is best to cut them down the centre and press them open. In this case care must be taken to oversew the cut edges carefully to prevent them from fraying; this must also be done when the darts have to be slashed (for instance, waist darts in a very tightly fitting jacket) or they will not lie flat.

The finishing touches to a knitted garment can mean a great deal in the way of comfort and appearance, and the following notes on the use of elastic and buttons

and so on may prove useful in helping you to give your knitted garments a professional appearance.

Fringe Edging.—A very simple way of making a fringe for the ends of scarves or edges of shawls is as follows: Cut lengths of yarn slightly more than double the required length of fringe. Take two or more strands according to the thickness desired and fold in half. With a crochet hook draw the loop through the edge of the knitting, draw the ends through the loop and tighten.

Zipps.—Zipp fasteners, when they can be procured, are probably the simplest way of fastening knitted garments as they do not need bands or borders. The zipp must be sewn in very carefully, preferably by hand, keeping it taut and slightly easing in the knitting to prevent it from bulging. The opening should be slightly longer than the zipp.

Buttons

Knitted buttons are very satisfactory for all kinds of knitted garments. They are easily made, wash and wear well, and you do not have the difficulty of matching the colour or finding suitable sizes and shapes. There are several ways of making these buttons.

Round Knitted Buttons.—These are made by knitting a square in either moss stitch or stocking stitch, rather larger than the diameter of the button or mould to be covered, using wool in 2-ply, 3-ply or 4-ply and No. 14 needles to produce a really close fabric. Run a thread all round the square and draw it up, to cover either a button mould or cuttings of wool; it is not advisable to use a cotton stuffing as it becomes lumpy and shapeless when washed. Fasten off securely. When sewing on the garment, attach a small linen button to the inside of the garment to take the strain—or the fabric will wear in holes.

Square Tailored Buttons.—Knit two

small squares for each button as described above; oversew them together leaving a small opening for the stuffing. Stuff with cuttings of wool; close the opening with oversewing, and finish the button with a firm line of back stitch a short distance in from the edge.

Dome - shaped Crochet Buttons.— Make five chain with a medium-sized crochet hook; make it into a ring with a slip stitch; then work about nine double crochet into the ring. Work about four more rounds of double crochet without

increasing. Stuff it with cut wool or cover a button mould as described in 1. This button can be made to any size, according to the number of double crochets and the number of rows worked. A very small button made with a fine hook will not need stuffing.

Ring Buttons.—Work a row of double crochet tightly all round a small bone or metal ring. Fill in the centre with threads crossing from side to side and finish off with several stitches in the centre. A very small button can be made by simply buttonholing round the edge of the ring.

Cover linen buttons either by oversewing or buttonholing with matching or contrasting yarn.

1. *Square tailored button, made by knitting two squares, sewing them together and stuffing it.* 2. *Dome-shaped crochet button, made by working double crochet into a crochet ring of chain stitch.* 3. *Round knitted button, made by knitting a square and fitting it over a round button mould.* 4. *Linen buttons can be covered by oversewing or buttonholing.* 5. *Ring buttons made by working double crochet round a ring and filling the centre with threads.*

Elastic

ELASTIC can be used in many ways in knitted garments.

Elastic Braid.—It is the most satisfactory material for the tops of knickers, skirts and so on. It is especially good for babies' and children's knickers, as it holds the garment in place without constriction. (This is an open-mesh braid made of elastic and covered with cotton, wool or rayon.)

The best way of using it to preserve its elasticity is by knitting into a row of holes at one edge as if picking up a row of knitted stitches. Use double wool for this process, breaking off one strand at the end of the row before continuing with the knitting in the usual way.

Casing for Elastic.—To apply elastic to waists of skirts, etc., the best way is to make a crochet casing on the wrong side of the garment. Make a slip stitch at the top edge of the ribbing or edge to which the elastic is to be added, * make 4, 5, 6 or more chain, according to the width of the elastic, miss 1 or more ribs, make a slip stitch into a rib several rows below, once again according to the width of the elastic, make a length of chain the same

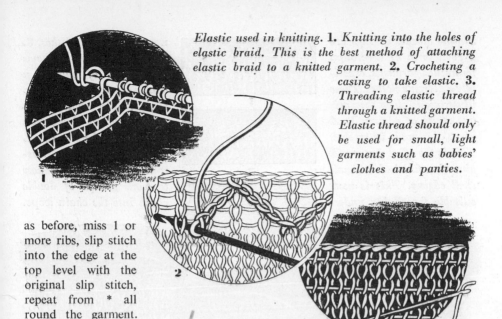

Elastic used in knitting. **1.** *Knitting into the holes of elastic braid. This is the best method of attaching elastic braid to a knitted garment.* **2.** *Crocheting a casing to take elastic.* **3.** *Threading elastic thread through a knitted garment. Elastic thread should only be used for small, light garments such as babies' clothes and panties.*

as before, miss 1 or more ribs, slip stitch into the edge at the top level with the original slip stitch, repeat from * all round the garment.

Threading with Fine Elastic. — Fine elastic can be threaded through ribbing to support the tops of skirts, etc. It will be found very suitable for children's garments, and much more comfortable than the ordinary tape elastic. Use a large-eyed wool needle and thread the elastic through one loop of each rib for the number of rows required. Fasten off securely by oversewing the end and turning it back so that it does not slip out.

Decoration

KNITTED garments as a general rule require little or no decoration, particularly if they are knitted in elaborate patterns. However, a little decoration can add a great deal of interest and can add a touch of smartness or glamour to the appearance of a plain garment. Oddments of wool in contrasting colours can be used for simple embroidery, though special embroidery wools can easily be obtained. Any of the stitches illustrated on page 35 could be used, and in addition a zigzag running stitch working on moss stitch can be very effective. If several rows are worked it has the appearance of smocking.

There are several useful edgings in crochet which not only help to lighten the appearance of a knitted garment, but will at the same time prevent the edges from curling. If the edges curl very badly it is best to work a row of double crochet before beginning the proper edge. The simplest edges are picot edge, shell or scallop edge and loop edging.

Picot Edge.—This is a very popular edging for babies' garments. 1 single crochet into first stitch, * 3 chain, 1 double crochet into first of these chain stitches, miss 1 stitch, 1 single crochet into next stitch; repeat from * to end.

Shell or Scallop Edge. — This is worked by doing 1 single crochet and 2 treble into the same stitch, leaving a small space and repeating all along the edge. A larger edge can be made by working 3 or more treble instead of 2.

Loop Edge.—This is worked either directly into the edge of the fabric or on the basis of a row of double crochet. Begin by making 1 double crochet, then work 2 or more chain according to the

Simple crochet edgings are a good form of decoration for knitted garments, especially children's clothes. These illustrations show the various styles of edging. 1. A picot edge made in crochet. This is the effect that it will give when finished. 2. Small shell edging. This is most suitable for edging under-

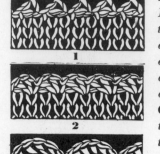

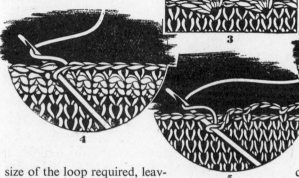

wear and babies' clothes. 3. Large shell edging. 4 shows the method of making a double crochet edge. 5. Loop edging. The chain loops attached to the foundation edge by a double chain. 6. Loop edging. The illustration below shows how to work groups of double chain into the chain loops.

size of the loop required, leaving a space and working another double crochet, the loop should lie fairly flat on the edge. Break off wool and work several double crochets into each loop.

Laundering

CARELESS washing can completely ruin a knitted garment long before it is really worn out, and in order to avoid this it is well worth while making a note of the following points, which, if followed carefully, should ensure that the shape and texture of your garment are not spoilt in the process.

1. Wet knitted garments very often look completely dejected with no shape at all, and before washing it is well worth while to make a record of the measurements of your garment so that it can be patted into size while it is still wet. Trying to press it back into shape when it is dry is not to be recommended, as it would necessitate using a very hot iron and a very damp cloth, both of which would be injurious to most yarns.

2. Wash knitted garments before they are dirty enough to require rubbing, because rubbing will felt the wool.

3. Use plenty of warm water, at a temperature comfortable to the hands; both very cold and very hot water are bad for wool and will shrink it.

4. Use good quality soap flakes and avoid all soap preparations containing soda.

5. Do not rub the garment between your hands, but move it about in the soapy water and squeeze it, rubbing very dirty spots only when absolutely necessary and as lightly as possible.

6. Rinse in at least two lots of clear water of the same temperature as the washing water. If the dye is fast use a little ammonia in the second rinse. Ammonia counteracts the smell of perspiration in woollen garments.

7. Never wring knitted garments by hand, squeeze them between the hands

or put them through a slack wringer.

8. Dry as quickly as possible; if woollen garments are left about when wet they will felt and shrink. Always dry as flat as possible, either in the open air or in a current of air. Never hang a wet knitted garment by its shoulders or it will drop completely out of shape. If you cannot dry it flat fold it over a line, moving its position from time to time.

9. Do not iron; press carefully in the same way as described in MAKING UP.

Cotton and silk garments require more shaping after washing than woollen garments; but if this is done carefully they will wash and wear indefinitely.

Finally, when you are laundering any kind of knitted garment, don't feel in despair if it comes out of the final rinsing water looking completely shapeless and in a word "awful." Careful pushing and putting into shape, and careful pressing will soon restore it to its former beauty.

Reknitting Garments

IN times of wool shortage you cannot afford to discard a partly worn knitted garment. The section beginning on page 225 will give you plenty of ideas of how to renovate and remake knitteds, but these few general points may help.

You should not attempt to unravel any garment that has become "felted."

Unravelled wool if dirty, should be washed in the skein before being reknitted.

If you want to wash skeins of wool that have been unravelled, put the skeins into the top compartment of a steamer and steam for about ten minutes. Hang up the skeins to dry, shaking them occasionally, then wind them in the ordinary way. You can knit up the wool into a new design, which will last as long as the original garment.

Consider how much wool you have after unravelling and do not plan a garment that uses as much wool as the orig-

inal garment—some wool is bound to be wasted in unpicking. Stripes, contrasting sleeves, or contrasting yokes will often provide a solution to your problem if you have not enough wool of the main shade in which to knit the whole jumper. The difference in quantities needed for making long and short sleeves is considerable.

Simple stitches for wool embroidery.

" Why haven't we met before?" For years you've been looking for a
knitted tailored shirt to wear with slacks or with a sports skirt. Well,
here it is, knitted in a simple rib. The last word in tailored smartness.

AN IDEA THAT NEVER GROWS OLD

Trim Tailored Shirt

IN TWO- OR THREE-PLY WOOL

MATERIALS

9 oz. 3-ply knitting wool.
2 No. 12 knitting needles.
3 buttons.
N.B.—For a light-weight shirt use 5 oz. of 2-ply wool and substitute No. 11 needles for No. 12 throughout, to obtain the correct tension.

MEASUREMENTS

Length, 21½ ins.
Bust size, 36 ins.
Sleeve seam, 5 ins.

TENSION

9 sts. to 1 in.

The Pocket Lining.—Cast on 28 sts. and work in following patt.:—

1st row.—P. 1, * k. 8, p. 1; rep. from * to end.

2nd row.—P. to end.

Rep. these 2 rows for 3¼ ins., ending with a first patt. row. Break off wool and leave sts. on a spare needle.

The Front.—Cast on 162 sts. and work 1 in. in k. 1, p. 1 rib.

Continue in patt. thus:—

1st row.—K. 4, p. 1, * k. 8, p. 1; rep. from * to last 4 sts., k. 4.

2nd row.—P. to end.

Rep. these 2 rows until work measures 15 ins. from lower edge, ending with a p. row.

Shape Armholes and Divide for Front Opening thus:—

Next row.—Cast off 8 sts., patt. to end.

Next row.—Cast off 8 sts., p. 68 sts., counting st. already on right-hand needle after casting off, turn, leaving remaining 78 sts. on a spare needle.

Continue in patt. on this set of sts., dec. 1 st. at armhole edge on each of the next 6 rows, then dec. 1 st. at same edge on every alternate row until 58 sts. remain.

Continue in patt. without shaping until work measures 19½ ins. from lower edge, ending at front opening edge.

Shape Neck and Shoulder thus:—

Continue in patt., cast off 3 sts. at beg. of the next row, then dec. 1 st. at neck edge on every row until 41 sts. remain.

Continue without shaping until work measures 21½ ins. from lower edge, ending at armhole edge.

Next row.—Cast off 10 sts., patt. to end.

Next row.—Patt. to end.

Rep. last 2 rows twice.

Cast off remaining sts.

Rejoin wool to second set of sts. at front edge and work thus:—

1st row.—K. 2, patt. to end.

2nd row.—K. 2 tog., patt. to last 2 sts., k. 2.

3rd row.—K. 2, patt. to last 2 sts., k. 2 tog.

Rep. last 2 rows twice.

Continue in patt. with g.st. front border, dec. 1 st. at armhole edge on every alternate row until 69 sts. remain, ending at armhole edge.

Next row.—K. 2 tog., patt. 12 sts., cast off next 28 sts., patt. to last 2 sts., k. 2.

Next row.—K. 2, p. 25, sl. sts. for pocket lining on to left-hand needle and p. across these sts., p. to end.

Continue in patt. without shaping until work measures 19½ ins. from lower edge, ending at front edge and retaining g.st. front border throughout.

Shape Neck and Shoulder thus :—Continuing in patt., cast off 3 sts. at beg. of next row, then dec. 1 st. at neck edge on every row until 41 sts. remain. Proceed without shaping until work measures 21½ ins. from lower edge, ending at armhole edge.

Shape shoulder as given for first shoulder.

The Back.—Work exactly as given for front until armhole shaping is reached and work measures 15 ins. from lower edge.

Shape Armholes thus:—Continue in patt., cast off 8 sts. at beg. of next 2 rows, then dec. 1 st. at each end of next 6 rows. Now dec. 1 st. at each end of every alternate row until 126 sts. remain.

Proceed without shaping until work measures 21½ ins. from lower edge, ending with a p. row.

Shape Neck and Shoulders thus:—

Next row.—Cast off 10 sts., patt. 35 sts., counting st. already on right-hand needle after casting off, k. 2 tog., cast off next 32 sts., patt. to end.

Work on last set of sts. thus:—

Next row.—Cast off 10 sts., patt. to last 2 sts., k. 2 tog.

Next row.—K. 2 tog., patt. to end.

Rep. last 2 rows twice.

Cast off remaining sts.

Rejoin wool to second set of sts. at needle point and work thus:—

1st row.—K. 2 tog., patt. to end.

2nd row.—Cast off 10 sts., patt. to last 2 sts., k. 2 tog.

3rd row.—As 1st row.

Rep. last 2 rows once.

Cast off remaining sts.

The Sleeves.—Cast on 116 sts. and work 1 in. in k. 1, p. 1 rib, inc. 1 st. at end of last row.

Continue in patt. as given for front until work measures 5 ins. from commencement.

Shape Top thus:—Continuing in patt., dec. 1 st. at each end of next 5 rows, then work 1 row without shaping.

Rep. these 6 rows until 47 sts. remain.

Cast off remaining sts.

The Collar.—Cast on 149 sts. and work in k. 1, p. 1 rib thus:—

1st row.—K. 2, * k. 1, p. 1; rep. from * to last 3 sts., k. 3.

2nd row.—K. 2, * p. 1, k. 1; rep. from * to last 3 sts., p. 1, k. 2.

3rd row.—K. 2, k. 2 tog., work in rib to last 4 sts., k. 2 tog., k. 2.

4th row.—K. 2 rib to last 2 sts., k. 2.

Rep. last 2 rows until work measures 2 ins. from commencement, then shape top edge thus:—

Continuing in rib, cast off 30 sts. at beg. of next 2 rows, then cast off 6 sts. at beg. of next 4 rows.

Cast off remaining sts. in rib.

The Front Over-wrap.—With right side of work facing and using No. 12 needles, pick up and k. 40 sts. evenly along right front edge.

Work ½ in. in k. 1, p. 1 rib, ending at neck edge.

Make buttonholes in next 2 rows:—

Next row.—Rib 3, * cast off 3 sts., rib 12 sts. counting st. already on right-hand

"My wool's 3-ply—What's yours?" With hasty apologies in passing to the dog for any hurt he may feel at this reference to his coat, let us explain that this is the 3-ply version of the sports shirt.

needle after casting off; rep. from * once; cast off 3 sts., rib to end.

Next row.—Rib 4, * cast on 3 sts., rib 12; rep. from * once; cast on 3 sts., rib 3.

Work ½ in. in rib.

Cast off loosely in rib.

The Pocket Border.—Cast on 28 sts. and work ½ in. in k. 1, p. 1 rib.

Cast off loosely in rib.

Make-up.—Press work, excepting ribbing, lightly on wrong side with a hot iron and damp cloth.

Join side, shoulder and sleeve seams.

Stitch sleeves into armholes, matching seams with side seams.

Stitch lower edge of the ribbed overwrap across the under-wrap.

Stitch cast-off edge of the collar round neck edge, beginning and ending about ½ in. from each front edge.

Sew on buttons to match buttonholes.

Stitch cast-on edge of the pocket border along cast-off edge of the pocket, stitching the border down at each side. Now stitch all round pocket lining on wrong side of work. Press all seams.

Because it's comfortable, because it's smart, because it's inevitable that it will become the close companion of that "pottering around the house and garden" day, you will fall for this knitted shirt. This version is made in 2-ply navy blue wool. The slightly heavier shirt photographed on page 39 is made in 3-ply and knitted in a natural shade.

LONG AND SHORT
Ribbed Sports Jersey
IN THREE-PLY WOOL

MATERIALS

5 oz. 3-ply wool.
2 No. 8, 2 No. 10 and a set of 4 No. 10 knitting needles, and 1 spare needle.

MEASUREMENTS

Length, 18½ ins.
Bust size, 34 ins.
Sleeve seam, 5½ ins.

TENSION

1 complete patt., i.e., 18 sts. to 2½ ins.

ABBREVIATIONS

(Used in these instructions only)
T. 10 = sl. 4 sts. on to a spare needle and leave at the back of the work, k. the next st., then k. the 4 sts. from the spare needle, sl. the next st. on to a spare needle and leave at the front of the work, k. next 4 sts., then k. st. from the spare needle; T. 5 (at the beg. of a row) = sl. 1 st. on to a spare needle and leave at the front of the work, then k. next 4 sts., then k. st. from spare needle; T. 5 (at the end of a row) = sl. 4 sts. on to a spare needle and leave at the back of the work, k. 1, then k. 4 sts. from the spare needle.

The Front.—Using No. 8 needles cast on 102 sts. Change to No. 10 needles and proceed in patt. as follows:—

1st row (working into the back of the sts.).—K. 2, * p. 2, k. 4, p. 2, t. 10; rep. from * to last 10 sts., then p. 2, k. 4, p. 2, k. 2.

2nd row.—P. 2, * k. 2, p. 4, k. 2, p. 10; rep. from * to last 10 sts., then k. 2, p. 4, k. 2, p. 2.

Rep. these 2 rows until work measures 3½ ins. from the beginning, ending with a row on the wrong side of the work. Change to No. 8 needles and continue in patt. inc. as follows:—

1st row.—Inc. in 1st st., k. 1, * p. 2, k. 4, p. 2, t. 10; rep. from * to last 10 sts., then p. 2, k. 4, p. 2, k. 1, inc. in last st.

2nd row.—P. 3, * k. 2, p. 4, k. 2, p. 10; rep. from * to last 11 sts., then k. 2, p. 4, k. 2, p. 3.

3rd row.—K. 3, * p. 2, k. 4, p. 2, t. 10; rep. from * to last 11 sts., then p. 2, k. 4, p. 2, k. 3.

4th and 5th rows.—Rep. 2nd and 3rd rows.

6th row.—Inc. in 1st st., p. 2, * k. 2, p. 4, k. 2, p. 10; rep. from * to last 11 sts., then k. 2, p. 4, k. 2, p. 2, inc. in last st.

7th row.—K. 4, * p. 2, k. 4, p. 2, t. 10; rep. from * to last 12 sts., then p. 2, k. 4, p. 2, k. 4.

8th row.—P. 4, * k. 2, p. 4, k. 2, p. 10; rep. from * to last 12 sts., k. 2, p. 4, k. 2, p. 4.

9th and 10th rows.—Rep. 7th and 8th rows.

11th row.—Inc. in 1st st., k. 3, * p. 2, k. 4, p. 2, t. 10; rep. from * to last 12 sts., then p. 2, k. 4, p. 2, k. 3, inc. in last st.

12th row.—P. 5, * k. 2, p. 4, k. 2, p. 10; rep. from * to last 13 sts., then k. 2, p. 4, k. 2, p. 5.

13th row.—T. 5, * p. 2, k. 4, p. 2, t. 10; rep. from * to last 13 sts., then p. 2, k. 4, p. 2, t. 5.

14th and 15th rows.—Rep. 12th and 13th rows.

And that's the long and short of it! Hip length or the newest "pulled down below the hips" length. Take your choice. The jerseys are knitted in an attractive fancy rib which is, nevertheless, perfectly simple to knit.

16th row.—Inc. in 1st st., p. 4, * k. 2, p. 4, k. 2, p. 10; rep. from * to last 13 sts., then k. 2, p. 4, k. 2, p. 4, inc. in last st.

17th row.—K. 1, t. 5, * p. 2, k. 4, p. 2, t. 10; rep. from * to last 14 sts., then p. 2, k. 4, p. 2, t. 5, k. 1.

18th row.—P. 6, * k. 2, p. 4, k. 2, p. 10; rep. from * to last 14 sts., then k. 2, p. 4, k. 2, p. 6.

19th and 20th rows.—Rep. 17th and 18th rows.

21st row.—Inc. in 1st st., t. 5, * p. 2, k. 4, p. 2, t. 10; rep. from * to last 14 sts., p. 2, k. 4, p. 2, t. 5, inc. in last st.

28th row.—P. 8, * k. 2, p. 4, k. 2, p. 10; rep. from * to last 16 sts., then k. 2, p. 4, k. 2, p. 8.

29th and 30th rows.—Rep. 27th and 28th rows.

31st row.—Inc. in 1st st., k. 2, t. 5, * p. 2, k. 4, p. 2, t. 10; rep. from * to last 16 sts., p. 2, k. 4, p. 2, t. 5, k. 2, inc. in last st.

32nd row.—P. 9, * k. 2, p. 4, k. 2, p. 10; rep. from * to last 17 sts., then k. 2, p. 4, k. 2, p. 9.

33rd row.—K. 4, t. 5, * p. 2, k. 4, p. 2, t. 10; rep. from * to last 17 sts., then p. 2, k. 4, p. 2, t. 5, k. 4.

A close-up of the fancy rib alternating with plain rib in which the sports jersey is knitted. The stitches are twisted as in a cable pattern.

22nd row.—P. 7, * k. 2, p. 4, k. 2, p. 10; rep. from * to last 15 sts., then k. 2, p. 4, k. 2, p. 7.

23rd row.—K. 2, t. 5, * p. 2, k. 4, p. 2, t. 10; rep. from * to last 15 sts., then p. 2, k. 4, p. 2, t. 5, k. 2.

24th and 25th rows.—Rep. 22nd and 23rd rows.

26th row.—Inc. in 1st st., p. 6, * k. 2, p. 4, k. 2, p. 10; rep. from * to last 15 sts., then k. 2, p. 4, k. 2, p. 6, inc. in last st.

27th row.—K. 3, t. 5, * p. 2, k. 4, p. 2, t. 10; rep. from * to last 16 sts., then p. 2, k. 4, p. 2, t. 5, k. 3.

34th and 35th rows.—Rep. 32nd and 33rd rows.

36th row.—Inc. in 1st st., p. 8, * k. 2, p. 4, k. 2, p. 10; rep. from * to last 17 sts., k. 2, p. 4, k. 2, p. 8, inc. in last st.

37th row.—T. 10, * p. 2, k. 4, p. 2, t. 10; rep. from * to last 18 sts., p. 2, k. 4, p. 2, t. 10.

38th row.—P. 10, * k. 2, p. 4, k. 2, p. 10; rep. from * to last 18 sts., then k. 2, p. 4, k. 2, p. 10.

39th and 40th rows.—Rep. 37th and 38th rows.

41st row.—Inc. in 1st st., t. 4 (sl. 3 sts.

Knitteds worn with a suit are the order of the day, and this type of jersey with turn-down collar is both smart and practicable.

on to spare needle, keeping them at the back of the work, k. 1, then k. 3 sts. from spare needle), t. 5, * p. 2, k. 4, p. 2, t. 10; rep. from * to last 18 sts., then p. 2, k. 4, p. 2, t. 5, t. 4 (sl. 1 st. on to spare needle and keep at the front of the work, k. 3, then k. st. on spare needle), inc. in last st.

42nd row.—K. 1, p. 10, * k. 2, p. 4, k. 2, p. 10; rep. from * to last 19 sts., then k. 2, p. 4, k. 2, p. 10, k. 1.

43rd row.—P. 1, t. 10, * p. 2, k. 4, p. 2, t. 10; rep. from * to last 19 sts., p. 2, k. 4, p. 2, t. 10, p. 1.

44th and 45th rows.—Rep. 42nd and 43rd rows.

46th row.—Inc. in 1st st., p. 10, * k. 2, p. 4, k. 2, p. 10; rep. from * to last 19 sts., k. 2, p. 4, k. 2, p. 10, inc. in last st. There are now 122 sts. on the needle.

47th row.—P. 2, t. 10, * p. 2, k. 4, p. 2, t. 10; rep. from * to last 2 sts., p. 2.

48th row.—K. 2, p. 10, * k. 2, p. 4, k. 2, p. 10; rep. from * to last 2 sts., k. 2.

Rep. these 2 rows without further shaping until the work measures 12½ ins. from the beginning, ending with a row on the wrong side of the work.

Shape Armholes thus:—Keeping patt. correct cast off 10 sts. at the beginning of each of the next 2 rows, then dec. 1 st. at each end of every alternate row until there are 94 sts. on the needle.

Continue in patt. and without further shaping until the work measures 17½ ins. from the beginning, ending with a row on the wrong side of the work.

Shape Neck and Shoulders thus:—

Next row.—K. 38 sts. in patt., turn.

Continue working on these 38 sts., dec. 1 st. at the neck edge on every row, until 29 sts. remain. Now continue without further shaping until the work measures 18½ ins. from the beginning, ending at the armhole edge.

Next row.—Cast off 7, work in patt. to end.

Next row.—Work to the end of the row.

Rep. these 2 rows twice more, then cast off remaining sts.

Sl. the centre 18 sts. on to a spare needle and leave for the neck. Join the wool at the needle point and continue working on the remaining 38 sts., dec. 1 st. at the neck edge on every row until 29 sts. remain, then complete the shoulder as given for the left front.

The Back.—Work exactly as the front until the armhole shapings are completed and there are 94 sts. on the needle. Then continue without further shaping until the work measures 18½ ins. from the beginning, ending with a row on the wrong side of the work.

Shape Neck and Shoulders thus:—

1st row.—Cast off 7, k. 27, k. 2 tog., turn.

2nd row.—K. 2 tog., work to the end.

3rd row.—Cast off 7, work to the end, k. 2 tog.

4th row.—K. 2 tog., work to the end.

Rep. these last 2 rows once more, then cast off remaining sts.

Sl. the centre 22 sts. on to a spare needle and leave for the neck. Join the wool at the needle point and complete the other shoulder in the same way.

The Sleeve.—Using No. 8 needles cast on 72 sts.

Change to No. 10 needles and proceed in patt. as follows:—

1st row.—K. 2, * p. 2, t. 10, p. 2, k. 4; rep. from * to the last 16 sts., then p. 2, t. 10, p. 2, k. 2.

2nd row.—P. 2, * k. 2, p. 10, k. 2, p. 4; rep. from * to the last 16 sts., then k. 2, p. 10, k. 2, p. 2.

Rep. these 2 rows until the work measures 1 in., ending with a row on the wrong side of the work. Change to No. 8 needles and keeping the patt. correct, inc. 1 st. at both ends of the next and every

following 4th row until there are 86 sts. on the needle.

Now proceed without further shaping until the work measures 5½ ins.

Shape Top thus:—Dec. 1 st. each end of every alternate row until there are 58 sts. on the needle; then dec. 1 st. at each end of every row until there are 28 sts. on the needle.

Cast off loosely.

The Collar.—Join the shoulder seams.

With the right side of the work facing and using the 4 No. 10 needles commence at the left shoulder seam and work thus:—

Pick up and k. 20 sts. along the neck edge, 18 sts. from the spare needle, 20 sts. to the right shoulder seam, 9 sts. along the neck edge, 22 sts. from the spare needle and 9 sts. to the left shoulder seam.

There are now 98 sts. on the needles. Arrange these sts. on the 3 needles, and beginning at the centre front work in a rib of k. 1, p. 1 for 1 in.

Now divide for the collar thus:—

Work to centre front, k. 2 tog., turn and work back. Continue working backwards and forwards without any shaping until the collar measures 2½ ins. from the neck edge. Change to No. 8 needles and work another inch in rib.

Cast off in rib very loosely.

Make-up.—Press all the work, with the exception of the collar, very lightly on the wrong side of the work, using a hot iron over a damp cloth.

Join the side and sleeve seams; stitch sleeves into armholes, placing seams to side seams.

Press all seams.

This jersey can be knitted in any variety of rib that pleases you—or it can be knitted in cable. It is better, by the way, to knit this pattern in rib rather than in plain fabric. To be effective, the jersey should fit fairly snugly, and this result is best gained by knitting in a rib or a cable.

Knitteds Hit a New Low

The line below the hips is now the correct thing; so here is the long version of the short yellow jumper. Wear it pulled well down and without a belt. It's a grand line for the slim. If you are doubtful about the hipline, don't chance it, stick to the short line or wear it tucked inside your skirt or slacks.

MATERIALS
6 oz. 3-ply wool.
2 No. 8, 2 No. 10 and a set of 4 No. 10 knitting needles, and 1 spare needle.

MEASUREMENTS
Length, 21½ ins. Bust size, 34 ins.
Sleeve seam, 5½ ins.

TENSION
1 complete patt., i.e., 18 sts. to 2½ ins.

ABBREVIATIONS
See abbreviations for original jersey.

This is the "below the hip line" version of the jersey. If you like it the instructions for making it are on this page.

The Front.—Using No. 8 needles cast on 102 sts. and proceed in patt., as given for the shorter jersey until the work measures 3 ins. from the beginning. Change to No. 10 needles and continue in patt. until work measures 6½ ins. from the beginning.

Change to No. 8 needles and continue in patt. inc. 1 st. at the beginning and end of the 1st and every following 5th row, as given in instructions for the shorter jersey, until there are 122 sts. on the needle.

Now continue without shaping until work measures 15½ ins. from the beginning.

Complete the armhole shaping as given in the original instructions, and continue in patt. until work measures 20½ ins. from the beginning, ending with a row on the wrong side of work.

Shape the neck as given in the original instructions, shaping the shoulders when the work measures 21½ ins. from the beginning.

The Back.—Work exactly as given for the front until the armhole shapings have been completed and there are 94 sts. on the needle. Continue without further shaping until work measures 21½ ins. from the beginning, ending with a row on the wrong side of the work.

Shape the neck and shoulders as given in the instructions for the original jersey.

The Sleeve.—This is worked exactly as the sleeve for the shorter jersey.

For the collar and the instructions for making up the garment refer to the original instructions.

Roll Collar Jersey

IN CRÊPE WOOL

MATERIALS

3 oz. 3-ply crêpe wool in dark blue.
5 oz. 3-ply crêpe wool in light blue.
2 No. 8, 2 No. 10 and 2 No. 12 knitting needles.

MEASUREMENTS

Length, 18½ ins.
Bust size, 34 ins.
Sleeve seam, 5 ins.

TENSION

About 7½ sts. to 1 in. measured over patt. worked on No. 8 needles.

The Front.—Using No. 12 needles and light blue wool cast on 108 sts. and work 3 ins. in k. 1, p. 1 rib.

Change to No. 8 needles and the patt.:

1st row.—K. to end.

2nd row.—P. to end.

3rd row.—K. to end.

4th row.—P. 2, * sl. 1 p.w., p. 2, sl. 1 p.w., p. 6; rep. from * to end, ending last rep. with p. 2 instead of p. 6.

5th row.—K. 2, * sl. next st. off left-hand needle, draw up to form a long loop and leave at front of work, k. the third st. on left-hand needle, then k. the first and second sts. and sl. all sts. off the needle tog., now k. the dropped st. (the crossing of these 4 sts. will be referred to as "cross next 4 sts."), k. 6; rep. from * to end, ending last rep. with k. 2 instead of k. 6.

6th row.—P. to end.

7th row.—K. to end.

8th row.—P. 7, * sl. 1 p.w., p. 2, sl. 1 p.w., p. 6; rep. from * to last st., p. 1.

9th row.—K. 7, * cross next 4 sts., k. 6; rep. from * to last st., k. 1.

10th row.—P. to end.

The last 8 rows (i.e., rows 3rd to 10th inclusive) form the patt. Continue in patt., inc. 1 st. at both ends of next row and of every following 6th row until there are 128 sts. on the needle, working the extra sts. at each side in st.st. (1 row k., 1 row p.) until they can be included in the patt. Now continue in patt. across all sts. until work measures 12½ ins. from lower edge, ending with a 5th or 9th patt. row.

Shape Armholes thus:—Keeping continuity of the patt., cast off 8 sts. at beg. of each of the next 2 rows, then dec. 1 st. at both ends of every row until 98 sts. remain.

Continue in patt. across all sts. without shaping until work measures 17 ins. from lower edge, ending with row on wrong side of work.

Shape Neck and Shoulders thus:—

Next row.—Work in patt. across 38 sts., turn.

Continue in patt. on this set of sts., dec. 1 st. at neck edge on the next 8 rows. Proceed without shaping until work measures 18½ ins. from lower edge, ending at armhole edge.

Next row.—Cast off 10 sts., patt. to end.

Next row.—Patt. to end.

Rep. last 2 rows once.

Cast off remaining sts.

Return to main set of sts. and sl. centre 22 sts. on to a spare needle and leave for the collar, join wool to needle point and work on remaining 38 sts. to match the first side.

Be lavish with colour if you must save on wool. Look at this jumper! The original was knitted in light blue, but lacking sufficient for the whole jumper, sleeves and collar were knitted in dark blue.

The Front Neck Band and Roll Collar.— With right side of work facing and using No. 10 needles and light blue wool, commence at left shoulder edge and k. up 25 sts. along neck edge, k. 22 sts. from spare needle, pick up and k. 25 sts. along neck edge to right shoulder edge.

Work 18 rows in k. 1, p. 1 rib, thus ending with row on right side of work, so that wrong side of work will be facing when working next row.

Change to No. 8 needles and dark blue wool and k. 1 row.

Work 1 in. in k. 1, p. 1 rib.

Cast off loosely in rib.

The Back.— Work as given for front to completion of the armhole shapings (98 sts.). Continue in patt. across all sts. until work measures 18½ ins. from lower edge, ending with a p. row.

Shape Neck and Shoulders thus:—

Next row.— Cast off 10 sts., patt. across 24 sts., counting st. already on right-hand needle after casting off, turn.

Work on this set of sts. only thus:—

1st row.— K. 2 tog., patt. to end.

2nd row.— Cast off 10 sts., patt. to last 2 sts., k. 2 tog.

3rd row.— As 1st row.

Cast off remaining sts.

Return to main set of sts. and sl. centre 30 sts. on to a spare needle, join wool to needle point and work 1 row to armhole edge.

Proceed thus:—

1st row.— Cast off 10 sts., patt. to last 2 sts., k. 2 tog.

2nd row.— K. 2 tog., patt. to end.

Rep. last 2 rows once.

Cast off remaining sts.

The jumper is knitted in a crêpe wool and in an attractive "cross-stitch" stripe, easy-to-knit pattern that makes a firm fabric. A brooch worn in the collar will give the jumper an air!

The Back Neck Band and Roll Collar.—With right side of work facing and using No. 10 needles and light blue wool, commence at right shoulder edge and pick up and k. 9 sts. along neck edge, k. 30 sts. from spare needle, then k. up 9 sts. along neck edge to left shoulder edge (48 sts.).

Work in k. 1, p. 1 rib on these sts. exactly as given for front band and collar.

The Sleeves.—Using No. 10 needles and dark blue wool, cast on 84 sts. and work 1 in. in k. 1, p. 1 rib.

Change to No. 8 needles.

Continue in k. 1, p. 1 rib, inc. 1 st. at both ends of next row and of every following 4th row until there are 96 sts. on the needle.

Continue in rib without shaping until work measures 5 ins. from commencement.

Shape Top thus:—

1st row.—K. 2 tog., work in rib to last 2 sts., k. 2 tog.

2nd row.—As 1st row.

3rd row.—Work in rib to end.

Rep. the last 3 rows until 36 sts. remain. Cast off remaining sts. in rib.

To Make-up.—Press work very lightly on wrong side with a hot iron and damp cloth, taking care not to stretch the ribbing.

Join side seams. Sew up shoulder and collar seams, stitching the shoulder seam and about ¾ in. of the neck band on wrong

This is the long-sleeved, below the hipline version of the roll collar jersey. Notice how smart the ribbed sleeves, collar and the broad band at the bottom look in contrast with the pattern of the main part of the jersey.

It's an idea, isn't it?—to knit the crêpe wool jumper with long-ribbed sleeves—this time in the same colour as the main part of the garment to add colour contrast at neck, wrists and waist band, and to make it long by adding wide ribbing.

Stitch of the roll collar jersey.

side of work, then st. the collar seams neatly on right side of work, afterwards turning the collar down on to right side of work for about 2 ins.

Join sleeve seams and sew into armholes, matching seams with side seams.

Press all seams.

Or do you like it this way

This variation of the crêpe wool jumper has long sleeves, and a wide band of dark blue at the waist helps to lengthen it to the fashionable hip length.

MATERIALS

1 oz. 3-ply wool in dark blue.
7 oz. 3-ply wool in light blue.
2 No. 8, 2 No. 10 and 2 No. 12 knitting needles.

MEASUREMENTS

Length, 22 ins. Bust size, 34 ins.
Sleeve seam, 18 ins.

The Front.—Using No. 10 needles and light blue wool cast on 108 sts. and work in a rib of k. 1, p. 1 for 4 ins. Change to No. 12 needles and continue in rib for a further inch, ending with a row on the wrong side of the work; the work will now measure 5 ins. from the beginning. Change to dark blue wool and k. 1 row plain. Continue in rib in dark wool until work measures $6\frac{1}{2}$ ins. from the beginning, ending with a row on the wrong side of the work.

Now change to No. 8 needles and light blue wool and proceed in patt., as given in the instructions for the short-sleeved jersey in crêpe wool. Follow these instructions, commencing the armhole shapings when the work measures 16 ins. from the beginning, and the neck and shoulder shapings when the work measures 21 ins. ; cast off for shoulders when the work measures 22 ins. from the beginning of the work.

Work the front neck band and roll collar as given in the original instructions.

The Back.—Work as given for the front, commencing the armhole shapings when the work measures 16 ins. from the beginning, and the neck and shoulder shapings when the work measures 22 ins., following the instructions given for the short-sleeved jersey.

The back neck band and roll collar are worked from the original instructions beginning on page 48.

The Sleeve.—Using No. 10 needles and dark blue wool cast on 60 sts. and work in a rib of k. 1, p. 1 for 1 in. Change to light blue and continue in rib for a further 2 ins. Change to No. 8 needles, continuing in rib, inc. 1 st. at both ends of the next and every following 6th row until there are 96 sts. on the needle. Continue without shaping until sleeve measures 18 ins. from the beginning.

Shape the top as given in the instructions for the short-sleeved jersey.

Follow the original instructions for making up the jersey (*see* page 50).

Moss Stitch Cardigan

FOR SPORTS OR DRESS OCCASIONS

MATERIALS

10 oz. 4-ply wool.
2 No. 14, 2 No. 12 and 2 No. 8 knitting needles. 10 buttons.

MEASUREMENTS

Length, 21 ins.
Bust size, 34 ins. to 36 ins.
Sleeve seam, 18 ins.

TENSION

7 sts. to 1 in.

The Fronts (both alike).—Using No. 8 needles cast on 48 sts. and work in double moss st. as follows:—

1st row.—* K. 1, p. 1; rep. from * to end.

2nd row.—Rep. 1st row.

3rd row.—* P. 1, k. 1; rep. from * to end.

4th row.—Rep. 3rd row.

These 4 rows form the patt. used throughout the cardigan. Rep. them until work measures 4 ins. from the beginning. Change to No. 12 needles and continue in patt. until work measures 6 ins. from the beginning. Change back to No. 8 needles and inc. 1 st. at the beginning of the next and every following 6th row until there are 56 sts. on the needle. Continue without shaping until work measures 14½ ins. from the beginning, ending with a row at the increased edge.

Shape Armholes thus:—Cast off 7 sts. at the beginning of the next row. Then dec. 1 st. at this edge on every row until there are 42 sts. on the needle. Continue without shaping until work measures 19 ins. from the beginning, ending with a row at the centre front.

Shape Neck and Shoulders thus:—Dec. 1 st. at the beginning of the next row. Then dec. 1 st. at this edge on every row until there are 28 sts. on the needle. Continue without shaping until work measures 21 ins. from the beginning, ending with a row at the armhole edge.

Next row.—Cast off 7 sts., work to the end.

Next row.—Work to the end.

Rep. these 2 rows twice more, then cast off remaining sts.

The Back.—Using No. 8 needles cast on 104 sts. and work in patt. as given for the fronts until the work measures 4 ins. from the beginning. Change to No. 12 needles and continue until work measures 6 ins. from the beginning. Change back to

Details of the stitch of the cardigan.

Have it your own way—not an argument but an invitation. This cardigan can serve so many purposes. Wear it with a blouse underneath or with a little collar, or buttoned up to neck as here.

There's a secret about this cardigan. To shape it at the waist and
the wrists, change on to smaller needles to constrict the fabric.

No. 8 needles and inc. 1 st. at both ends of the next and every following 6th row until there are 118 sts. on the needle. Continue without shaping any further until work measures 14½ ins. from the beginning.

Shape Armholes thus:—Cast off 7 sts. at the beginning of each of the next 2 rows. Then dec. 1 st. at both ends of every row until there are 90 sts. on the needle. Continue without shaping until work measures 21 ins. from the beginning.

Shape Shoulders thus:—Cast off 7 sts. at the beginning of each of the next 8 rows. Cast off remaining sts.

The Sleeves.—Using No. 12 needles cast on 56 sts. and work in pattern as given for the fronts until the work measures 2 ins. Change to No. 8 needles and continue in patt., inc. 1 st. at both ends on the next and every following 6th row until there are 90 sts. on the needle. Continue without shaping until work measures 17 ins. from the beginning.

Shape Top thus:—Dec. 1 st. at both ends of every alternate row until there are 56 sts. on the needle. Then dec. 1 st. at both ends of every row until there are 20 sts. on the needle. Cast off.

The Right Front Band.—Using No. 14 needles cast on 9 sts. and work in g.st. (k.

every row) for $1\frac{1}{2}$ ins. Make a buttonhole in the next 2 rows as follows:—

Next row.—K. 3, cast off 3, k. to end.

Next row.—K. 3, cast on 3, k. to end.

Continue in g.st., making buttonholes at intervals of 2 ins. measured from the *cast-off* edge of the previous buttonhole, until the band measures 19 ins. from the

An old and tried friend pops up among the ingenious ideas presented to you for giving the cardigan a new face, as it were. Here is a classic twin set, and both are knitted from the cardigan instructions.

beginning, and 9 buttonholes have been worked. Cast off.

The Left Front Band.—Work exactly as given for the right front band omitting the buttonholes.

The Neck Band.—Using No. 14 needles cast on 124 sts. and work in g.st. for $\frac{1}{2}$ in. Make a buttonhole in the next 2 rows.

Next row.—K. 3, cast off 3, k. to the end.

Next row.—K. to the edge of the cast-off sts., cast on 3, k. 3. Continue in g.st. until the band measures 1 in. Cast off loosely.

The Sleeve Bands.—Using No. 14 needles cast on 9 sts. and work in g.st. for 7 ins. Cast off.

Make-up.—Press all knitting lightly on the wrong side, using a warm iron over a damp cloth. Join side, sleeve and shoulder seams and set the sleeves into the arm-holes. Stitch the right front band to the right front and the left band to the left front. Stitch the neck band to the edge of the neck and the sleeve bands to the bottom of the sleeves. Press all seams. Attach buttons to the left front to correspond with the buttonholes.

A very good partnership

Don't you think the cardigan looks well, worn as part of a twin set over the classic jersey? The jersey, by the way, can have a straight neckline as in the jumper on page 82 or the same round neck that the cardigan has itself. If you are making the cardigan part of a twin set, knit it in stocking stitch in 3-ply wool.

You can make the cardigan less fitting by omitting to knit the band at the waist on smaller needles.

These are the days when ingenuity counts for more than a large income when it comes to dressing oneself. The cardigan can be worn as a perfectly straight forward sports garment with a tweed skirt. You can wear quite a dressy blouse beneath it and decorate it with a brooch if you need it for a more formal occasion. You can make your friends swear they've never seen it before if you wear it with a skirt that contrasts or even argues with it. Give your clothes as many new faces as you can, and select styles that will last.

Larger Size Cardigan

FOR THE OLDER WOMAN

MATERIALS

12 oz. 4-ply wool.
2 No. 14, 2 No. 12 and 2 No. 8 knitting
needles. 10 buttons.

MEASUREMENTS

Length, 23 ins.
Bust size, 38 ins. to 40 ins.
Sleeve seam, 18 ins.

TENSION

7 sts. to 1 in.

The Fronts (both alike).—Using No. 8
needles cast on 56 sts. and work in double
moss st. as follows:—

1st row.—* K. 1, p. 1; rep. from * to
end.

2nd row.—Rep. 1st row.

3rd row.—* P. 1, k. 1; rep. from * to
end.

4th row.—Rep. 3rd row.

These 4 rows form the patt. used
throughout the cardigan. Rep. them until
work measures 4½ ins. from the beginning.
Change to No. 12 needles and continue in
patt. until work measures 6½ ins. Change
back to No. 8 needles and continue in
patt., inc. 1 st. at the beginning of the
next and every following 6th row until
there are 62 sts. on the needle. Continue
without shaping until work measures 16
ins. from the beginning, ending with a
row at the increased edge.

Shape Armholes thus:—Cast off 7 sts.
at the beginning of the next row. Then
dec. 1 st. at this edge on every row until
there are 48 sts. on the needle. Continue
without shaping until work measures
21 ins. from the beginning, ending with a
row at the centre front.

Shape Neck and Shoulders thus:—
Change to No. 12 needles and dec. 1 st.
at the beginning of the next row, and on
every row at this edge until there are 34 sts.
on the needle. Continue without shaping
until work measures 23 ins. from the
beginning, ending with a row at the armhole edge.

Next row.—Cast off 8 sts., work to the
end.

Next row.—Work to the end.
Rep. these 2 rows once more.

Next row.—Cast off 9 sts., work to the
end.

Next row.—Work to the end.
Cast off remaining sts.

The Back.—Using No. 8 needles cast
on 120 sts. and work in patt. as given for
the fronts until the work measures 4½ ins.
from the beginning. Change to No. 12
needles and continue in patt. until work
measures 6½ ins. Change back to No. 8
needles and continue in patt., inc. 1 st. at
both ends of the next and every following
6th row until there are 132 sts. on the
needle. Continue without shaping until
work measures 16 ins. from the beginning.

Shape Armholes thus:—Cast off 7 sts.
at the beginning of the next 2 rows.
Then dec. 1 st. at both ends of every
row until there are 104 sts. on the needle.
Continue without shaping until work
measures 21 ins. from the beginning.
Change to No. 12 needles and continue
without shaping until work measures 23
ins. from the beginning.

Shape Shoulders thus:—Cast off 8 sts.
at the beginning of the next 4 rows.
Then cast off 9 sts. at the beginning of
the next 4 rows.
Cast off remaining sts.

Keep the lines of your knitteds simple—and you'll be smart even if
approaching the forties in bust and hip measurements. If you need the
larger size in cardigans wear a blouse and aim for a softer neckline.

The Sleeves.—Using No. 12 needles cast on 62 sts. and work in patt. as given for the fronts until the work measures 2 ins. Change to No. 8 needles and inc. 1 st. at both ends of the next and every following 6th row until there are 98 sts. on the needle. Continue without shaping until sleeve measures 17 ins. from the beginning.

Shape Top thus :—Dec. 1 st. at both ends of every alternate row until 62 sts. remain. Then dec. 1 st. at both ends of the right front band, omitting the button-holes.

The Neck Band.—Using No. 14 needles cast on 130 sts. and work in g.st. for ½ in. Make a buttonhole in the next 2 rows.

Next row.—K. 3, cast off 3, k. to end.

Next row.—K. to edge of cast-off sts., cast on 3, k. 3.

Continue in g.st. until neck band measures 1 in. from the beginning. Cast off loosely.

The Sleeve Bands.—Using No. 14

*The classic shapes are excellent for every type of figure.
Here is the larger size in cardigans in a dark colour.*

every row until 26 sts. remain. Cast off.

The Right Front Band.—Using No. 14 needles cast on 9 sts. and work in g.st. (k. every row) for 1½ ins. Make a buttonhole in the next 2 rows as follows:—

Next row.—K. 3, cast off 3, k. to end.

Next row.—K. 3, cast on 3, k. to end.

Continue in g.st., making buttonholes at intervals of 2 ins. measured from the *cast-off* edge of the previous buttonhole, until the band measures 21 ins. and 10 buttonholes have been worked. Cast off.

The Left Front Band.—Work exactly as needles cast on 9 sts. and work in g.st. for 9 ins. Cast off.

Make-up.—Press all the knitting lightly on the wrong side, using a warm iron over a damp cloth. Join side, sleeve and shoulder seams and set the sleeves into the armholes. Stitch the right front band to the right front and the left band to the left front. Stitch the neck band to the edge of the neck and the sleeve band to the bottom of the sleeves. Press all seams. Attach buttons to the left front to correspond with the buttonholes.

Expressing warm sentiments: The letter? Undoubtedly, but we were thinking of the vest and pantie set. They're right—and they're so cosy. Come wind, come weather, you'll be warm and with that lovely "well-dressed all through" feeling.

Vest and Pantie Set

IN TWO-PLY WOOL

MATERIALS

5 oz. 2-ply wool for the set, or
3 oz. 2-ply wool for the vest, and
2 oz. 2-ply wool for the panties.
2 No. 8 and 2 No. 12 knitting needles.
¾ yd. elastic for the panties.

MEASUREMENTS

Vest: Length, 28 ins.
Bust size, 34 ins.
Panties: Waist to crutch, 14 ins.
To stretch to fit a 38-in. hip.

TENSION

Using No. 8 needles, 5½ sts. to 1 in.,
measured over the stretched rib.

THE VEST

The Back and Front Alike.—Using No.
8 needles cast on 105 sts. loosely with
double wool. Break off 1 strand of wool
and continue in single wool in moss st. for
1 in. With the right side of the work facing
continue in the following rib:—

1st row.—K. 2, * p. 1, k. 4; rep. from
* to last 3 sts., p. 1, k. 2.

2nd row.—P. 2, * k. 1, p. 4; rep. from
* to last 3 sts., k. 1, p. 2.

Rep. these 2 rows until the work measures 14 ins. from the beginning.

Change to No. 12 needles and continue
in rib until work measures 18½ ins. from
the beginning. Change back to No. 8
needles and continue in rib until work
measures 23 ins. from the beginning of
the work. Change to moss st. and work
1 in.

Shape Top and Make Shoulders thus:—
Next row.—Cast off 7, moss st. to end.

Next row.—Cast off 7, moss st. 45,
including st. already on needle when
casting off has been done, turn.

Continue working on these 45 sts., dec.
1 st. at both ends of every row until there
are 11 sts. on the needle. Continue working on these 11 sts. for the shoulder straps
until they measure 5 ins. Cast off in moss
st.

Rejoin wool at needle point and dec.
1 st. at the beginning of the next row,
work in moss st. to the end. Now continue
to shape this side to correspond with the
one already completed, dec. 1 st. at both
ends of the next row and every following
row until there are 11 sts. on the needle.
Complete this side to correspond with the
right side.

Make Up.—Press the work lightly on
the wrong side, using a warm iron over a
damp cloth. Join the side and shoulder
seams and work a picot edge round the
neck and armhole edges as follows:—

1 s.c. into the first st., * 3 ch., 1 d.c. into
the first of these ch., miss 1 st., 1 s.c. into
the next; rep. from * to end.

THE PANTIES

The Left Leg.—Using No. 8 needles and
double wool cast on 114 sts. Break off 1
strand of wool and change to No. 12
needles and work in a rib of k. 1, p. 1 for
¾ in., inc. 1 st. at the end of the last row
of ribbing. There are now 115 sts. on
the needle.

Change to No. 8 needles and continue
in rib as follows:—

1st row.—K. 2, * p. 1, k. 4; rep. from
* to last 3 sts., p. 1, k. 2.

2nd row.—P. 2, * k. 1, p. 4; rep. from * to last 3 sts., k. 1, p. 2. Rep. these 2 rows until work measures 3½ ins. from the beginning.

Begin Decreasings:—

Keeping the rib correct dec. 1 st. at both ends of the next and every following 6th row until there are 91 sts. on the needle. Continue without shaping until work measures 12½ ins. from the beginning, ending with a row on the wrong side of the work.

Shape Waist thus:—

Next row.—Work 45 sts. in rib, turn.

Next row.—Work in rib to end.

Next row.—Work 36 sts. in rib, turn.

Next row.—Work in rib to end.

Continue in this way, working 9 sts. less on every alternate row until all 45 sts. have been worked. Now change to No. 12 needles and dec. 1 st. at the beginning of the 1st row, work 2 ins. in rib of k. 1, p. 1.

Cast off very loosely in rib.

The Right Leg.—Work exactly as given

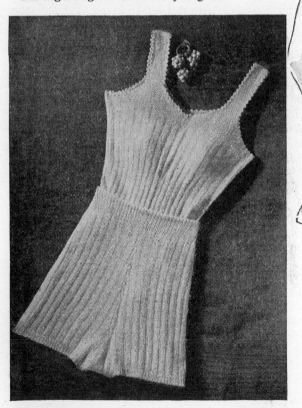

That odd ball of 2-ply— must do something with it. You knit the moss stitch bits with it, and thread ribbon where the colours meet.

The set is knitted in rib with bands of moss stitch to edge the panties, and a moss stitch yoke and straps for the vest finished with a picot edge.

for the left leg until the work measures 12½ ins. from the beginning, but ending with a row on the *right* side of the work. Shape the waist and complete the ribbing as given for the left leg.

The Gusset.—Using No. 8 needles and single wool cast on 1 st. K. 3 times into this st. Now work in st.st., inc. 1 st. at each end of every k. row 12 times. There are now 27 sts. on the needle. Now dec. 1 st. at each end of every k. row until 3 sts. remain. K. 3 tog. and fasten off.

Make-up.—Press the work on the wrong side, using a warm iron over a damp cloth. Join the back and front seams as far as the first decreasing, thus leaving 3½ ins. free for the gusset. Stitch the gusset into position, placing the cast-on and cast-off points of the gusset to the centre back and front. Make a casing for the elastic at the waist as follows:—

Commence at the centre front with 1 s.c. into the top edge of the ribbing, * 5 ch., 1 d.c. into the ribbing about ½ in. along and about ½ in. down, 5 ch., 1 d.c. into the top edge of ribbing about ½ in. along. Rep. from * to end.

Thread the elastic through this casing, fastening end securely. Press all seams.

Add a little colour

by adding it to your lingerie. Why have your vest and pantie set in one colour only! The top of the vest and the hem of the panties would look very charming in a deeper shade or in a contrasting pastel colour. Where the two colours meet, run a narrow ribbon through and finish off with little ribbon bows.

Vest and Panties

WITH A LACY LOOK !

Sometimes you can't help feeling that there is too much of this utility business about clothes. Especially does that go for underclothes. Even if we have to wear strictly practical frocks and suits that will go on until doomsday, we like to let ourselves go all frivolous when it comes to underclothes—and yet, we must keep warm. Well, here's the best that can be done in the way of meeting all requirements and you'll admit that it's a pretty good best. Here is the vest and panties set again—yet it is different. It is still practical, warm, snug and slim fitting and yet with its ribbon straps and its lace insertions as dainty as you please.

You can choose yourself whether you'll wear the vest inside or outside the panties. In either case they're designed to be completely unobtrusive under the most streamlined of frocks, and not a soul would guess that you're actually wearing hand-knitted woollen underwear!

MATERIALS
> 5 oz. 2-ply wool for the set, or
> 3 oz. 2-ply wool for the vest, and
> 2 oz. 2-ply wool for the panties.
> 2 No. 8 and 2 No. 12 knitting needles.
> 1 yd. ribbon for the shoulder straps.
> ¾ yd. elastic for the panties.

MEASUREMENTS
Vest: Length, 26 ins.
Bust size, 34 ins.
Panties: Waist to crutch, 14 ins.
To stretch to fit a 38-in. hip.

TENSION
Using No. 8 needles, 5½ sts. to 1 in., when measured over the stretched rib.

*Flowers to the fair! And a very charming picture she makes in the " glamour "
edition of the vest and pantie set. The vest has ribbon straps, instead of knitted,
as in the set on page 60, and an airy fairy lace inset on both of the garments.*

THE VEST

The Front.—Using No. 8 needles cast on 105 sts. loosely with double wool. Break off 1 strand of wool and continue in single wool in moss st. (k. 1, p. 1 on every row) for 1 in. With the right side of the work facing continue in rib as follows:—

1st row.—K. 2, * p. 1, k. 4; rep. from * to last 3 sts., p. 1, k. 2.

2nd row.—P. 2, * k. 1, p. 4; rep. from * to last 3 sts., k. 1, p. 2.

Rep. these 2 rows until work measures 14 ins. from the beginning.

Change to No. 12 needles and continue in rib for the waist until the work measures $18\frac{1}{2}$ ins. from the beginning. Change to No. 8 needles and work 1 more in. in rib, ending with a row on the wrong side of the work.

Begin Lacy Inset thus:—

1st row.—K. 2, *, p. 1, k. 4; rep. from * 5 times more, p. 1, then ** k. 1, m. 1, k. 2 tog., p. 1, k. 1, p. 1; rep. from ** 5 times more, k. 1, m. 1, k. 2 tog., then p. 1, *** k. 4, p. 1; rep. from *** to last 2 sts., k. 2.

2nd row.—P. 2, * k. 1, p. 4; rep. from * 5 times more, k. 1, then ** k. 1, m. 1, k. 2 tog., p. 1, k. 1, p. 1; rep. from ** 5 times more, k. 1, m. 1, k. 2 tog., then *** k. 1, p. 4; rep. from *** to last 3 sts., k. 1, p. 2.

Rep. these 2 rows until work measures 26 ins. from the beginning, ending with a row on the wrong side of the work. Cast off loosely.

The Back.—Work exactly as given for the front until the waist shaping has been worked and the work measures $18\frac{1}{2}$ ins. from the beginning. Change to No. 8 needles and continue in rib until work measures 28 ins. from the beginning, ending with a row on the wrong side of the work. Cast off the back very loosely.

This variation of the vest and pantie set has ribbon straps and a simple but very effective lace stitch insertion on the vest top and the panties. The vest and the panties are also finished with picot edging.

Make-up.—Press work on the wrong side, using a warm iron over a damp cloth. Join side seams. Finish the top of the vest with a picot edge as follows:—

1 s.c. into the first st., * 3 ch., 1 d.c. into the first of these ch., miss 1 st., 1 s.c. into the next; rep. from * to end.

Sew ribbon to the top in the required position at the back and front.

A detail of the lace stitch.

THE PANTIES

The Left Leg.—Using No. 8 needles cast on 115 sts. loosely with double wool. Break off 1 strand of wool and continue with single wool in moss st. for $\frac{1}{2}$ in. Then with right side of the work facing continue in rib as follows:—

1st row.—K. 2, * p. 1, k. 4; rep. from * 6 times more, p. 1, then ** k. 1, m. 1, k. 2 tog., p. 1, k. 1, p. 1; rep. from ** 5 times more, k. 1, m. 1, k. 2 tog., then *** p. 1, k. 4; rep. from *** to last 3 sts., p. 1, k. 2.

2nd row.—P. 2, * k. 1, p. 4; rep. from * 6 times more, k. 1, then ** k. 1, m. 1, k. 2 tog., p. 1, k. 1, p. 1; rep. from ** 5 times more, k. 1, m. 1, k. 2 tog., then *** k. 1, p. 4; rep. from *** to last 3 sts., k. 1, p. 2.

Rep. these 2 rows until work measures $3\frac{1}{2}$ ins. from the beginning.

Begin Decreasings: Keeping the rib and the lace inset correct dec. 1 st. at both ends of the next and every following 6th row until the work measures $6\frac{1}{2}$ ins. from the beginning. Continue working in the rib of k. 4, p. 1 right across, dec. as before until there are 91 sts. on the needle. Continue without shaping until work measures $12\frac{1}{2}$ ins. from the beginning, ending with a row on the wrong side of the work.

Shape Waist thus:—

Next row.—Work 45 sts. in rib, turn.

Next row.—Work in rib to the end.

Next row.—Work 36 sts. in rib, turn.

Next row.—Work in rib to end.

Continue in this way, working 9 sts. less on every alternate row until all 45 sts. have been worked.

Now change to No. 12 needles and dec. 1 st. at the beginning of the 1st row, work 2 ins. in a rib of k. 1, p. 1.

Cast off very loosely in rib.

The Right Leg.—Work exactly as given for the left leg until the work measures $12\frac{1}{2}$ ins. from the beginning, but ending with a row on the *right* side of the work. Shape the waist and complete the ribbing as given for the left leg.

The Gusset.—Using No. 8 needles and single wool cast on 1 st. K. 3 times into this st. Now work in st.st., inc. 1 st. at each end of every k. row 12 times. There are now 27 sts. on the needle. Now dec. 1 st. at each end of every k. row until 3 sts. remain. K. 3 tog., and fasten off.

Make-up.—Press the work on the wrong side, using a warm iron over a damp cloth. Join the back and front seams as far as the first decreasing, thus leaving $3\frac{1}{2}$ ins. free for the gusset. Stitch the gusset into position, placing the cast-on and cast-off points of the gusset to the centre back and front. Stitch the edges of the gusset to the leg edges, bringing the widest part of the gusset to the edge of the legs.

Make a casing for the elastic at the waist as follows:—

Commence at the centre front with 1 s.c. into the top edge of the ribbing, * 5 ch., 1 d.c. into the ribbing about $\frac{1}{2}$ in. along and about $\frac{1}{2}$ in. down, 5 ch., 1 d.c. into top edge of ribbing about $\frac{1}{2}$ in. along. Rep. from * to end.

Thread elastic through this casing, fastening end securely. Press all seams. Work a picot edge round the legs of the panties to match top of vest.

Lace Rib Camiknickers

IN TWO-PLY WOOL

MATERIALS

4 oz. of 2-ply wool.

2 No. 9 and 2 No. 12 knitting needles.

A fine crochet hook.

6 press studs.

1 yd. ribbon.

MEASUREMENTS

Length at side edge (not including gusset or shoulder straps), 24 ins.

Bust size, stretching to fit a 37-in. to 40-in. bust.

TENSION

About 7 sts. to 1 in. measured over slightly stretched pattern.

Front and Back Both Alike.—Using No. 9 needles cast on 28 sts. and work in g.st. (each row k.) for 3 ins. for the gusset.

Next row.—Cast on 64 sts. for one leg, k. to end of row, cast on 64 sts. for the second leg (156 sts.).

Continue in g.st. for 1 in., then work in following patt.:—

1st row.—* P. 2, k. 2 tog., m. 1, k. 1, m. 1, sl. 1, k. 1, p.s.s.o.; rep. from * to last 2 sts., k. 2.

2nd row.—* K. 2, p. 5; rep. from * to last 2 sts., p. 2.

3rd row.—* P. 2, k. 5; rep. from * to last 2 sts., p. 2.

4th row.—As the 2nd row.

These 4 rows form the patt. Continue in patt. shaping as follows:—

5th row.—As the 1st row.

6th row.—As the 2nd row.

7th row.—* P. 2, k. 5; rep. from * to 7 sts. before the centre 2 sts., p. 2, k. 3, k. 2 tog., p. centre 2 sts., k. 2 tog., k. 3, p. 2, ** k. 5, p. 2; rep. from ** to end.

8th row.—* K. 2, p. 5; rep. from * to 6 sts. before the centre 2 sts., k. 2, p. 4, k. 2 centre sts., p. 4, k. 2, ** p. 5, k. 2; rep. from ** to end.

9th row.—* P. 2, k. 2 tog., m. 1, k. 1, m. 1, sl. 1, k. 1, p.s.s.o.; rep. from * to 6 sts. before the centre 2 sts., p. 2, k. 2 tog., m. 1, k. 2, p. the 2 centre sts., k. 2, m. 1, sl. 1, k. 1, p.s.s.o., p. 2, ** k. 2 tog., m. 1, k. 1, m. 1, sl. 1, k. 1, p.s.s.o., p. 2; rep. from ** to end.

10th row.—As the 8th row.

11th row.—* P. 2, k. 5; rep. from * to 6 sts. before the centre 2 sts., p. 2, k. 2, k. 2 tog., p. 2 centre sts., k. 2 tog., k. 2, p. 2, ** k. 5, p. 2; rep. from ** to end.

12th row.—* K. 2, p. 5; rep. from * to 5 sts. before centre 2 sts., k. 2, p. 3, k. 2 centre sts., p. 3, k. 2, ** p. 5, k. 2; rep. from ** to end.

13th row.—* P. 2, k. 2 tog., m. 1, k. 1, m. 1, sl. 1, k. 1, p.s.s.o.; rep. from * to 5 sts. before the centre 2 sts., p. 2, k. 2 tog., m. 1, k. 1, p. 2 centre sts., k. 1, m. 1, sl. 1, k. 1, p.s.s.o., p. 2, ** k. 2 tog., m. 1, k. 1, m. 1, sl. 1, k. 1, p.s.s.o., p. 2; rep. from ** to end.

14th row.—As the 12th row.

15th row.—* P. 2, k. 5; rep. from * to 5 sts. before the centre 2 sts., p. 2, k. 1, k. 2 tog., p. 2 centre sts., k. 2 tog., k. 1, p. 2, ** k. 5, p. 2; rep. from ** to end.

16th row.—* K. 2, p. 5; rep. from * to 4 sts. before the centre 2 sts., k. 2, p. 2, k. 2 centre sts., p. 2, k. 2, ** p. 5, k. 2; rep. from ** to end.

17th row.—* P. 2, k. 2 tog., m. 1, k. 1,

"*This is perfect at any rate.*" And that doesn't go only for the stockings. She is wearing the smaller size in camiknickers, and you can see how attractive they look, and how perfectly fitting they are.

m. 1, sl. 1, k. 1, p.s.s.o.; rep. from * to 4 sts. before the centre 2 sts., p. 2, k. 2, p. 2 centre sts., k. 2, p. 2, ** k. 2 tog., m. 1, k. 1, m. 1, sl. 1, k. 1, p.s.s.o., p. 2; rep. from ** to end.

18th row.—As the 16th row.

Continue thus, working in patt. and dec. 1 st. on each side of the 2 centre p. sts. on next row and on every following 4th row until 114 sts. remain.

Continue without shaping until the work measures 13 ins. from the cast-on leg sts., ending with row on wrong side of work.

Change to No. 12 needles and work in k. 1. p. 1 rib for 3½ ins., ending with row on wrong side of work.

Change back to No. 9 needles and continue in the patt. for 6½ ins. (Work measures 23 ins. from cast-on leg sts.)

Work in g.st. for 1 in.

Cast off.

Work a second piece in the same way.

Make - up. — Press work lightly on wrong side with hot iron and damp cloth.

Join side seams.

Work the following picot edge all round top thus: Commence at a side seam with 1 s.c. into the seam, * 3 ch., 1 d.c. into the first of these ch., miss 1 st., 1 s.c. into next st.; rep. from * to end.

Work this edging all round lower edge of the legs. Overwrap the gusset pieces so that the gusset is double and fasten across with 3 press studs back and

front. Stitch the press studs to a ribbon facing for extra strength.

Sew on ribbon for shoulder straps in required position. Press the seams.

Have You a Smaller Size?

Camiknickers are specially recommended to those with larger figures, it is true, because they are all in one piece and there is nothing to make bulky folds round the waist and hips. Perhaps because of that they are universally popular, and so instructions for a smaller size are included.

Fine wool camiknickers are ideal for fuller figures which particularly need a straight, unbroken line, and no bulkiness around the hips, which vest and panties are apt to give.

MEASUREMENTS

Length at side edge (not including gusset or shoulder straps), $21\frac{1}{2}$ ins.

Bust size, stretching to fit 32-in. to 36-in. bust.

The smaller size takes just over 3 oz. so that 10 oz. will make three pairs.

Back and Front Both Alike.—Using No. 9 needles cast on 28 sts. for the gusset and work in g.st. for only $2\frac{1}{2}$ ins. instead of 3 ins.

Next row.—Cast on 57 sts. for one leg instead of 64 sts., k. to end of row, cast on 57 sts. for the second leg (142 sts.).

Work in g.st. for 1 in., then continue in patt. exactly as given for the larger size, dec. until only 100 sts. remain instead of 114 sts.

Continue without shaping until work measures 12 ins. instead of 13 ins. from the cast-on leg sts.

Change to No. 12 needles and work the waist ribbing as given, then change back to No. 9 needles and continue in patt. for 5 ins. instead of $6\frac{1}{2}$ ins. (Work measures $20\frac{1}{2}$ ins. from cast-on leg sts.)

Work 1 in. in g.st.

Cast off.

Work a second piece in the same way.

Make Up.—As given for the larger size camiknickers (*see* page 69).

If you don't feel like knitting your camiknickers in lace rib or you prefer something a little more solid, try knitting them in a fairly wide rib. Finish the neck and leg edges with picot edging.

The lace rib of the camiknickers.

Open Rib Stockings

IN TWO-PLY WOOL

MATERIALS

3 oz. of 2-ply wool.

2 No. 14 knitting needles.

2 No. 10 knitting needles.

MEASUREMENTS

Length from top to bottom of heel, 27 ins.

Length of foot, 9½ ins. (adjustable).

TENSION

9 sts. to 1 in.

N.B.—To fit a leg measuring more than 13½ ins. round the calf, substitute No. 13 needles for No. 14.

With No. 10 needles and the wool used double, cast on 102 sts.

Break off 1 strand of wool and change to No. 14 (or No. 13) needles, continuing with single wool.

Work in k. 1, p. 1 rib for 2 ins., then continue in following patt.:—

1st row.—K. 1, k. into the back of each of the next 2 sts., * m. 1, k. 2 tog., k. into the back of each of the next 3 sts.; rep. from * to last 4 sts., m. 1, k. 2 tog., k. into the back of the next st., k. 1.

2nd row.—K. 1, p. 2, * w.o.n., k. 2 tog., p. 3; rep. from * to end, ending the last rep. with p. 2 instead of p. 3.

These 2 rows form the fancy rib patt. Continue in patt. until the work measures 11 ins. ending with a second patt. row, then shape the leg thus:—

1st row.—K. 1, k. 2 tog., work in fancy

The stockings are knitted in an open rib which takes away the "solid" look that hand-knitted woollen stockings are apt to have. They are really meant for sports wear, and look grand worn turned down below the knees.

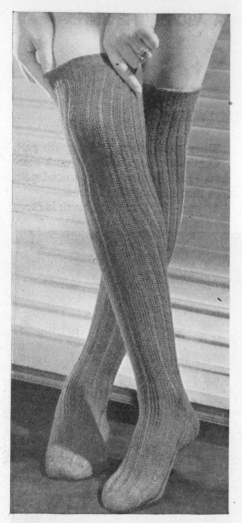

If you don't like the knee-length sock appearance, wear the stockings pulled right up. The pair only needs 3 oz. of wool.

rib to the last 4 sts., m. 1, k. 3 tog., k. 1.

Work 5 rows in patt. allowing for the decreased sts.

7th row.—K. 1, k. 2 tog., k. 1, k. into the back of each of the next 3 sts., work in fancy rib to the last 3 sts., k. 2 tog., k. 1.

Work 5 rows in patt. allowing for the decreased sts.

13th row.—K. 1, k. 2 tog., k. into the back. of the next 3 sts., work in fancy rib to the last 7 sts., m. 1, k. 2 tog., k. into the back of each of the next 2 sts., k. 2 tog., k. 1.

Work 5 rows in patt. allowing for the decreased sts.

19th row.—K. 1, k. 2 tog., k. into the back of each of the next 2 sts., work in fancy rib to the last 6 sts., m. 1, k. 2 tog., k. into the back of the next st., k. 2 tog., k. 1.

Work 5 rows in patt. allowing for the decreased sts.

25th row.—K. 1, k. 2 tog., k. into the back of the next st., work in fancy rib to the last 5 sts., m. 1, k. 2 tog., k. 2 tog., k. 1.

26th row.—As the second patt. row.

27th and 28th rows.—Rep. the first and second patt. rows once.

29th and 30th rows.—As the 27th and 28th rows.

Rep. the last 30 rows 3 times more (62 sts. remain).

Continue in patt. without shaping until the work measures 23 ins. from the cast-on edge, ending with a second patt. row, then commence the foot thus:—

Next row.—Work in fancy rib across 47 sts., turn.

Next row.—Work in fancy rib across 32 sts., turn.

Continue in patt. on these 32 sts. for $8\frac{1}{2}$ ins. ending with a second patt. row, then shape the toe. (*N.B.*—For a 9-in. foot work for only 8 ins., for a 10-in. foot work for 9 ins.)

Shape the Toe thus:—

Next row.—K. 1, sl. 1, k. 1, p.s.s.o., k. to last 3 sts., k. 2 tog., k. 1.

Next row.—P. to end.

Rep. last 2 rows 8 times.

Leave the remaining 14 sts. on a spare needle.

With right side of work facing, place the two sets of heel sts. on to one needle with the side seams in the centre forming the back seam.

Work for the heel thus:—

Next row.—K. to end.
Next row.—P. to end.
Rep. the last 2 rows 24 times.
Turn Heel thus:—
1st row.—K. 20, k. 2 tog., turn.
2nd row.—P. 11, p. 2 tog., turn.
3rd row.—K. 11, k. 2 tog., turn.
4th row.—As the 2nd row.
Rep. the last 2 rows until all of the side sts. are worked in and 12 sts. remain.

Now on to this same needle pick up and p. 15 sts. along side of heel flap, leaving the remaining 2 ins. of the flap to be stitched to top part of foot.

Next row.—K. to end, then k. up 15 sts. along the second side of the heel flap leaving the spare 2 ins. to match the first side (42 sts.).

Next row.—P. to end.

Shape Instep thus:—
1st row.—K. 1, sl. 1, k. 1, p.s.s.o., k. to last 3 sts., k. 2 tog., k. 1.
2nd row.—P. to end.
Rep. the last 2 rows 4 times (32 sts.).
Continue in st.st. until the work measures the same as the top part of the foot to the commencement of the toe shapings, ending with a p. row.

Shape the Toe as given for the top part of the foot, then graft or cast off the two sets of sts. tog. Make the second stocking in exactly the same way.

Make-up.—Press work lightly on the wrong side with a hot iron over a damp cloth, taking care not to stretch the fabric.

Join foot seams neatly, then narrowly backstitch the centre back of leg seams. Press the seams.

FOR GOOD FOOTWORK

Ribbed Ankle Socks

IN THREE-PLY WOOL

MATERIALS
2 oz. 3-ply wool.
2 No. 12 knitting needles.

MEASUREMENTS
Length of leg, 7 ins.
Length of foot, 9 ins. (adjustable).

TENSION
8½ sts. to 1 in. (measured over slightly stretched rib).

Cast on 67 sts. loosely and work in k. 1, p. 1 rib as follows:—

1st row.—Sl. 1, k. 1, * p. 1, k. 1; rep. from * to last st., k. 1.

2nd row.—Sl. 1, * p. 1, k. 1; rep. from * to end.

Rep. these 2 rows until the work measures 4½ ins. ending with a second row of rib, then divide for heel and foot thus:—

Next row.— Rib across 51 sts., turn.
Next row.—Rib 35 sts., turn.

Continue in rib on the 35 sts. for the instep for 6½ ins. for a 9-in. foot (for an 8-in. foot work for 5½ ins., for a 10-in foot work for 7½ ins.), ending with row on wrong side of work, then shape toe thus:—

Next row.—K. 1, sl. 1, k. 1, p.s.s.o., k. to last 3 sts., k. 2 tog., k. 1.

Next row.—P. to end.
Rep. last 2 rows 11 times.
Leave these 11 sts. on a spare needle. **Break off wool.**

Now sl. the two sets of heel sts. on to one needle with the side edges to the centre to form the back seam and with right side of work facing proceed thus:—

1st row.—* Sl. 1, k. 1; rep. from * to end.

2nd row.—P. to end.

Rep. these 2 rows 18 times.

Turn Heel thus:—

1st row.—K. 20, k. 2 tog., turn.

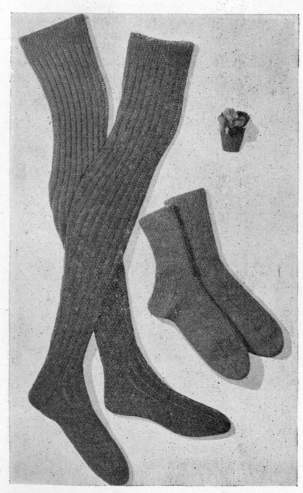

The stockings are made in an open rib and are knitted in 2-ply wool. The socks are knitted in 3-ply in a close rib, so that they fit snugly round the ankle. They are meant to be worn without turnover tops.

2nd row.—P. 9, p. 2 tog., turn.

3rd row.—K. 9, k. 2 tog., turn.

4th row.—As the 2nd row.

Rep. the last 2 rows until all the side sts. are worked off.

Next row.—K. to end, then pick up and k. 16 sts. along side of heel flap, leaving about ½ in. of flap free to be stitched to top part of foot.

Next row.—P. to end, then pick up and p. 16 sts. down second side of heel flap, leaving the last ½ in. free to match the first side.

Work on these 42 sts. thus:—

Next row.—K. 1, sl. 1, k. 1, p.s.s.o., k. to last 3 sts., k. 2 tog., k. 1.

Next row.—P. to end.

Rep. the last 2 rows 3 times.

Continue in st.st. on 34 sts. until the work measures the same as the top part of the foot to the commencement of the toe shaping, ending with a p. row.

Shape Toe thus:—

Next row.—K. 1, sl. 1, k. 1, p.s.s.o., k. to last 3 sts., k. 2 tog., k. 1.

Next row.—P. to end.

Rep. the last 2 rows 10 times.

Next row.—K. 1, sl. 1, k. 1, p.s.s.o., k. to end.

Next row.—P. to end.

Now graft or cast off the two sets of toe sts. tog.

Make a second sock in the same way.

Make-up.—Press work lightly with hot iron and damp cloth.

Join foot and leg seams neatly.

Press the seams.

Cardigan and Jumper

IN TWO-PLY WOOL

MATERIALS

6 oz. 2-ply wool.
2 No. 14, 2 No. 12 and 2 No. 11 knitting needles.
11 buttons.

MEASUREMENTS

Length, 19 ins.
Bust size, 34 ins.
Sleeve seam, 18 ins.

TENSION

Using No. 11 needles, 8 sts. to 1 in.

The Back.—Using No. 12 needles cast on 127 sts. and proceed in patt. as follows:

1st row.—P. 3, * w.r.n., p. 4; rep. from * to end of row.

2nd row.—* K. 3, w.fd., sl. 1 p.w., dropping the made st. of the previous row, w.o.n.; rep. from * to last 3 sts., k. 3.

3rd row.—* P. 3, sl. the next 2 sts. p.w., w.r.n.; rep. from * to last 3 sts., p. 3.

4th row.—* K. 3, w.fd., sl. next 3 sts. p.w., w.o.n.; rep. from * to last 3 sts., k. 3.

5th row.—* P. 3, sl. next 4 sts. p.w., w.r.n.; rep. from * to last 3 sts., p. 3.

6th row.—* K. 3, (p. 1, k. 1, p. 1) through the next group of 5 sts.; rep. from * to last 3 sts., k. 3.

7th row.—P. 2, * k. 2 tog., p. 1, sl. 1 k.w., k. 1, p.s.s.o., p. 1; rep. from * to last 2 sts., p. 2.

8th row.—K.

These 8 rows form the patt. used throughout the cardigan. Rep. them until work measures 3 ins. from the beginning, ending with the 8th row of patt. Change

to No. 11 needles and begin side increasings. Inc. 1 st. at both ends of the next and every following 16th row until 4 increasings have been worked on each side. These 4 extra sts. can now be incorporated in the patt. Continue without shaping until work measures 12 ins. from beginning, ending with the 7th row of patt.

Shape Armholes thus: Cast off 7 sts. at beginning of next 2 rows. Keeping patt. correct dec. 1 st. at the end of every row until 103 sts. remain. Continue without shaping until work measures $17\frac{1}{2}$ ins., ending with the 7th row of patt.

Shape Neck thus:—

Next row.—K. 31, cast off 49, k. to end.

Continue working on this last set of 31 sts. until work measures 19 ins. (about 8 rows), ending at armhole edge.

Shape Shoulders thus:—

Next row.—Cast off 8 sts., work in patt. to end.

Next row.—Work to end.

Rep. these 2 rows twice more, then cast off remaining sts.

Rejoin wool at needle point and work on the remaining 31 sts. to correspond.

Pocket Linings.—Using No. 11 needles cast on 30 sts. and work in st.st. for 3 ins. ending with a p. row. Leave these 30 sts. on a spare needle for the present. Work a second lining to correspond.

The Left Front.—Using No. 12 needles cast on 59 sts. and work in patt. as given for the back for 3 ins., ending with the 8th patt. row. Change to No. 11 needles and begin side increasings.

Next row.—Inc. in 1st st., work in patt. to end. Work 6 rows in patt. without inc.

A Breath of Spring: That was the idea in mind when this cardigan was designed. Not too heavy in design or stitch yet warm and close fitting, it is ideal for the "'tween seasons" part of the year.

This simple stitch makes an open yet firm fabric. Square neck and pocket borders are worked in garter stitch. Gilt buttons make a gay finish.

Insert Pocket thus:—

Next row.—K. 18, cast off 30, k. to end.

Next row.—Patt. 12, k. across 30 sts. for pocket lining from spare needle, patt. to end.

Work 7 rows in patt. without inc. Then inc. 1 st. at the beginning of the next row and every following 16th row until 4 increasings have been worked. These sts. may now be incorporated in the patt. Continue without shaping until work measures 12 ins. from beginning, ending with the 8th patt. row, at armhole edge.

Shape Armhole thus:—

Next row.—Cast off 7, patt. to end.

Now dec. 1 st. at the end of the next and every alternate row until 51 sts. remain. Continue without shaping until work measures 15½ ins., ending with the 7th patt. row, at centre front.

Shape Neck: Cast off 20 sts. at beginning of next row, k. to end. Continue in patt. on remaining 31 sts. without shaping until work measures 19 ins. from beginning, ending with the 8th patt. row at armhole edge.

Shape Shoulders thus:—

Next row.—Cast off 8 sts., work in patt. to end.

Next row.—Work in patt. to end.

Rep. these 2 rows twice more. Cast off remaining sts.

The Right Front.—Using No. 12 needles cast on 59 sts. and work in patt. as given for the back until the work measures 3 ins., ending with the 8th patt. row. Change to No. 11 needles and begin side increasings.

Next row.—Patt. to end, inc. in last st. Work 6 rows in patt. without shaping.

Insert Pocket thus:—

Next Row.—K. 12, cast off 30, k. to end.

Next row.—Patt. 18 sts., k. across 30 sts. for pocket lining, from spare needle, patt. to end.

Work 7 rows in patt. without shaping. Then inc. 1 st. at the end of the next row and every following 16th row, until 4 increasings have been worked, and complete the front as given for left front, beg. the armhole shaping at the end of the 7th row of patt. and the neck shaping at the end of the 8th row of patt.

The Sleeves. — Using No. 12 needles cast on 59 sts. and work in patt. as given for back for 3 ins., ending with the 8th row of patt. Change to No. 11 needles and continue in patt., inc. 1 st. at both ends of every 8th row until there are 99 sts. on needle. Continue without shaping until work measures 18 ins. from beginning, ending with the 8th row of the pattern.

A detail of the cardigan stitch. This makes a light firm fabric.

Shape Top: Cast off 7 sts. at beginning of each of next 2 rows. Now dec. 1 st. at the end of every row until 31 sts. remain. Cast off.

Work a second sleeve to correspond.

Pocket Bands.—Using No. 14 needles cast on 42 sts. and work in g.st. for 1 in. Cast off. Make a second band to correspond.

Left Front Band and Neck Band.—

Using No. 14 needles cast on 14 sts. and work in g.st. for 15½ ins.

Next row.—K. 14, turn and cast on 30 sts. for neck band.

Work on these 44 sts. for 1 in., ending with a row at centre front.

Next row.—Cast off 32 sts. k. to end. Continue on these 12 sts. for a further 3 ins., finishing with a row at neck edge. Place these sts. on a spare needle and leave for present.

Right Front and Neck Band. — Using No. 14 needles cast on 14 sts. and work in g.st. for 1 in. Make a buttonhole in the next 2 rows as follows:—

Next row.—K. 4, cast off 6, k. to end.

Next row.—K. 4, cast on 6, k. to end.

Continue in g.st., making a buttonhole every 1½ ins. measured from the cast-off edge of the previous buttonhole until 10 buttonholes have been worked. Work a further 1 in. Band should now measure 15½ ins. from beg.

Next row.—K. 14, turn and cast on 30 sts. for neck band of the cardigan.

Work for ½ in. on these 44 sts. and make a buttonhole in the neck band in the next 2 rows.

Continue in g.st. until neck band measures 1 in. from cast-on edge, ending with a row at centre front.

Next row.—Cast off 32 sts., k. to end. Continue on these 12 sts. for a further 3 ins., finishing with a row at neck edge.

Giving a backwards glance—just to admire the buttoned effect. Here is the jersey knitted from the same instructions as the cardigan, but turned back to front. Notice how well the simple lines suit the older woman.

Next row.—Cast on 36 sts., k. across 12 sts. left on spare needle for left front band (60 sts.).

Work in g.st. on these 60 sts. for 1 in. Cast off.

Make-up.—Press all knitting lightly on the wrong side, using a warm iron over a damp cloth. Join side, shoulders and sleeve seams, and st. sleeves into armholes. Sew pocket linings into position on the wrong side, and sew pocket bands to the tops of pockets on the right side, and to cardigan along side edges. St. front and neck bands to cardigan, slightly stretching the bands. Attach buttons to left front to correspond to buttonholes. Press all seams.

Turn Your Back

if you want the world to get the real joy of this jumper. It's the same design as the cardigan except that you wear it, so to speak, back to front. Just omit the pockets, and all the buttons go down the back. The high, square neck is a very good line for most people, and you'll do all the buttoning up and unbuttoning with a good grace when you remember that it does prevent you from pulling the neck out of shape.

The jumper is worked from the same instructions as the cardigan—but it is 3 ins. longer.

You can make it a bigger size by working it on larger sized needles. This plan was followed with the jersey photographed on page 79. The fabric obtained by knitting in this particular stitch is very elastic, too, and will stretch quite a lot if it is called upon to do so.

It is interesting too, to notice that the simple, square-necked design is equally as charming for an older, bigger woman, as it is for quite a young girl. The girl makes the neckline a little more severe by wearing a tailored shirt blouse underneath her cardigan. The older woman softens the neckline by wearing a string of pearls.

The cardigan and jersey were called a twin set, and maybe you're wondering where that comes in, since they appear to be about as separate as they can be. If you knit the jersey the same size as the cardigan and do not add the extra 3 ins. to the length, the two can be worn as a very charming twin set. If you adopt this idea, see that the buttons on the back of the jersey are fairly flat, or they will make too much of a bulge under the cardigan. You may prefer to fasten the back with press studs, or have only two or three buttons at the top.

Here are instructions for a jersey made to the same measurements as the cardigan, but with 3 extra ins. on to the length.

The Front.—Cast on 127 sts. as for the back of the cardigan, but using No. 11 needles and work for a depth of 3 ins. in patt. Change to No. 12 needles and work exactly as given, from commencement of instructions, i.e., after the 3 ins. on 11's work 3 ins. on 12's, then change to 11's and begin side increasings. Allow for the extra 3 ins. by shaping armholes at 15 ins. instead of 12 ins., neck at 20½ ins. instead of 17½ ins. and shoulders at 22 ins. instead of 19 ins.

The Back.—Work this in two pieces as the front of the cardigan, working an extra 3 ins. at the bottom on No. 11 needles, and omitting the pockets. In this case, of course, the instructions for the "left front" of the cardigan will apply to the "right back" of the jumper.

Work exactly as given for the cardigan fronts, but allowing for the extra 3 ins., until the armhole shapings have been worked. Then continue without shaping until work measures 20½ ins. from the beginning, ending with a row at front edge.

Shape Neck: Cast off 20 sts. Continue on remaining 31 sts. until work measures 22 ins. from the beginning, ending with a row at the armhole edge.

Shape shoulders as given in instructions for cardigan fronts.

The Sleeves.—Work exactly as in the

instructions given for the cardigan.

The Right Back Band and Neck Band.—
Using No. 14 needles cast on 14 sts. and
work in g.st. for $\frac{1}{4}$ in. Make a buttonhole
in the next 2 rows as given in instructions
for cardigan. Continue in g.st., making a
buttonhole every $1\frac{3}{4}$ ins. measured from
the cast-off edge of the previous one, until
the work measures $20\frac{1}{2}$ ins. when slightly
stretched and the 12th buttonhole has
been worked. Work another 1 in. in g.st.,
ending with a row at the centre front.

Next row.—K. 14, turn and cast on 30
sts. for neck band.

Work on these 44 sts. for $\frac{3}{4}$ in. Make a
buttonhole. Work a further $\frac{1}{4}$ in. on these
sts., ending with a row at centre front.

Next row.—Cast off 32 sts., k. to end.

Continue on these 12 sts. for $1\frac{1}{2}$ ins.,
ending with a row at neck edge.

Place these sts. on a spare needle and
leave for the present.

The Left Back and Neck Band.—Work
as given for the right back band, omitting
the buttonholes, until the shoulder is
reached, finishing with a row at the neck
edge.

Next row.—Cast on 36 sts., k. across
12 sts. left on spare needle for right back
band. There are now 60 sts. on the needle.
Work in g.st. on these 60 sts. for 1 in.
Cast off.

Make up the jumper in the same way
as the cardigan, attaching the buttons, to
correspond to the buttonholes, to the
left back band.

*The jersey—the twin of the cardigan on page 76, buttons down
the back, and has a high, square neck. Made in the same size
as the cardigan the two can be worn together as a set.*

The Classic Jumper

IN TWO-PLY WOOL

MATERIALS

6 oz. 2-ply wool.

2 No. 12, 2 No. 13 and 2 No. 14 knitting needles.

1½ yds. ribbon. 7 buttons.

MEASUREMENTS

Length, 21 ins. Bust size, 34 ins.

Sleeve seam, 18 ins.

TENSION

Using No. 12 needles, 9 sts. to 1 in.

The Back.—Using No. 12 needles cast on 132 sts. and work in a rib of k. 1, p. 1 for 1 in. Change to st.st. and continue until work measures 2 ins. from the beginning. Change to No. 13 needles and continue until work measures 4 ins. from the beginning. Change to No. 14 needles and continue until work measures 6 ins. from the beginning. Change to No. 12 needles and commence the side increasings, inc. 1 st. at both ends of the next and every following 6th row until there are 156 sts. on the needle. Continue without shaping until work measures 15 ins. from the beginning, ending with a p. row.

Shape Armholes thus : Cast off 9 sts. at beginning of each of the next 2 rows. Then dec. 1 st. at both ends of every row until there are 118 sts. on the needle.

Divide for Neck thus :—

Next row.—K. 59, turn. Place the remaining sts. on a spare needle and leave for the present, and continue working on these 59 sts. without shaping until work measures 21 ins. from the beginning, ending with a row at the armhole edge.

Shape Shoulders thus :—

Next row.—Cast off 10 sts., work to end.

Next row.—Work to end.

Rep. these 2 rows once.

Next row.—Cast off 9 sts., work to end.

Next row.—Work to end.

Cast off remaining 30 sts.

Rejoin wool at needle point and work the other back to correspond.

The Front.—Work exactly as given for the back until the armhole shapings have been completed and there are 118 sts. on needle. Continue on these 118 sts. without shaping until work measures 21 ins. from the beginning.

Shape Shoulders thus: Cast off 10 sts. at beginning of each of the next 4 rows. Cast off 9 sts. at the beginning of each of the next 2 rows. Cast off remaining 60 sts.

The Sleeves.—Using No. 14 needles cast on 62 sts. and work in a rib of k. 1, p. 1 for 1 in. Change to No. 12 needles and continue in st.st. until work measures 3 ins. from the beginning. Now begin side increasings by inc. 1 st. at the beginning and end of the next and every following 6th row until there are 108 sts. on the needle. Continue without shaping until work measures 18 ins. from the beginning.

Shape Top thus : Dec. 1 st. at both ends of every alternate row until 60 sts. remain. Then dec. 1 st. at both ends of every row until 18 sts. remain. Cast off.

Work a second sleeve to correspond.

Make-up.—Press all knitting, with the exception of the ribbing, with a warm iron over a damp cloth. Bind the neck and shoulders of the jersey with a ribbon bind

Plain stocking stitch with a plain straight neckline: where does it differ from the rest? Well, look at the ribbon-bound shoulder-line and neck. Just a little touch, but it makes all the difference.

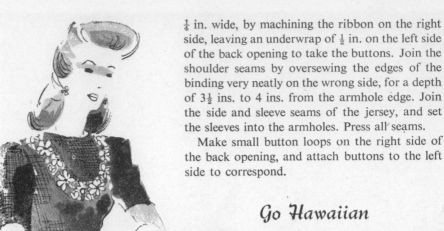

¼ in. wide, by machining the ribbon on the right side, leaving an underwrap of ½ in. on the left side of the back opening to take the buttons. Join the shoulder seams by oversewing the edges of the binding very neatly on the wrong side, for a depth of 3½ ins. to 4 ins. from the armhole edge. Join the side and sleeve seams of the jersey, and set the sleeves into the armholes. Press all seams.

Make small button loops on the right side of the back opening, and attach buttons to the left side to correspond.

Go Hawaiian

Honestly, nothing is lacking except the ukelele, and it's so simple too. You embroider a leis (Hawaiian for garland of flowers) in bright-coloured lazy daisies—the brighter, the better—on the front of your plain, dark-coloured jumper. The result ought to give you a kind of Sunny South Seas feeling.

The result can be seen in the sketch on the left. It has the same straight neckline as the classic and opens down the back in the same way but the neckline and the placket at the back of the jersey are not bound with ribbon.

By the way, you'd like to see what the opening of the jumper is like, wouldn't you? It opens down the back with seven little buttons.

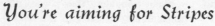

You're aiming for Stripes

One way and another stripes are in the air. If you wish to brighten the outlook a bit you might try this method with the plain classic jersey. Use six different colours—1 oz. of each. In these hard times, who cares if they're not the six colours in the world that agree best together. Just try to keep actual combatants apart. Clothes, and that includes knitteds, must be simple and enduring these days, but they don't have to be dreary. Try to get as much colour into them as you can.

If you like your styles simple and your colours strong, this is the jersey for you. It is knitted in six fairly wide stripes each a different colour.

Classic in Checks

First reaction on seeing this lively edition of the plain classic is "How marvellous! How lovely! How difficult!" The first two statements will pass. The last isn't true. It's simple and can be achieved by any person past the "knit one, knot one" stage.

For this jersey a specially fine 2-ply yarn of very light weight was used as the check pattern involves the use of double yarn. If an ordinary 2-ply yarn were used, as in the plain jersey, the result would be a much heavier fabric, though the size of the garment will be found to be the same.

The original check jersey used 1½ oz. of fine 2-ply wool in each of 3 colours, red, green and yellow; if ordinary 2-ply wool

were used you would require about 3 oz. of each colour. In either case you will need 2 No. 12, 2 No. 13 and 2 No. 14 needles.

TENSION

Using the yarn double, 9 sts. to 1 in.

Note.—The colour not in use should be woven loosely across the back of the work (*see* BASIC PRINCIPLES OF KNITTING, FAIR ISLE KNITTING).

Front and Back (both alike).—Using No. 12 needles and green wool cast on 132 sts. and work in a rib of k. 1, p. 1 for 1 in. Change to check patt. as follows:—

1st row.—* Using red and green wool tog., k. 12, using red wool only, k. 12;

rep. from * to last 12 sts., using red and green wool, k. 12.

2nd row.—* Using red and green wool, p. 12, using red wool, p. 12; rep. from * to last 12 sts., using red and green wool, p. 12.

Rep. these 2 rows 7 times more. Change to No. 13 needles.

17th row.—* Using green wool, k. 12, using green and yellow wool, k. 12; rep. from * to last 12 sts., using green wool, k. 12.

18th row.—* Using green wool, p. 12, using green and yellow wool, p. 12; rep. from * to last 12 sts., using green wool, p. 12.

Rep. these 2 rows 7 times more.

33rd row.—* Using red and yellow wool, k. 12, using yellow wool, k. 12; rep. from * to last 12 sts., using red and yellow wool, k. 12.

34th row.—* Using Red and yellow wool, p. 12, using yellow wool, p. 12; rep. from * to last 12 sts., using red and yellow wool, p. 12.

Rep. these 2 rows 7 times more. These 48 rows form the patt.

Change to No. 14 needles and rep. rows 1 to 16. Change to No. 12 needles and, keeping the coloured squares correct, continue in patt., inc. 1 st. at both ends of the next and every following 6th row until there are 156 sts. on the needle. Continue without shaping until work measures 15 ins. from the beginning.

Shape Armholes thus : Cast off 9 sts. at beginning of each of the next 2 rows. Then dec. 1 st. at both ends of every row until 118 sts. remain. Continue without shaping until work measures 21 ins. from the beginning.

Detail of the arrangement of the checks.

Shape Shoulders thus : Cast off 10 sts. at beginning of each of the next 6 rows. Change to green wool and work in rib of k. 1, p. 1 on the remaining 58 sts. for ½ in. Cast off very loosely in rib.

The Sleeves.—Using No. 12 needles and green wool cast on 62 sts. and work in a rib of k. 1, p. 1 for 1 in. Continue in check patt. as follows:—

1st row.—Using red and green wool, k. 13, * using red wool, k. 12, using red and green wool, k. 12; rep. from * to last st., k. 1.

2nd row. — Using red and green wool, p. 13, * using red wool, p. 12, using red and green wool, p. 12; rep. from * to last st., p. 1.

Rep. these 2 rows 7 times more.

17th row.—Using green wool, k. 13, * using green and yellow wool, k. 12, using green wool, k. 12; rep. from * to last st., k. 1.

18th row.—Using green wool, p. 13, * using green and yellow wool, p. 12, using green wool, p. 12; rep. from * to last st., p. 1.

Rep. these 2 rows 5 times more.

29th row.—Using green wool, inc. in first st., * k. 12, using green and yellow wool, k. 12; rep. from * to last 13 sts., using green wool, k. 12, inc. in last st.

30th row.—Using green wool, p. 14, * using green and yellow wool, p. 12, using green wool, p. 12; rep. from * to last 2 sts., p. 2.

31st row.—Using green wool, k. 14, * using green and yellow wool, k. 12, using green wool, k. 12; rep. from * to last 2 sts., k. 2.

32nd row.—Rep. 30th row.

33rd row.—Using yellow wool, k. 2, *

"It's a very bright outlook!" It certainly is, and you might say,
*variegated, too. The check edition of the classic is knitted in
only three colours but so woven and blended as to seem more.
The yarn of which it is made is especially fine, and is used double.*

using yellow and red wool, k. 12, using yellow wool, k. 12; rep. from * to last 14 sts., using yellow and red wool, k. 12, using yellow wool, k. 2.

34th row.—Using yellow wool, p. 2, * using yellow and red wool, p. 12, using yellow wool, p. 12; rep. from * to last 14 sts., using yellow and red wool, p. 12, using yellow wool, p. 2.

35th row.—Using yellow wool inc. in first st., k. 1, * using yellow and red wool, k. 12, using yellow wool, k. 12; rep. from * to last 14 sts., using yellow and red wool, k. 12, using yellow wool, k. 1, inc. in last st.

36th row.—Using yellow wool, p. 3, * using yellow and red wool, p. 12, using yellow wool, p. 12; rep. from * to last 14 sts., using yellow and red wool, p. 12, using yellow wool, p. 3.

37th row.—Using yellow wool, k. 3, * using yellow and red wool, k. 12, using yellow wool, k. 12; rep. from * to last 14 sts., using yellow and red wool, k. 12, using yellow wool, k. 3. Rep. last 2 rows once more, then rep. 36th row.

Keeping the patt. correct in this way continue in check patt. inc. 1 st. at both ends of the next and every following 6th row until there are 108 sts. on the needle. Continue without shaping until the work measures 18 ins. from the beginning.

Shape Top thus: Dec. 1 st. at both ends of every alternate row until 60 sts. remain; then dec. 1 st. at both ends of every row until 18 sts. remain. Cast off.

Make-up.—Press all the work lightly on the wrong side, using a warm iron over a damp cloth. Join side, shoulder and sleeve seams. Stitch sleeves into armholes. Press all seams.

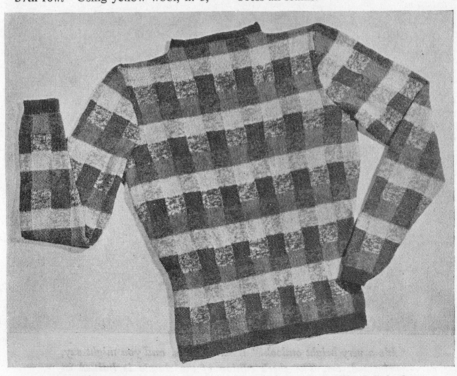

The check version of the classic was knitted in a specially fine 2-ply, and a double yarn was used which gives the variegated appearance.

Twisted Yoke Jumper

IN THREE COLOURS

MATERIALS

4 oz. 2-ply wool in main colour, a small quantity of 2-ply wool in 3 other colours for the yoke.

2 No. 10 and 2 No. 14 knitting needles.

MEASUREMENTS

Length, 19 ins.
Bust size, 34 ins.
Sleeve seam, 5 ins.

TENSION

Using No. 10 needles, 8 sts. to 1 in.

The Back.—Using No. 10 needles cast on 115 sts. Change to No. 14 needles and work in the following patt., which is used throughout the jumper, except the yoke.

1st row (right side of work facing).—P.

2nd row.—* K. 3, p. 1; rep. from * to last 3 sts., k. 3.

Rep. these 2 rows until work measures 4 ins. from the beginning. Change to No. 10 needles and continue in patt., inc. 1 st. at both ends of the next and every following 6th row, until there are 137 sts. on the needle. Continue without further shaping until work measures 13 ins. from the beginning.

Shape Armholes thus : Cast off 8 sts. at beginning of each of the next 2 rows. Then dec. 1 st. at both ends of the next 8 rows. There will now be 105 sts. on the needle. Continue without shaping until work measures 19 ins. from the lower edge.

Shape Shoulders thus : Cast off 8 sts. at beginning of each of the next 8 rows. Cast off remaining sts.

The Front.—Work exactly as given for the back until the armhole shaping has been completed and there are 105 sts. on the needle. Work in patt. for 1 in. beyond the end of the armhole shaping on these sts.

Shape Yoke thus : Cast off 32 sts. at beginning of each of the next 2 rows. Then dec. 1 st. at both ends of the next 3 rows; now dec. 1 st. at both ends of every alternate row until 25 sts. remain. Cast off.

The Sleeves.—Using No. 10 needles cast on 87 sts. Change to No. 14 needles and work in patt. as given for the back for 1½ ins. Change to No. 10 needles and continue in patt., inc. 1 st. at both ends of the next and every following 4th row until there are 101 sts. on the needle. Continue without shaping until work measures 5 ins. from the beginning.

Shape Top thus: Cast off 8 sts. at beginning of each of next 2 rows. Then dec. 1 st. at both ends of every alternate row until 29 sts. remain. Cast off.

The Yoke Bands.—Using No. 14 needles and one of the colours to be used for the yoke, cast on 22 sts. and work in the following patt.:—

1st row.—* K. 1, w.fd., sl. 1, w.b.; rep. from * to end of row.

2nd row.—* P. 1, w.b., sl. 1, w.fd.; rep. from * to end of row.

Rep. these 2 rows until band measures 17 ins. from the beginning. Cast off.

Work 2 more bands in the other 2 colours in the same way.

Make-up.—Press all knitting lightly on the wrong side, using a warm iron over a

"I'm dressed up with a big bow!" And it makes all the difference to this simple jersey, which, apart from the yoke, is plain and unadorned. The yoke is knitted in one straight piece, twisted and sewn in place.

The rib stitch of the twisted yoke jersey.

The lace yoke of the evening jersey.

Detail of the stitch of the twisted yoke.

damp cloth. Join side and sleeve seams.

To make yoke, begin at the left-hand side, and with the wrong side of the bands facing, join the 3 bands together for 5 ins. Now plait the centre 7 ins. of the bands, finishing at a point 5 ins. from the opposite end, so that the band which was at the top of the yoke on the left-hand side will be at the bottom on the right-hand side, and the bottom band will be the top, leaving the centre band the same.

Stitch this yoke to the shaped top of the front, and to the back shoulders for 4 ins. from the armhole edge. Sew sleeves into armholes, easing in as you do, any fullness towards the top. Press all seams of the garment.

Foundation for Effect

A black lace jumper is the ideal thing for somewhat more formal wear. You give it a build up according to the kind of function you're attending, or may be just the mood you're in. You can go all exotic, with flowers in your hair, bright-coloured necklaces, earrings, and bracelets. Wear it, then, with a long, sweeping, rustling skirt, if you can. You can wear heavy gold jewellery borrowed for the occasion from your grandmother or other obliging friends or relations, old enough to qualify for the possession of such knick-knacks, or you can contrive other fascinating accessories. In any case, you can use a little imagination to get a stunning effect with this lace yoke and sleeve variation of the twisted yoke jumper.

In the photograph on page 93, the evening jersey is worn with a straight neckline and a treble row of beads. You can get quite a different effect by putting a heavy gold ornament or brooch in the neck, so that a folded V-neckline is produced.

MATERIALS

6 oz. 2-ply wool (1½ oz. for yoke and sleeves only).

2 No. 8, 2 No. 10, 2 No. 12, and 2 No. 14 knitting needles.

MEASUREMENTS

Length, 21½ ins. Bust size, 34 ins. Sleeve seam, 11 ins.

The Back.—Using No. 10 needles cast on 115 sts. and work in the patt. used for the original jersey until the work measures 4 ins. from the beginning. Change to No. 14 needles and work in patt. until the work measures 6 ins. from the beginning. Change to No. 10 needles and proceed as given for the back of the original jersey, shaping the armholes when the work measures 15½ ins. from the beginning, and the shoulders when the work measures 21½ ins.

The Front.—Work exactly as given for the back of this jersey, until the armhole shaping has been completed and there are 105 sts. on the needle. Complete the front as given in the instructions for the original jersey.

Sleeves and Front Yoke.—Using No. 12 needles cast on 63 sts. K. 1 row, then proceed in the following patt. :—

Next row.—K. 1, * m. 1, k. 2 tog. ; rep. from * to end of row. Rep. this row until work measures 3 ins. from the beginning.

Continuing in patt., change to No. 8 needles and proceed until work measures 11 ins. from the beginning.

Shape Top of Sleeve and Begin Yoke thus : Dec. 1 st. at both ends of the next and every following row until there are 43 sts. on the needle.

Next row.—K. 2 tog., work to the end of the row.

Next row.—Work to the last 2 sts., k. 2 tog.

Rep. these 2 rows until there are 25 sts. on the needle. Continue in patt. on these 25 sts. for the front yoke until it measures 6½ ins. from the end of the dec. Cast off very loosely, or leave sts. on spare needle to be grafted.

Work a second sleeve in the same way.

Make-up.—Join side seams and sleeve seams. Join shaped edge of sleeve top to back armhole on each side. Stitch or graft the ends of the two yoke pieces in centre front. Now stitch lower edge of yoke to shaped top of bodice front slightly easing in the edge of the yoke. Stitch edges of back shoulders to a corresponding length of top edge of yoke. The garment may be worn with the high straight neckline, or the centre of the yoke may be drawn into folds with a clip.

Very "Off the Shoulder"

is the effect given by this edition of the evening jumper. The yoke and sleeves are knitted in bright-coloured stripes. Notice that the stripes are up and down and not across. The yoke can be knitted in ordinary stocking stitch if you prefer not to knit it in the more complicated lace stitch.

Bright-coloured stripes rise vertically to form the yoke and sleeves of this jumper.

If it's glamour you're aiming at, this evening jersey will give you a very good beginning on which to work. It's simple in itself but so effective, with its open work lace stitch yoke and sleeves.

"*I say, talking of substitutes——*" Well, if you are talking about
them, the little jumper on the right is knitted in rayon yarn and
that on the left in bouclé with a yoke in a contrasting colour.

IT NEEDN'T BE WOOL !

Afternoon Jumper

IN RAYON OR BOUCLÉ

MATERIALS

6 oz. Rayon yarn equal to 3-ply wool in thickness, or 5 oz. 3-ply wool.
2 No. 9 and 2 No. 11 knitting needles.
A fine crochet hook.
4 small buttons.

MEASUREMENTS

Length, 18½ ins.
Bust size, 32 ins. to 34 ins.
Sleeve seam, 4 ins.

TENSION

About 6 sts. to 1 in., measured over the drop-st. rib on No. 9 needles.

The Front.— Using No. 11 needles cast on 87 sts. and work in rib and drop-st. patt. thus:—

1st row.—K. 8, * p. 1, k. 9; rep. from * to last 9 sts., p. 1, k. 8.

2nd row.—P. 8, k. 1, * p. 9, k. 1; rep. from * to last 8 sts., p. 8.

3rd and 4th rows.—As 1st and 2nd rows.

5th row.—K. 1, winding yarn twice round needle for each st., work in rib to the last st., k. 1.

6th row.—P. 1, dropping extra loops, work in rib to last st., p. 1.

Rep. the last 4 rows (i.e., rows 3 to 6 inclusive), until work measures 3 ins. from commencement.

Change to No. 9 needles and continue in the rib and drop-st. patt., inc. 1 st. at both ends of the 5th row and every following 4th row until there are 105 sts. on needle. Proceed without shaping until work measures 12½ ins. from lower edge, ending with row on wrong side of work.

Shape Armholes thus: Continuing in rib and drop st., cast off 8 sts. at beg. of next 2 rows, then dec. 1 st. at both ends of every row until 81 sts. remain, thus ending with row on wrong side of work.

Commence Yoke thus:—

1st row.—K. 1, * m. 1, k. 3, sl. 1, k. 2 tog., p.s.s.o., k. 3, m. 1, k. 1; rep. from * to end.

2nd row.—P. 2, * m. 1, p. 2, p. 3 tog., p. 2, m. 1, p. 3; rep. from * to end, ending last rep. with p. 2 instead of p. 3.

3rd row.—K. 3, * m. 1, k. 1, sl. 1, k. 2 tog., p.s.s.o., k. 1, m. 1, k. 5; rep. from * to end, ending last rep. with k. 3 instead of k. 5.

4th row.—P. 4, * m. 1, p. 3 tog., m. 1, p. 7; rep. from * to end, ending last rep. with p. 4 instead of p. 7.

5th row.—K. 2 tog., * k. 3, m. 1, k. 1, m. 1, k. 3, sl. 1, k. 2 tog., p.s.s.o.; rep. from * to end, ending last rep. with k. 2 tog. instead of sl. 1, k. 2 tog., p.s.s.o.

6th row.—P. 2 tog., * p. 2, m. 1, p. 3, m. 1, p. 2, p. 3 tog.; rep. from * to end, ending last rep. with p. 2 tog. instead of p. 3 tog.

7th row.—K. 2 tog., * k. 1, m. 1, k. 5, m. 1, k. 1, sl. 1, k. 2 tog., p.s.s.o.; rep. from * to end, ending last rep. with k. 2 tog. instead of sl. 1, k. 2 tog., p.s.s.o.

8th row.—P. 2 tog., * m. 1, p. 7, m. 1, p. 3 tog.; rep. from * to end, ending last rep. with p. 2 tog. instead of p. 3 tog.

Rep. the last 8 rows 4 times more.

Shape Neck and Shoulders thus:—

Next row.—K. 1, * (m. 1, k. 3, sl. 1, k. 2 tog., p.s.s.o., k. 3, m. 1, k. 1) 3 times,

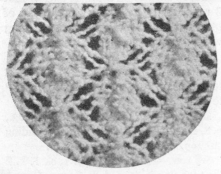

(above) Drop stitch rib of the jumper, and (below) detail of the lace stitch yoke.

* cast off next 19 sts., there now being 1 st. on right-hand needle after casting off; rep. from * to * once.

Work on last set of 31 sts. thus:—

1st row.—P. 2, * m. 1, p. 2, p. 3 tog., p. 2, m. 1, p. 3; rep. from * once, m. 1, p. 2, p. 3 tog., p. 2, m. 1, p. 2 tog.

2nd row.—K. 2 tog., * m. 1, k. 1, sl. 1, k. 2 tog., p.s.s.o., k. 1, m. 1, k. 5; rep. from * to end, ending last rep. with k. 3 instead of k. 5.

3rd row.—P. 4, * m. 1, p. 3 tog., m. 1, p. 7; rep. from * to end, ending last rep. with p. 2 tog. instead of p. 7.

4th row.—K. 2 tog., k. 1, m. 1, k. 3, sl. 1, k. 2 tog., p.s.s.o., k. 3, m. 1. k. 1, m. 1, k. 3, sl. 1, k. 2 tog., p.s.s.o., k. 3, m. 1, k. 1, m. 1, k. 3, k. 2 tog.

5th row.—P. 2 tog., * p. 2, m. 1, p. 3, m. 1, p. 2, p. 3 tog.; rep. from * once, p. 2, m. 1, p. 1, p. 2 tog.

6th row.—K. 2 tog., k. 1, m. 1, k. 1, sl. 1, k. 2 tog., p.s.s.o., * k. 1, m. 1, k. 5, m. 1, k. 1, sl. 1, k. 2 tog., p.s.s.o.; rep. from * once, ending rep. with k. 2 tog. instead of sl. 1, k. 2 tog., p.s.s.o.

7th row.—P. 2 tog., * m. 1, p. 7, m. 1, p. 3 tog.; rep. from * once, m. 1, p. 3.

8th row.—K. 2 tog., k. 2, m. 1, k. 1, * m. 1, k. 3, sl. 1, k. 2 tog., p.s.s.o., k. 3, m. 1, k. 1; rep. from * to end.

9th row.—Cast off 8 sts., there now being 1 st. on right-hand needle, p. 3, m. 1, p. 2, p. 3 tog., p. 2, m. 1, p. 3, m. 1, p. 1, p. 2 tog.

10th row.—K. 2 tog., m. 1, k. 5, m. 1, k. 1, sl. 1, k. 2 tog., p.s.s.o., k. 1, m. 1, k. 5.

11th row.—Cast off 8 sts., there now being 1 st. on right-hand needle, p. 8.

12th row.—K. 3, sl. 1, k. 2 tog., p.s.s.o., k. 3.

Cast off remaining sts.

Rejoin wool at needle point and work thus:—

1st row.—P. 2 tog., * m. 1, p. 2, p. 3 tog., p. 2, m. 1, p. 3; rep. from * to end, ending last rep. with p. 2 instead of p. 3.

2nd row.—K. 3, * m. 1, k. 1, sl. 1, k. 2 tog., p.s.s.o., k. 1, m. 1, k. 5; rep. from * to end, ending last rep. with k. 2 tog. instead of k. 5.

3rd row.—P. 2 tog., * m. 1, p. 3 tog., m. 1, p. 7; rep. from * to end, ending last rep. with p. 4 instead of p. 7.

4th row.—K. 2 tog., * k. 3, m. 1, k. 1, m. 1, k. 3, sl. 1, k. 2 tog., p.s.s.o.; rep. from * once, k. 3, m. 1, k. 1, k. 2 tog.

5th row.—P. 2 tog., p. 1, m. 1, p. 2, p. 3 tog., * p. 2, m. 1, p. 3, m. 1, p. 2, p. 3 tog.; rep. from * once, ending rep. with p. 2 tog. instead of p. 3 tog.

6th row.—K. 2 tog., * k. 1, m. 1, k. 5 m. 1, k 1, sl. 1, k. 2 tog., p.s.s.o.; rep. from * once, k. 1, m. 1, k. 1, k. 2 tog.

7th row.—P. 3, m. 1, p. 3 tog., * m. 1, p. 7, m. 1, p. 3 tog.; rep. from * to end, ending last rep. with p. 2 tog. instead of p. 3 tog.

8th row.—Cast off 8 sts., there now

being 1 st. on right-hand needle, k. 1, m. 1, k. 1, m. 1, k. 3, sl. 1, k. 2 tog., p.s.s.o., k. 3, m. 1, k. 3, k. 2 tog.

9th row.—P. 2 tog., p. 3, m. 1, p. 2, p. 3 tog., p. 2, m. 1, p. 5.

10th row.—Cast off 8 sts., there now being 1 st. on right-hand needle, k. 2, m. 1, k. 3, k. 2 tog.

11th row.—P. 8. Cast off remaining sts.

The Back.—Work exactly as given for front to completion of the armhole shaping, ending with row on wrong side of work (81 sts.).

Commence Yoke and Divide for Front Opening thus:—

Next row.—(K. 1, m. 1, k. 3, sl. 1, k. 2 tog., p.s.s.o., k. 3, m. 1) 4 times, k. twice into next st., (m. 1, k. 3, sl. 1, k. 2 tog., p.s.s.o., k. 3, m. 1, k. 1) 4 times.

Next row.—P. 2, (m. 1, p. 2, p. 3 tog., p. 2, m. 1, p. 3) 3 times, m. 1, p. 2, p. 3 tog., p. 2, m. 1, p. 2, turn, leaving remaining 41 sts. on a spare needle.

Continue in patt. on these 41 sts., working patt. rows 3 to 8 inclusive, as given for front yoke, once, then rep. patt. rows 1 to 8 inclusive 4 times, then patt. rows 1 to 7 inclusive, once. Thus ending at armhole edge.

Shape Shoulder thus:—

1st row.—Cast off 8 sts., work in patt. to end.

2nd row.—Work in patt. to end.

Rep. last 2 rows twice.

Cast off remaining sts.

Replace second set of sts. on to the No. 9 needle and work thus:—

Rep. patt. rows 2 to 8 inclusive once, then rep. patt. rows 1 to 8 inclusive 5 times. Shape shoulder as given for first shoulder.

The Sleeves.—Using No. 11 needles cast on 63 sts. and work in rib and drop st. thus:—

1st row.—K. 1, * p. 1, k. 9; rep. from * to last 2 sts., p. 1, k. 1.

You can make these enchanting afternoon blouses from the same set of instructions—and neither of them is knitted in wool. The rayon blouse on the left is photographed to show the fastening at the back.

2nd row.—P. 1, * k. 1, p. 9; rep. from * to last 2 sts., k. 1, p. 1.

3rd and 4th rows.—As 1st and 2nd rows.

5th row.—K. 1, winding yarn twice round needle for each st., work in rib to last st., k. 1.

6th row.—P. 1, dropping extra loops, work in rib to last st., p. 1.

Rep. rows 3 to 6 inclusive for 1½ ins.

Change to No. 9 needles and continue in rib and drop-st. patt. inc. 1 st. at both ends of next row and every following 4th row until there are 71 sts. on the needle. Proceed without shaping until work measures 4 ins. from commencement.

To simplify matters, knit the whole jumper in the drop-stitch rib. This is the effect!

Shape Top thus: Keeping rib and drop-st. patt. throughout, dec. 1 st. at both ends of every row until 11 sts. remain. Cast off remaining sts.

The Neck Band.—Using No. 11 needles cast on 5 sts. and work in g.st. for 13½ ins. Cast off.

To Make Up.—Press work lightly on wrong side with hot iron and damp cloth. Join side, shoulder and sleeve seams. Sew in sleeves, matching seams to side seams.

Stitch neck band round neck edge, turning it over and stitching down again to give a "bound" effect.

Work 2 rows of d.c. down each back opening edge, making 4 small button loops on one side at regular intervals.

Sew on buttons to match the loops.

Press all seams.

This idea deserves attention!

That odd two ounces of bouclé—what can one do about it? Here's one idea. The very fetching little jumper (page 97 right) is knitted to exactly the same design as the jumper in rayon yarn, but the yarn used is bouclé. The yoke knitted in a contrasting colour gives a very charming effect.

Quantities required are 5 oz. of yarn for the main part and the sleeves and 2 oz. in a contrasting colour for the yoke. If the yarn is thicker than a normal 3-ply wool, substitute No. 10 needles for No. 9 and No. 12 for No. 11 to obtain the correct tension. Change to the contrasting colour for the yoke on the first row of the lacy pattern.

A fairly heavy bouclé yarn or a 4-ply wool, used with No. 9 and No. 11 needles, as in the original garment, will give a 34-in. to 36-in. bust measurement.

You drop everything

when you make this variation of the lace yoke jumper. And that's quite a correct instruction, you know. The jumper is knitted in the simple drop-stitch rib of the main part of the jersey.

You will get some idea of how it will look from the sketch on the left. This jersey, by the way, can be worn equally well tucked into the skirt, or worn outside it. You will notice that in the photograph on page 94, it is worn both ways and both, you will admit, are equally successful.

Gloves in Boucle

KNITTED SIDEWAYS

MATERIALS

1 oz. bouclé wool.
1 oz. 4-ply knitting wool.
2 No. 12 and 2 No. 13 knitting needles.

TENSION

Using 4-ply wool and No. 13 needles, 8½ sts. to 1 in.

Back of Right- and Left-hand Gloves.— Commence at the side of the hand and work thus:—

Using No. 12 needles and bouclé wool cast on 58 sts.

1st row.—K. to last 2 sts., k. twice into next st., k. 1.
2nd row.—K. to end.
3rd row.—As the 1st row.
4th row.—K. to the last 16 sts., turn.
5th row.—K. to end.
6th row.—K. to end.
7th row.—K. to the last 2 sts., k. 2 tog.
8th row.—K. to end.
9th row.—As the 7th row.
10th row.—Cast off 16 sts., thus completing one finger, cast on 21 sts. for second finger, k. to end of row.

Now rep. 1st to 9th rows inclusive as given for the first finger, once more.

Next row.—Cast off 20 sts., thus completing the second finger, cast on 22 sts. for the third finger, k. to end of row.

Work for third finger thus:—

1st row.—K. to last 2 sts., k. twice into next st., k. 1.
2nd row.—K. to end.
3rd row.—As the 1st row.
4th row.—K. to end.
5th row.—K. to end.
6th row.—K. to last 16 sts., turn.
7th row.—K. to end.
8th row.—K. to end.
9th row.—K. to last 2 sts., k. 2 tog.
10th row.—K. to end.
11th row.—As the 9th row.
12th row.—Cast off 22 sts., thus completing the third finger, cast on 20 sts. for the fourth finger, k. to end of row.

Now rep. 1st to 11th rows inclusive as given for the third finger, once more.

Next row.—Cast off 29 sts., thus completing the fourth finger, cast on 18 sts. for the thumb and proceed as follows:—

1st row.—K. 20 sts., turn.
2nd row.—K. to last 2 sts., k. twice into next st., k. 1.
3rd row.—K. 23 sts., turn.
4th row.—K. to last 2 sts., k. twice into next st., k. 1.
5th row.—K. 26 sts., turn.
6th row.—K. to end.
7th row.—K. 28 sts., turn.
8th row.—K. to end.
9th row.—K. 30 sts., turn.
10th row.—K. to last 2 sts., k. 2 tog.
11th row.—K. 31 sts., turn.
12th row.—As the 10th row.
Cast off loosely.

Work the second piece in exactly the same way.

Palm of Right- and Left-hand Gloves.— Using No. 13 needles and 4-ply wool cast on 58 sts.

1st row.—K. to end.
2nd row.—K. to last 2 sts., k. twice into next st., k. 1.
3rd row.—K. to end.
4th row.—As the 2nd row.

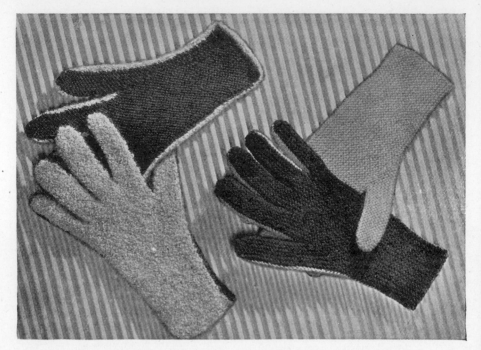

*The palm of your gloves is a vivid contrast to the back. One
pair (left) is in bouclé and wool, the other all 4-ply wool.*

5th row.—K. to last 16 sts., turn.

6th row.—K. to last 2 sts., k. 2 tog.

7th row.—K. to end.

8th row.—As the 6th row.

9th row.—Cast off 16 sts., thus completing the first finger, cast on 21 sts. for the second finger, k. to end of row.

Now rep. 2nd to 8th rows inclusive as given for the first finger, once more.

Next row.—Cast off 20 sts., thus completing the second finger, cast on 20 sts., k. to end of row.

The Third Finger:—

1st row.—K. to last 2 sts., k. twice into next st., k. 1.

2nd row.—K. to end.

3rd row.—As the 1st row.

4th row.—K. to last 16 sts., turn.

5th row.—K. to end.

6th row.—K. to end.

7th row.—K. to the last 2 sts., k. 2 tog.

8th row.—K. to end.

9th row.—As the 7th row.

10th row.—Cast off 22 sts., thus completing the third finger, cast on 20 sts. for the fourth finger, k. to end of row.

Now rep. 1st to 9th rows inclusive as given for the third finger, once more.

Next row.—Cast off 29 sts., thus completing the fourth finger, cast on 18 sts. for the thumb and work as follows:—

1st row.—K. 20 sts., turn.

2nd row.—K. to last 2 sts., k. twice into next st., k. 1.

3rd row.—K. 23 sts., turn.

4th row.—K. to last 2 sts., k. twice into next st., k. 1.

5th row.—K. 26 sts., turn.

6th row.—K. to end.

7th row.—K. 28 sts., turn.

8th row.—K. to last 2 sts., k. 2 tog.

9th row.—K. 29 sts., turn.

10th row.—As the 8th row.

Cast off loosely.

Work the second piece in exactly the same way.

Make-up.—Press work lightly with hot iron and damp cloth.

Place one back and one palm piece together with right sides of work facing and stitch neatly all round hand and fingers. Press the seams then turn out to right sides.

Concerning Your Hands

Don't hide the fact that you have knitted your own gloves. If you fall for the particular colour scheme suggested here, you'll shout it aloud. This variation of the bouclé-backed gloves are knitted all in 4-ply wool, the backs in black and the palms in red.

MATERIALS

1 oz. 4-ply wool for back of gloves and 1 oz. of 4-ply wool in contrasting colour for the palms.

2 No. 13 knitting needles.

Back of Right- and Left-hand Gloves.—Commence at side edge using the 4-ply wool and cast on 64 sts. instead of 58 sts. with the No. 13 needles.

Work as given for first finger of the glove back in bouclé to the completion of the 9th row.

10th row.—Cast off 17 sts. instead of 16 sts., thus completing the first finger, cast on 21 sts. for second finger, k. to end.

Work for the second finger as given for second finger of the glove back in bouclé, but cast on 23 sts. for the third finger instead of 22 sts.

Work for third finger as given for third finger of the glove back in bouclé to the completion of the 11th row.

12th row.—Cast off 23 sts. instead of 22 sts., thus completing the third finger, cast on 21 sts. instead of 20 sts. for the fourth finger, k. to end of row.

Work for the fourth finger as given for fourth finger of the glove back in bouclé, but cast off 30 sts. instead of 29 sts. to complete the finger.

Work for thumb exactly as given for the thumb of glove back in bouclé.

Work a second piece in exactly the same way.

Palm of Right- and Left-hand Gloves.—Using the contrasting wool work two more pieces exactly the same as glove back.

Make-up.—As given for gloves with bouclé backs.

Gauntlet Gloves

PLAIN OR DECORATED!

MATERIALS

3 oz. 4-ply wool.

2 No. 12 knitting needles.

TENSION

$8\frac{1}{2}$ sts. to 1 in.

RIGHT-HAND GLOVE

Use two balls of wool and working with double wool cast on 56 sts.

Work in double moss st. thus:—

1st row.—* K. 2, p. 2; rep. from * to end.

2nd row.—As the 1st row.

3rd row.—* P. 2, k. 2; rep. from * to end.

4th row.—As the 3rd row.

Rep. these 4 rows until the work measures $3\frac{1}{4}$ ins., dec. 1 st. at each end of the last row (54 sts. remain).

Break off 1 strand of wool and using single wool work 6 rows in st.st. (1 row k., 1 row p.).

Shape for Thumb Gusset thus:—

1st row.—(K. 2, p. 2) 7 times, inc. in next st., k. 2, inc. in next st., (k. 2, p. 2) 5 times, k. 2.

2nd row.—(P. 2, k. 2) 5 times, p. to last 28 sts., (k. 2, p. 2) 7 times.

3rd row.—(P. 2, k. 2) 7 times, k. to last 22 sts., (p. 2, k. 2) 5 times, p. 2.

4th row.—(K. 2, p. 2) 5 times, k. 2, p. to last 28 sts., (p. 2, k. 2) 7 times.

5th row.—Patt. 28 sts., inc. in next st., k. to last 23 sts., inc. in next st., patt. 22 sts.

6th row.—Patt. 22 sts., p. to last 28 sts., patt. 28 sts.

7th row.—Patt. 28 sts., k. to last 22 sts., patt. 22.

8th row.—As the 6th row.

Rep. 5th to 8th rows inclusive 5 times (68 sts.).

Next row.—Patt. 28 sts., k. 18 sts., turn and cast on 2 sts.

Next row.—P. 20 sts., turn and cast on 2 sts.

Work in st.st. on these 22 sts. for the thumb for 2 ins., ending with a p. row.

Shape Top thus:—

Next row.—(K. 1, k. 2 tog.) 7 times, k. 1.

Next row.—P. to end.

Next row.—(K. 2 tog.) 7 times, k. 1.

Break off the wool leaving a long end, thread this through a wool needle, slip through remaining sts., draw up and fasten off, then st. down side edges of thumb to base.

With right side of work facing and using the right-hand needle, k. up 4 sts. through the 4 cast-on sts. at base of thumb, work in patt. to end.

Continue in patt. for 1½ ins. on 54 sts., ending with row on wrong side of work.

Commence the Fingers thus:—

First Finger: Next row.—K. 34 sts., turn, cast on 1 st.

Next row.—P. 15 sts., turn, cast on 1 st.

Work in st.st. on these 16 sts. for 2½ ins., ending with a p. row.

Shape the Top thus:—

Next row.—(K. 1, k. 2 tog.) 5 times, k. 1.

Next row.—P. to end.

Next row.—(K. 2 tog.) 5 times, k. 1.

Break off the wool and complete as given for thumb.

Second Finger: With right side of work facing and using right-hand needle, k. up 2 sts. at base of the first finger, k. next 7 sts., turn, cast on 1 st.

Next row.—P. 17 sts., turn, cast on 1 st.

Work in st.st. on these 18 sts. for 3 ins., ending with a p. row.

Shape the Top thus:—

Next row.—(K. 1, k. 2 tog.) 6 times.

Next row.—P. to end.

Next row.—(K. 2 tog.) 6 times.

Break off the wool and complete as given for thumb.

Third Finger: Work as given for the second finger, knitting up 2 sts. at the base of the second finger instead of the first finger, and working for only 2½ ins. instead of 3 ins. before shaping the top.

Fourth Finger: With right side of work facing and using right-hand needle, k. up 4 sts. at base of the third finger, k. to end.

Work in st.st. on these 16 sts. for 2¼ ins., ending with a p. row.

Shape the Top as given for the first finger, stitching down side of hand to edge of gauntlet.

Left-hand Glove.—Work as given for right-hand glove to commencement of the thumb shapings, proceed thus:—

1st row.—(K. 2, p. 2) 5 times, k. 2, inc. in next st., k. 2, inc. in next st., (p. 2, k. 2) 7 times.

2nd row.—(P. 2, k. 2) 7 times, p. to last 22 sts., (p. 2, k. 2) 5 times, p. 2.

3rd row.—(P. 2, k. 2) 5 times, p. 2, k. to last 28 sts., (k. 2, p. 2) 7 times.

4th row.—(K. 2, p. 2) 7 times, p. to last 22 sts., (k. 2, p. 2) 5 times, k. 2.

5th row.—Patt. 22 sts., inc. in next st.,

Cover your wrists, and your hands will keep really warm. That's why we suggest gauntlets. They can be decorated with fringes, or plain. And don't you think the mittens a good idea for indoors? Knit them from the glove pattern.

k. to last 29 sts., inc. in next st., patt. 28 sts.

6th row.—Patt. 28 sts., p. to last 22 sts., patt. 22.

7th row.—Patt. 22 sts., k. to last 28 sts., patt. 28.

8th row.—As the 6th row.

Rep. 5th to 8th rows inclusive 5 times (68 sts.).

Next row.—Patt. 22 sts., k. 18 sts., turn and cast on 2 sts.,

Next row.—P. 20 sts., turn and cast on 2 sts.

Work as given for thumb of right-hand glove.

With right side of work facing and using right-hand needle, k. up 4 sts. through the 4 cast-on sts. at base of thumb, work in patt. to end.

Continue in patt. on 54 sts. and complete the glove as given for right-hand glove.

Make-up.—Press work lightly with hot iron and damp cloth.

The Tufted Trimming: (Work a tuft into each st. where the decoration is required). Thread a wool needle with a length of wool, place the needle through centre of st. and bring out at left-hand side of st. leaving a ½-in. length of wool at front of work. Now place needle into the right-hand side of st. and bring out at the centre. Cut wool, leaving a ½-in. length. This makes one tuft.

In the original glove the "tufting" was worked to form a border at the edge of the gauntlet. Then 3 single lines of tufts were worked along the back of the hand, these were afterwards cut off close to the fabric.

You must make Mittens

Really, the very latest thing, and so sensible too. When heating isn't what it was in our young days, it's essential to morale to keep the hands warm, and then by some divine providence, the nose won't

go too purple—which brings us right back to mittens. Not the sort of black things, but in gay colours and stripes, so that they warm the heart as well as the wrists. This pair is adapted from the gloves. It's all so easy. Look and see!

MATERIALS

2 oz. 4-ply wool.

2 No. 12 knitting needles for average to large size.

2 No. 13 knitting needles for smaller size.

Right-hand Mitten.—Using single wool cast on 54 sts. and work 2½ ins. in k. 1, p. 1 rib.

Work 6 rows in st.st., then shape for thumb gusset as given for right-hand glove, until there are 68 sts. on the needle.

Continue for thumb as given, but work only ¾ in. in st.st. instead of 2 ins., ending with a p. row.

Work 4 rows in k. 1, p. 1 rib.

Cast off loosely in rib, and st. down to base of thumb.

Continue exactly as given for right-hand glove to commencement of the fingers.

Continue for first finger as given, but work only ¾ in. in st.st. instead of 2½ ins., ending with a p. row.

Work 4 rows in k. 1, p. 1 rib.

Cast off loosely in rib, and st. down to base of finger.

Continue for second, third and fourth fingers exactly as given, but work only ¾ in. in st.st., with 4 rows in k. 1, p. 1 rib to match the first finger, instead of the original length.

Left-hand Mitten.—Work the wrist ribbing as given for right-hand mitten.

Work 6 rows in st.st., then shape for thumb gusset as given for left-hand glove, until there are 68 sts. on the needle.

Continue for thumb and complete the hand and fingers, as given for right-hand mitten.

Make-up.—As given.

Open Work Gloves

IN COTTON OR WOOL

MATERIALS

2 oz. knitting cotton,
2 No. 13, knitting needles; or
1½ oz. 4-ply wool,
2 No. 12 knitting needles.

TENSION

8½ sts. to 1 in. measured over st.st.
N.B.—This makes an average to large-size glove. For a smaller size use No. 14 needles with cotton or No. 13 needles with 4-ply wool.

The Right-hand Glove.—Cast on 42 sts. and work 3½ ins. in k. 1, p. 1 rib. Inc. 1 st. at the end of the last row (43 sts. on the needle).

Continue in the following patt.:—

1st row.— K. 1, * m. 1, k. 2 tog.; rep. from * to end.

Rep. this row 3 times.

Shape Thumb Gusset thus:—

1st row.— K. 1, (m. 1, k. 2 tog.) 11 times, (k. twice into the next st.) twice, k. 2, (m. 1, k. 2 tog.) 8 times.

2nd row.—K. 1, (m. 1, k. 2 tog.) 8 times, p. 5, k. 1, (m. 1, k. 2 tog.) 11 times.

3rd row.—K. 1, (m. 1, k. 2 tog.) 11 times, k. 6, (m. 1, k. 2 tog.) 8 times.

4th row.—Rep. 2nd row.

5th row.—K. 1 (m. 1, k. 2 tog.) 11 times, k. twice into the next st., k. 2, k. twice into the next st., k. 2, (m. 1, k. 2 tog.) 8 times.

6th row.—K. 1, (m. 1, k. 2 tog.) 8 times, p. 7, k. 1, (m. 1, k. 2 tog.) 11 times.

7th row.—K. 1, (m. 1, k. 2 tog.) 11 times, k. 8, (m. 1, k. 2 tog.) 8 times.

8th row.—Rep. 6th row.

9th row.—K. 1, (m. 1, k. 2 tog.) 11 times, k. twice into the next st., k. 4, k. twice into the next st., k. 2, (m. 1, k. 2 tog.) 8 times.

10th row.—K. 1, (m. 1, k. 2 tog.) 8 times, p. 9, k. 1, (m. 1, k. 2 tog.) 11 times.

11th row.—K. 1, (m. 1, k. 2 tog.) 11 times, k. 10, (m. 1, k. 2 tog.) 8 times.

12th row.—Rep. 10th row.

Continue in this way, working in patt. with the thumb gusset in st.st., inc. 1 st. in the first and last st., but one in the gusset on the next row and on every following 4th row until there are 17 sts. in the gusset.

Work 1 row after the last inc. row.

Next row.—K. 1, (m. 1, k. 2 tog.) 11 times, k. 17, turn.

Next row.—P. 17, turn and cast on 3 sts.

Work in st.st. on these 20 sts. for the thumb for 2¼ ins. or required length, ending with a p. row.

Shape Top thus:—

1st row.—* K. 2 tog.; rep. from * to end.

2nd row.—P.

3rd row.—Rep. 1st row.

Break off the yarn and thread through the remaining sts.; draw up and fasten off securely; then st. down seam to base of thumb.

Rejoin yarn to right-hand needle and with right side of work facing, pick up and k. 5 sts. at base of thumb, k. 1, (m. 1, k. 2 tog.) 8 times. There are now 45 sts. on the needle.

Continue in patt. on these 45 sts. for 2 ins., ending with a row on the wrong side of the work.

Commence Fingers thus:—

The First Finger: Next row.—K. 1, (m. 1, k. 2 tog.) 14 times, k. 1, turn and cast on 1 st.

Next row.—P. 16, turn and cast on 1 st.

Work in st.st. on these 17 sts. for 2¾ ins. or required length, ending with a p. row.

Shape Top thus:—

1st row.—(K. 2 tog., k. 1) 5 times, k. 2 tog.

2nd row.—P.

3rd row.—(K. 2 tog) 5 times, k. 1.

Break off wool and complete to correspond with thumb.

The Second Finger.—Rejoin yarn at point of right-hand needle and with right side of work facing, pick up and k. 4 sts. at the base of the first finger, k. next 5 sts., turn and cast on 1 st.

Next row.—P. 15, turn and cast on 1 st.

Work in st.st. on these 16 sts. for 3 ins. or required length, ending with a p. row.

Shape top and complete to correspond with thumb.

The Third Finger.—Rejoin yarn at point of right-hand needle and with right side of work facing pick up and k. 4 sts. at the base of the second finger, k. next 5 sts., turn and cast on 1 st.

Next row.—P. 15, turn and cast on 1 st.

Work in st.st. on these 16 sts. for 2½ ins. or required length, ending with a p. row.

Shape top and complete to correspond with thumb.

The Fourth Finger.—Rejoin yarn at point of right-hand needle and pick up and k. 4 sts. at the base of the third finger, k. to end. Work in st.st. on these 14 sts. for 2¼ ins., or required length, ending with a p. row.

Shape Top thus:—

1st row.—(K. 2 tog., k. 1) 4 times, k. 2 tog.

2nd row.—P.

3rd row.—(K. 2 tog.) 4 times, k. 1.

Break off yarn and complete to correspond with the thumb, stitching down side edge of glove to wrist.

The Left-hand Glove.—Continue as given for the right-hand glove to the commencement of the thumb gusset, ending with the 4th row of patt. Continue to shape for thumb gusset exactly as given for the right-hand glove, but work 17 sts. in patt. before the incs. instead of 23 sts., and 23 sts. after the incs. instead of 17 sts. Thus the 1st row will read:—

K. 1, (m. 1, k. 2 tog.) 8 times, (k. twice into the next st.) twice, k. 2, (m. 1, k. 2 tog.) 11 times.

Continue in this way until there are 17 sts. in the gusset. Work 1 row after the last inc. row.

Rib stitch of the main part of the gloves.

Next row.—K. 1, (m. 1, k. 2 tog.) 8 times, k. 17, turn and cast on 3 sts.

Next row.—P. 20, turn.

Work in st.st. on these 20 sts. for 2¼ ins. or required length, ending with a p. row.

Shape top as given for thumb of right-hand glove.

Rejoin yarn at point of right-hand needle and with right side of work facing, pick up and k. 5 sts. at base of thumb, k. 1, (m. 1, k. 2 tog.) 11 times. There are now 45 sts. on the needle.

Continue in patt. on these 45 sts. for 2 ins., ending with a row on the wrong side of the work.

Work fingers as given for fingers of right-hand glove.

Press very lightly, using a warm iron over a damp cloth.

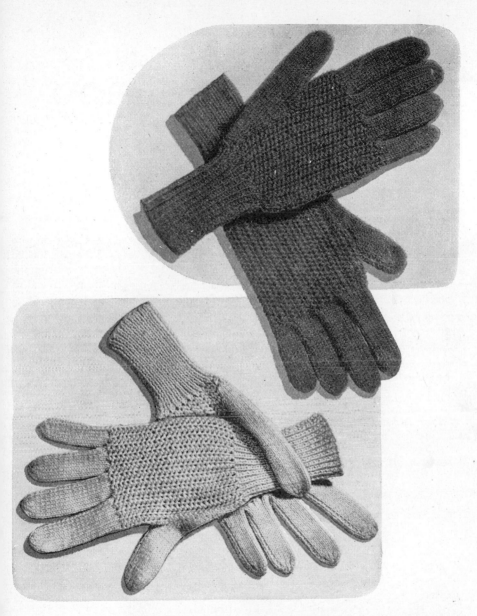

For finest day to day service this type of glove is strongly recommended. It fits well, and stays fitting well. It is sufficiently smart to be worn with one's "best" suit, and sufficiently inconspicuous to be worn with anything. The pair can be made in 4-ply as in the top illustration, or in cotton, as in the bottom picture. They are knitted in an open-work rib which is just a little exciting but isn't so open-work that you feel they're "draughty." For fun, work them in matching or contrasting shades for particular outfits.

Cable Rib Cap

IN FOUR-PLY WOOL

MATERIALS

2 oz. 4-ply wool.

2 No. 12 knitting needles.

¼ yd. of lining.

¼ yd. of stiffening.

MEASUREMENTS

Width round edge of head band, 21 ins.
Depth of head band at centre front, 4 ins.

TENSION

10 sts. to 1 in.

The Head Band.—Cast on 194 sts. and work in the following patt. :—

Make your hat with the crown in one colour and the head band in a contrasting shade. Then knit the gloves (page 101) with ribbed backs to match the hat.

1st row.—P. 2, * k. 4, p. 2; rep. from * to the end of the row.

2nd row.—* K. 2, p. 4; rep. from * to last 2 sts., k. 2.

3rd row.—P. 2, * sl. next 2 sts. on to a spare needle and leave at the back of the work, k. next 2 sts., then k. 2 sts. from the spare needle, p. 2; rep. from * to end of the row.

4th row.—Rep. 2nd row.

These 4 rows form the patt. Rep. them until the work measures 3 ins. from the beginning. Continuing in patt., cast off 11 sts. at the beginning of each of the next 12 rows. Cast off remaining sts.

The Crown.—Cast on 3 sts. and work in st.st., inc. 1 st. at both ends of the next and every alternate row until there are 47 sts. on the needle. Continue without shaping until work measures 6½ ins. from the beginning. Now dec. 1 st. at both ends of every alternate row until there are 11 sts. on the needle. Cast off.

Make-up.—Press the pieces of knitting on the wrong side, using a warm iron over a damp cloth. Stitch pieces of tailors canvas or some similar stiffening to the wrong side of the knitted pieces, cutting them to shape, and being careful not to stretch the knitting. Now cover the stiffening with lining, sewing neatly round the edges so that the stitches do not show on the right side. Join the back seam of the head band and press. Now stitch the shaped edge of the head band to the edge of the crown and press. Push the crown in and catch to the head band about ½ in. from the top if necessary.

Let your hats be gay and wear them with an air. Here's one that will please you. It has something of a martial air and is knitted in a firm cable rib. Wear it with the gloves on page 101.

"*Well suited.*" *It's something of a miracle to produce a knitted suit that is so absolutely right for the larger figure. But here it is; the skirt is knitted in a diagonal stripe which keeps it firm.*

Suit for the Matron

KNITTED IN BOUCLÉ

MATERIALS

27 oz. bouclé wool (equivalent to 3-ply wool in thickness) for the suit.
13 oz. for the skirt.
15 oz. for the jacket.
2 No. 10, 2 No. 11 and 2 No. 12 knitting needles.
A fine crochet hook.
¾ yd. elastic. 8 buttons.
1¼ yds. corded ribbon in matching shade, 1½ ins. wide.

MEASUREMENTS

The Skirt: Length, 26 ins.
Hips, 40 ins.
The Jacket: Length 24¼ ins.
Bust size, 38 ins.
Sleeve seam, 18 ins.

TENSION

Using No. 10 needles, 7 sts. to 1 in. (after light pressing).
N.B.—For a smaller size (bust 34-35, hips 37-38) use No. 11 needles throughout wherever No. 10 are stated, giving 7½ sts. to 1 in. after light pressing.

THE SKIRT

Front and Back Both Alike.—Using No. 10 needles cast on 183 sts. and work in following patt.:—

1st row.—*K. 3, p. 3; rep. from * to last 3 sts., k. 3.

2nd row.—* P 3, k. 3; rep. from * to last 3 sts., p. 3.

3rd row.—K. 2, (p. 3, k. 3) 14 times, p. 3, k. 5, p. 3, (k. 3, p. 3) 14 times, k. 2.

4th row.—P. 2, (k. 3, p. 3) 14 times, k. 3, p. 5, k. 3, (p. 3, k. 3) 14 times, p. 2.

5th row.—K. 1, (p. 3, k. 3) 15 times, p. 1, (k. 3, p. 3) 15 times, k. 1.

6th row.—P. 1, (k. 3, p. 3) 15 times, k. 1, (p. 3, k. 3) 15 times.

7th row.—* P. 3, k. 3; rep. from * to last 3 sts., p. 3.

8th row.—* K. 3, p. 3; rep. from * to last 3 sts., k. 3.

9th row.—P. 2, (k. 3, p. 3) 14 times, k. 3, p. 5, k. 3, (p. 3, k. 3) 14 times, p. 2.

10th row.—K. 2, (p. 3, k. 3) 14 times, p. 3, k. 5, p. 3, (k. 3, p. 3) 14 times, k. 2.

11th row.—P. 1, (k. 3, p. 3) 15 times, k. 1, (p. 3, k. 3) 15 times, p. 1.

12th row.—K. 1, (p. 3, k. 3) 15 times, p. 1, (k. 3, p. 3) 15 times, k. 1.

These 12 rows form the pattern.

Commencing again at the 1st row, continue in patt. until work measures 6 ins. from commencement.

Keeping continuity of the patt., dec. 1 st. at both ends of next row and every following 12th row until 175 sts. remain, then dec. at both ends of every 10th row until 167 sts. remain. Now dec. at both ends of every 8th row until work measures 16 ins. from lower edge.

Change to No. 11 needles and continue in patt., dec. on every 8th row as before until work measures 22½ ins. from lower edge.

Change to No. 12 needles and continue in patt., dec. on every 8th row as before until 143 sts. remain. Continue without shaping until work measures 24½ ins. from lower edge, ending with row on wrong side of work and dec. 1 st. at end of last row (142 sts.). Work 1½ ins. in k. 1, p. 1 rib. Cast off loosely in rib.

Work a second piece in the same way.

Make-up.—Press work lightly on wrong side with hot iron over a damp cloth. Join the side seams.

Make elastic casing at back of the waist ribbing as follows:—Using the crochet hook commence with 1 s.c. into the top edge of the ribbing at a side seam, * 7 ch., 1 s.c. into the ribbing about ¾ in. down and ¾ in. along, 7 ch., 1 s.c. into top edge of the ribbing about ¾ in. along; rep. from * all round. Thread elastic through the casing. Press the seams.

THE JACKET

The Back.—Using No. 10 needles cast on 130 sts. and work in g.st. (each row k.) for 1 in.

Continue in reversed st.st. thus:—

1st row.—P. to end.

2nd row.—K. to end.

Rep. the last 2 rows once.

5th row.—P. 22, p. 2 tog., p. 5, p. 2 tog., p. 68, p. 2 tog., p. 5, p. 2 tog., p. 22.

Work 13 rows in reversed st. st.

19th row.—P. 22, p. 2 tog., p. 3, p. 2 tog., p. 68, p. 2 tog., p. 3, p. 2 tog., p. 22.

Work 13 rows in reversed st.st.

33rd row.—P. 22, p. 2 tog., p. 1, p. 2 tog., p. 68, p. 2 tog., p. 1, p. 2 tog., p. 22.

Work 13 rows in reversed st.st.

47th row.—P. 22, p. 3 tog., p. 68, p. 3 tog., p. 22 (114 sts.).

The jacket of the suit has a fly front and no collar. It is shaped, but should be worn without a belt.

If necessary, continue in reversed st.st. without shaping until work measures 6 ins. from commencement.

Change to No. 12 needles and continue in reversed st.st. for 2 ins. (8 ins. from commencement). Change back to No. 10 needles and continue in reversed st.st., inc. 1 st. at both ends of the 5th row and every following 6th row until there are 130 sts. on the needle.

Continue without shaping until the work measures 18 ins. from the lower edge.

Shape Armholes thus: Cast off 6 sts. at beg. of the next 2 rows, then dec. 1 st.

at both ends of the next 10 rows (98 sts. remain).

Continue without shaping until work measures $24\frac{1}{2}$ ins. from lower edge, ending with row on wrong side of work.

Shape Neck and Shoulders thus: Cast off 11 sts. at beg. of the next 4 rows, then cast off 10 sts. at beg. of the next 2 rows.

Now continue in g.st. on the remaining 34 sts. for $\frac{3}{4}$ in., dec. 1 st. at each end of every alternate row.

Cast off loosely.

The Right Front.—Using No. 10 needles cast on 71 sts. and work in g.st. for 1 in., then work in reversed st.st. with g.st. front border thus:—

1st row.—K. 11, p. to end.

2nd row.—K. to end.

Rep. last 2 rows once.

5th row.—K. 11, p. 29, p. 2 tog., p. 5, p. 2 tog., p. 22.

Work 13 rows in reversed st.st. with g.st. front border.

19th row.—K. 11, p. 29, p. 2 tog., p. 3, p. 2 tog., p. 22.

Work 13 rows in reversed st.st. with g.st. front border.

33rd row.—K. 11, p. 29, p. 2 tog., p. 1, p. 2 tog., p. 22.

Work 13 rows in reversed st.st. with g.st. front border.

47th row.—K. 11, p. 29, p. 3 tog., p. 22.

If necessary, continue in reversed st.st. with g.st. front border without shaping until work measures 6 ins. from commencement, ending at the front edge.

Next row.—K. 11, turn.

Work 2 ins. in g.st. on these 11 sts., ending at the inside edge.

Now using No. 12 needles continue in reversed st.st. on the remaining 52 sts. for 2 ins., ending at the side edge.

Change back to No. 10 needles and continue working across all sts. in reversed st.st. with g.st. front border, inc. 1 st. at the side edge on the 5th row and on every following 6th row until there are 71 sts. on the needle.

Continue without shaping until work measures 18 ins. from lower edge, ending at the side edge.

Shape Armhole thus: Cast off 6 sts. at the beg. of the next row, then dec. 1 st. at this same edge on each of the next 10 rows (55 sts.).

Continue without shaping until work measures 20 ins. from lower edge, ending at the front edge.

Shape for Rever thus:—

1st row.—K. twice into first st., k. 11, p. to end.

2nd and each alternate row.—K. to end.

3rd row.—K. twice into first st., k. 12, p. to end.

5th row.—K. 15, p. to end.

7th row.—K. twice into first st., k. 14, p. to end.

9th row.—K. twice into first st., k. 16, p. to end.

11th row.—K. 18, p. to end.

13th row.—K. twice into first st., k. 18, p. to end.

15th row.—K. twice into first st., k. 19, p. to end.

17th row.—K. 22, p. to end.

19th row.—K. twice into first st., k. 21, p. to end.

21st row.—K. twice into first st., k. 23, p. to end.

23rd row.—K. 25, p. to end.

25th row.—K. twice into first st., k. 25, p. to end.

27th row.—K. twice into first st., k. 26, p. to end.

29th row.—K. 29, p. to end.

31st row.—K. twice into first st., k. 28, p. to end.

33rd row.—K. twice into first st., k. 30, p. to end.

35th row.—K. 32, p. to end.

37th row.—K. twice into first st., k. 32, p. to end.

39th row.—K. twice into first st., k. 33, p. to end.

41st row.—K. 36, p. to end.

Now continue in reversed st.st. and

g.st., inc. 1 st. at the outer edge on next row and every following 4th row until work measures 24½ ins. from lower edge, ending at armhole edge.

Shape the Shoulder thus:—

1st row.—Cast off 11 sts., k. to end.

2nd row.—K. twice into first st., k. to last 21 sts., p. 21.

3rd row.—Cast off 11 sts., k. to end.

4th row.—K. to last 10 sts., p. 10.

5th row.—Cast off 10 sts., k. to end.

6th row.—K. twice into first st., k. to end.

7th row.—Cast off 9 sts., k. to end.

8th row.—K. to end.

9th row.—As 7th row.

10th row.—As 6th row.

Rep. last 4 rows once.

Cast off remaining sts.

The Left Front.—Using No. 10 needles cast on 71 sts. and work in g.st. for 1 in.

Continue in reversed st.st. with g.st. front border thus:—

1st row.—P. to last 11 sts., k. 11.

2nd row.—K. to end.

Rep. last 2 rows once.

5th row.—P. 22, p. 2 tog., p. 5, p. 2 tog., p. 29, k. 11.

Work 13 rows in reversed st.st. with g.st. front border.

19th row.—P. 22, p. 2 tog., p. 3, p. 2 tog., p. 29, k. 11.

Work 13 rows in reversed st.st. with g.st. front border.

33rd row.—P. 22, p. 2 tog., p. 1, p. 2 tog., p. 29, k. 11.

Work 13 rows in reversed st.st. with g.st. front border.

47th row.—P. 22, p. 3 tog., p. 29, k. 11.

If necessary, continue in reversed st.st. with g.st. front border without shaping until work measures 6 ins. from commencement, ending at the front edge.

Next row.—K. 11, turn.

Work 2 ins. in g.st. on these 11 sts., ending at the inside edge.

Now using No. 12 needles continue in reversed st.st. on the remaining 52 sts.

for 2 ins., ending at the side edge.

Change back to No. 10 needles and continue working across all sts. exactly as given for the right front until the armhole shapings are completed and 55 sts. remain.

Continue without shaping until work measures 20 ins. from lower edge, ending at armhole edge.

Shape for Rever thus:—

1st row.—P. to last 12 sts., k. 10, k. twice into next st., k. 1.

2nd and each alternate row.—K. to end.

3rd row.—P. to last 13 sts., k. 11, k. twice into next st., k. 1.

5th row.—P. to last 15 sts., k. 15.

7th row.—P. to last 15 sts., k. 13, k. twice into next st., k. 1.

9th row.—P. to last 17 sts., k. 15, k. twice into next st., k. 1.

11th row.—P. to last 18 sts., k. 18.

13th row.—P. to last 19 sts., k. 17, k. twice into next st., k. 1.

15th row.—P. to last 20 sts., k. 18, k. twice into next st., k. 1.

17th row.—P. to last 22 sts., k. 22.

19th row.—P. to last 22 sts., k. 20, k. twice into next st., k. 1.

21st row.—P. to last 24 sts., k. 22, k. twice into next st., k. 1.

23rd row.—P. to last 25 sts., k. 25.

25th row.—P. to last 26 sts., k. 24, k. twice into next st., k. 1.

27th row.—P. to last 27 sts., k. 25, k. twice into next st., k. 1.

29th row.—P. to last 29 sts., k. 29.

31st row.—P. to last 29 sts., k. 27, k. twice into next st., k. 1.

33rd row.—P. to last 31 sts., k. 29, k. twice into next st., k. 1.

35th row.—P. to last 32 sts., k. 32.

37th row.—P. to last 33 sts., k. 31, k. twice into next st., k. 1.

39th row.—P. to last 34 sts., k. 32, k. twice into next st., k. 1.

41st row.—P. to last 36 sts., k. 36.

Now continue in reversed st.st. and g.st., inc. 1 st. at the outer edge on next row and every following 4th row until work measures 24½ ins. from lower edge, ending at armhole edge.

Shape Shoulders thus:—

1st row.—Cast off 11 sts., p. 21, counting st. already on right-hand needle after casting off, k. to last 2 sts., k. twice into next st., k. 1.

2nd and each alternate row.—K. to end.

3rd row.—Cast off 11 sts., p. 10, counting st. already on right-hand needle after casting off, k. to end.

5th row.—Cast off 10 sts., k. to last 2 sts., k. twice into next st., k. 1.

7th row.—Cast off 9 sts., k. to end.

8th row.—As 2nd row.

9th row.—Cast off 9 sts., k. to last 2 sts., k. twice into next st., k. 1.

10th row.—As 2nd row.

Rep. last 4 rows once.

Cast off remaining sts.

The Sleeves.—Using No. 10 needles, cast on 64 sts. and work 1 in. in g.st.

Continue in reversed st.st. for 2 ins., then inc. 1 st. at each end of next row and every following 8th row until there are 96 sts. on the needle. Continue without shaping until work measures 18 ins. from lower edge, ending with row on wrong side of work.

Shape Top thus: Dec. 1 st. at the beg. of the next 14 rows, then dec. 1 st. at both ends of every row until 22 sts. remain.

Cast off remaining sts.

The Pockets.—Using No. 10 needles, cast on 45 sts. and work in g.st. dec. 1 st. at both ends of the 9th and every following 10th row until 33 sts. remain. Cast off.

Work a second piece in the same way.

You can, if you wish, knit the suit in ordinary fingering rather than bouclé. Here it is. Cardigan and skirt are knitted alike in a simple cross-over rib.

A detail of the cross-over rib in which you may knit the suit if you use fingering. It makes a very firm fabric.

Page 115

Make-up.—Press work lightly on wrong side with hot iron over a damp cloth. Join the side, shoulder and sleeve seams and stitch the sleeves into the armholes. Stitch the pockets to the fronts, placing them about $\frac{1}{2}$ in. from the g.st. border, and placing the bottom of the pockets level with the top of the g.st. hem.

Take a piece of ribbon about 1 in. wide and about 20 ins. long; make 8 buttonholes in this ribbon, about $2\frac{1}{2}$ ins. apart. Stitch this strip to the inside of the right-hand front border and catch it down neatly between the buttonholes. Attach buttons to the left front to correspond with the buttonholes and press all seams.

More Ideas to Suit You

Perhaps you prefer to use ordinary fingering rather than bouclé for your suit. In that case choose a 4-ply wool—preferably one with a firm twist. This should produce the same tension as the bouclé knitted on the same size needles, for although bouclé is equivalent to 3-ply in thickness, its uneven texture makes it necessary to use needles one size finer than would be used for 3-ply fingering.

For 4-ply fingering, a simple pattern is more effective for the cardigan than plain stocking stitch and the same pattern can be substituted for the chevron rib of the skirt. The sketch on page 115 will give you an idea of how the suit would look.

Here are instructions for a simple cross-over rib which would be ideal for the suit knitted in 4-ply.

This pattern needs a number of stitches divisible by 4 plus 2.

1st row.—* K. 2, pass the needle purlwise through the next st. and k. into the front of the second stitch, then k. into the back of the first st. and slip both sts. off the needle together. Rep. from * to the last 2 sts., k. 2.

2nd row.—* K. 2, p. 2, rep. from * to the last 2 sts., k. 2.

While we are thinking of suits, let's consider what can be done in the way of small size suits. The next pattern (page 117) is for a frock. You can knit just the skirt of this, and wear it with a blouse, as in the sketch on the right. Make it into a complete suit with the cardigan (see p. 121).

White Collar Frock

KNITTED IN BOUCLÉ

MATERIALS

20 oz. bouclé wool, equivalent to 3-ply wool in thickness.
2 No. 10 and 2 No. 12 knitting needles. A circular needle size 10, or 4 No. 10 needles pointed at both ends. 1 collar. 2 buttons. ¾ yd. wide elastic for waist.

MEASUREMENTS

Length, 41 ins.
Bust measurement, 35 ins. To fit a 34-in. bust.
Short sleeve seam, 5 ins.
Long sleeve seam, 18 ins.

TENSION

7½ sts. to 1 in. measured over the wide rib.

Using the circular needle (or the 4 No. 10 needles) commence at lower edge by casting on 416 sts.

To avoid twisting the work continue in rows thus:—

1st row.—K. to end.

2nd row.—K. to end.

3rd row.—* P. 12, k. 1; rep. from * to end.

4th row.—* P. 1, k. 12; rep. from * to end.

Rep. the last 2 rows twice, then rep. the 3rd row once more, thus ending with row on right side of work.

Now continue to work in rounds with right side of work outside as follows:—

1st round.—* P. 12, k. 1; rep. from * to end. (It will be found helpful to mark the end of the round with a small piece of coloured wool.) Rep. this round 38 times.

Next round.—* P. 2 tog., p. 10, k. 1; rep. from * to end.

Next round.—* P. 11, k. 1; rep. from * to end. Rep. the last round 38 times.

Next round.—*P. 2 tog., p. 9, k. 1; rep. from * to end.

Next round.—* P. 10, k. 1; rep. from * to end. Rep. the last round 38 times.

Next round.—* P. 2 tog., p. 8, k. 1; rep. from * to end.

Next round.—* P. 9, k. 1; rep. from * to end. Rep. the last round 38 times.

Next round.—* P. 2 tog., p. 7, k. 1; rep. from * to end.

Next round.—* P. 8, k. 1; rep. from * to end. Rep. the last round 36 times.

Next round.—* P. 2 tog., p. 6, k. 1; rep. from * to end.

Next round.—* P. 7, k. 1; rep. from * to end.

Rep. the last round until work measures 24 ins. from lower edge, finishing at the end of the round.

Next round.—K. 2 tog., k. 10, * (k. 2 tog., k. 4) 4 times, k. 2 tog., k. 3; rep. from * 7 times, k. 2 tog., k. 10 (214 sts.).

This completes the skirt.

The work is now continued in two parts for back and front of bodice and waist band, working in rows as follows:—

The Back of the Bodice.—Using No. 12 needles and with wrong side of work facing, k. across 107 sts., turn.

Continue in g.st. on these 107 sts. for 1½ ins., ending with row on wrong side of work.

Change to No. 10 needles, and continue in p. 5, k. 1 rib thus:—

Next row.—K. 3, * k. 4, k. twice into

"New Standard" Styles mean simplicity and utility combined with smartness. And so this little frock in bouclé. And you make it look different every day! Ring the changes with different collars, belts and accessories.

next st., k. 8; rep. from * to end (115 sts.).

Next row.—* P. 1, k. 5; rep. from * to last st., p. 1.

Next row.—* K. 1, p. 5; rep. from * to last st., k. 1.

Rep. the last 2 rows once, then rep. the former row once more.

Continue in the rib, inc. 1 st. at both ends of next row and every following 8th row until there are 131 sts. on the needle, working the increased sts. into the rib.

Continue without shaping until work measures 9½ ins. above the g.st. waist band.

Shape Armholes thus: Continuing in rib, cast off 6 sts. at beg. of next 2 rows, then dec. 1 st. at each end of the next 9 rows (101 sts. remain).

Continue in rib without shaping until work measures 14½ ins. above the g.st. waist band, ending with row on wrong side of work.

Commence the Yoke thus: Change to No. 12 needles and continue in g.st. for 1 in., ending with row on wrong side of work.

Shape Neck and Shoulders thus:—

Continuing in g.st., cast off 8 sts. at beg. of next 6 rows, then cast off 9 sts. at beg. of next 2 rows. Cast off remaining 35 sts.

The Front of the Bodice: Using No. 12 needles and with wrong side of work facing, work in g.st. on the remaining 107 sts. for 1½ ins., ending with row on wrong side of work.

Change to No. 10 needles and continue in p. 5, k. 1 rib, dividing for the front opening thus:—

Next row.—K. 3, * k. 4, k. twice into next st., k. 8; rep. from * to end (115sts.).

Next row.—(P. 1, k. 5) 9 times, k. 7 sts. for front band, turn, leaving remaining sts. on a spare needle.

Continue on 61 sts. for right side of front in rib with g.st. front border:—

Next row.—K. 7, * p. 5, k. 1; rep. from * to end.

Next row.—* P. 1, k. 5; rep. from * to last 7 sts., k. 7. Rep. the last 2 rows once.

Continue in rib with g.st. front border, inc. 1 st. at the side edge on next row and on every following 8th row until there are 69 sts. on the needle, working the increased sts. into the rib.

Continue without shaping until work measures 9½ ins. above the g.st. waist band, ending at the side edge.

Shape Armhole thus: Cast off 6 sts. at beg. of next row, then dec. 1 st. at this same edge on the next 9 rows (54 sts.).

Continue without shaping until work measures 12 ins. above the g.st. waist band, ending at the front edge.

Shape the Neck thus:—

Next row.—K. 2 tog., k. 6, work in rib to end.

Next row.—Work in rib to last 8 sts., k. 6, k 2 tog. Rep. the last 2 rows 9 times.

Next row.—K. 2 tog., k. to end.

Next row.—K. to end.

Rep. the last row twice more (33 sts. remain).

Change to No. 12 needles and continue in g.st. until work measures 15½ ins. above the g.st. waist band, ending at armhole edge.

Shape Shoulder thus:—

Next row.—Cast off 8 sts., k. to end.

Next row.—K. to end.

Rep. last 2 rows twice.

Cast off remaining 9 sts.

With wrong side of work facing and using No. 10 needles, rejoin wool to remaining 54 sts. for left side of the front at the front edge and cast on 7 sts. for the underwrap.

Next row.—K. the 7 cast-on sts., * k. 5, p. 1; rep. from * to end.

Next row.—* K. 1, p. 5; rep. from * to last 7 sts., k. 7.

Next row.—K. 7, * k. 5, p. 1; rep. from * to end. Rep. last 2 rows once.

Continue in rib with g.st. underwrap, exactly as given for right side of the front.

The Short Sleeves.—Using No. 12 needles cast on 77 sts., work 1 in. in g.st.

The frock is knitted in a firm rib with the front fly opening in garter stitch.

Next row.—* P. 5, k. 1; rep. from * to last 5 sts., p. 5.

Next row.—* K. 5, p. 1; rep. from * to last 5 sts., k. 5.

Continue in rib, inc. 1 st. at both ends of next row and every following 4th row until work measures 2½ ins. from commencement.

Change to No. 10 needles and continue in rib inc. as before on every 4th row until there are 91 sts. on the needle, working the increased sts. into the rib.

Continue without shaping until work measures 5 ins. from commencement, ending with row on wrong side of the work.

Shape the Top thus:—

1st row.—K. 2 tog., work in rib to last 2 sts., k. 2 tog.

2nd to 3rd rows.—Rep. 1st row twice.

4th row.—Work in rib to end.

Rep. the last 4 rows 10 times.

Cast off remaining sts.

Alternative Instructions for Long Sleeves.—Using No. 12 needles cast on 53 sts. and work 1 in. in g.st.

Change to No. 10 needles and continue in the p. 5, k. 1 rib as given for the short sleeve, inc. 1 st. at both ends of the 5th row and every following 8th row until there are 91 sts. on the needle. Continue without shaping until work measures 18 ins. from commencement, ending with row on wrong side of work.

Shape the Top as given for the short sleeve.

Make-up.—Press work lightly on wrong side with a hot iron over a damp cloth.

Join side and shoulder seams of the bodice. Join sleeve seams and stitch sleeves into armholes matching seams with side seams. Stitch underwrap behind overwrap at lower edge. Stitch the outside edge of the underwrap to the inside edge of the overwrap (so that the outside edge of the overwrap is free) as far as about 3 ins. from the neck edge. Now make two small buttonloops on the wrong side of the fabric at the inside edge of the underwrap and sew two small buttons to the outside edge of the overwrap to correspond.

Make a crochet casing round the waist on the wrong side thus (*N.B.*—An odd piece of matching wool will be found easier to handle than the bouclé yarn for this purpose):—

Make a single crochet into one edge of the g.st. strip, then make a length of chain sufficient to reach to the other side of the strip diagonally. Join this chain to the opposite edge with another single crochet, then make a similar length of chain and join diagonally to the top edge, and so on all round, thus making a zig-zag of chain joined to top and bottom of the g.st. strip with single crochets. Cut the elastic to fit the waist firmly when slightly stretched and thread through the casing, stitching the ends together neatly.

Stitch the collar round the neck edge. Press the seams.

It suits you! Never mind the pun—it's true. The cardigan (page 53) worn with the frock makes a charming two-piece suit. Or you can make only the skirt (see page 116) and wear a blouse with this suit.

Chatting over tea, and talking of knitteds, don't you take to this afternoon jumper for the not so young and slim? The radiating ribs and tucked shoulder effect slim the bust line, and the frilling at the neck makes the perfect finish.

Fancy Rib Jumper

IN TWO-PLY WOOL

MATERIALS

5 oz. 2-ply wool.
2 No. 10 and 2 No. 12 knitting needles.
¾ yd. narrow frilling.

MEASUREMENTS

Bust size, 38 ins. to 40 ins.
Length, 22 ins.
Sleeve seam, 18 ins.

TENSION

8 sts. to 1 in.

The Front.—Using No. 12 needles cast on 154 sts. and work in following patt.:—

1st row.—P. 2, * k. 3, p. 5; rep. from * 6 times, (k. 3, p. 2) 7 times, k. 3, ** p. 5, k. 3; rep. from ** 6 times, p. 2.

2nd row.—K. 2, * p. 3, k. 5; rep. from * 6 times, (p. 3, k. 2) 7 times, p. 3, ** k. 5, p. 3; rep. from ** 6 times, k. 2.

3rd row.—P. 2, * take wool to the back, insert the needle p.w. through the first st. on left-hand needle and k. the second st., drop this st. off the needle and k. the third st. in the same way, now sl. the first st. from the needle (this will be referred to as "cross next 3 sts."), p. 5; rep. from * 6 times, (take wool to the back, cross next 3 sts., p. 2) 7 times, take wool to the back, cross next 3 sts., ** p. 5, take wool to the back, cross next 3 sts.; rep. from ** 6 times, p. 2.

4th row.—K. 2, * k. 1, m. 1, k. 6; rep. from * 6 times, (k. 1, m. 1, k. 3) 7 times, k. 1, m. 1, k. 1, ** k. 6, m. 1, k. 1; rep. from ** 6 times, k. 2.

5th row.—P. 2, * p. 1, keep wool to front of work, sl. next st. p.w. (the made st. of previous row), w.r.n., p. 6; rep. from * 6 times, (p. 1, keep wool to front of work, sl. next st. p.w., w.r.n., p. 3) 7 times, p. 1, keep wool to front of work, sl. next st. p.w., w.r.n., p. 1, ** p. 6, keep wool to front of work, sl. next st. p.w., w.r.n., p. 1; rep. from ** 6 times, p. 2.

6th row.—K. 2, * k. 1, p. the 2 made sts. tog., k. 6; rep. from * 6 times, (k. 1, p. the 2 made sts. tog., k. 3) 7 times, k. 1, p. the 2 made sts. tog., k. 1, ** k. 6, p. the 2 made sts. tog., k. 1; rep. from ** 6 times, k. 2.

These 6 rows form the patt.

Continue in patt. until work measures 6 ins. from commencement.

Change to No. 10 needles and continue in patt., inc. 1 st. at each end of the 7th row and every following 6th row until 8 increasings have been worked at each side, working these increased sts. into the patt. (170 sts.).

Continue in patt. without shaping until work measures 14½ ins. from lower edge, ending with row on wrong side of work.

Divide for the Front Opening, taking the centre panel up each side of the opening, as follows:—

Next row.—Work in patt. across 84 sts., p. 1, turn. Leave remaining 85 sts. on a spare needle.

Continue in patt. on the first set of 85 sts. until the work measures 15 ins. from lower edge, ending at the side edge.

Shape Armholes thus : Keeping continuity of patt., cast off 8 sts. at beg. of the next row, then dec. 1 st. at the same edge on each of the next 8 rows (69 sts.).

Continue in patt. without shaping until

work measures 19½ ins. from lower edge, ending at armhole edge, with a 6th patt. row.

Decrease for Shoulder Yoke thus:—

Next row.—P. 2, * k. 3, p. 3 tog., p. 2 tog.; rep. from * to last 19 sts., patt. 19 (51 sts.).

Next row.—Patt. 19 sts., * k. 2, p. 3; rep. from * to last 2 sts., k. 2.

Next row.—* P. 2, k. 3; rep. from * to last 21 sts., p. 2, patt. 19.

Rep. the last 2 rows for 1½ ins.

Change to No. 12 needles and continue in the rib with patt. panel until work measures 22 ins. from lower edge, ending at armhole edge.

Shape Shoulders thus :—

Next row.—Cast off 5 sts., work to end of row.

Next row.—Work to end of row.

Rep. last 2 rows 3 times.

Next row.—Cast off 6 sts., work to end of row.

Next row.—Work to end of row.

Rep. last 2 rows once.

Cast off remaining 19 sts.

Rejoin wool to second set of sts. at the neck edge and continue in patt. until work measures 15 ins. from lower edge, ending at the side edge.

Shape armhole as given for the first side, then continue in patt. without further shaping until work measures 19½ ins. from lower edge, ending at the front edge, with a 6th patt. row.

Decrease for Shoulder Yoke thus:—

Next row.—Patt. across 19 sts., * p. 2 tog., p. 3 tog., k. 3; rep. from * to last 2 sts., p. 2 (51 sts.).

Next row.—* K. 2, p. 3; rep. from * to last 21 sts., k. 2, patt. 19.

Next row. — Patt. 19 sts., * k. 2, p. 3; rep. from * to last 2 sts., k. 2.

Rep. last 2 rows for 1½ ins.

Change to No. 12 needles and continue in the rib with patt. panel until work measures 22 ins. from lower edge, ending at armhole edge.

The arrangement of the lacy ribs gives a slimming effect to this jumper designed for the larger figure. A detail of the stitch used is on the right.

If you want a more simple edition of this jumper, knit it in an ordinary plain and purl rib.

Shape shoulder as given for the first shoulder.

The Back.—Using No. 12 needles cast on 127 sts. and work in patt. as follows:—

1st row.—P. 2, * k. 3, p. 5; rep. from * to last 5 sts., k. 3, p. 2.

2nd row.—K. 2, * p. 3, k. 5; rep. from * to last 5 sts., p. 3, k. 2.

3rd row.—P. 2, * take wool to the back, cross next 3 sts., p. 5; rep. from * to last 5 sts., take wool to the back, cross next 3 sts., p. 2.

4th row.—K. 2, * k. 1, m. 1, k. 6; rep. from * to last 4 sts., k. 1, m. 1, k. 3.

5th row.—P. 2, * p. 1, keep wool to front of work, sl. next st. p.w., w.r.n., p. 6; rep. from * to end, ending last rep. with p. 2 instead of p. 6.

6th row.—K. 2, * k. 1, p. the 2 made sts. tog., k. 6; rep. from * to end, ending the last rep. with k. 2 instead of k. 6.

Rep. these 6 rows until the work measures 6 ins. from commencement.

Change to No. 10 needles and continue in patt., inc. 1 st. at each end of the 7th row and every following 6th row until 8 increasings are worked at each side, working these increased sts. into patt. (143 sts.).

Continue in patt. without shaping until work measures 15 ins. from lower edge, ending with row on wrong side of work.

Shape Armholes thus : Keeping continuity of patt., cast off 8 sts. at beg. of next 2 rows, then dec. 1 st. at each end of the next 8 rows (111 sts.).

Continue in patt. without shaping until work measures 22 ins. from lower edge, ending with row on wrong side of work.

Shape Neck and Shoulders thus : Keeping continuity of the patt., cast off 13 sts. at beg. of the next 4 rows, then cast off 12 sts. at beg. of the next 2 rows.

Cast off remaining 35 sts.

The Sleeves.—Using No. 12 needles cast on 63 sts. and work in patt. as given for the back for 2½ ins.

Change to No. 10 needles and continue in patt., inc. 1 st. at each end of the 7th row and every following 6th row until 23 increasings have been worked at each side, working the increased sts. into the patt. (109 sts.).

Continue in patt. without shaping until work measures 18 ins. from lower edge, ending with row on wrong side of work.

Shape the Top thus: Work 4 rows in patt., dec. 1 st. at each end of every row.

Work 1 row without shaping.

Rep. the last 5 rows until 29 sts. remain. Cast off remaining sts.

Make-up.—Press work lightly on wrong side with a warm iron over a damp cloth. Join side, shoulder and sleeve seams. Stitch sleeves into armholes, matching seams to side seams. Press the seams. Stitch frilling round neck edge.

It's not easy to be a glamour girl first thing in the morning, but in this enchanting bedjacket and hood, you simply can't help it. Jacket and hood are lined, and stitched to give a quilted effect.

FOR BRIGHT, FAIR MORNINGS

Quilted Bedjacket

IN RAYON, BOUCLÉ OR CRÊPE YARN

MATERIALS

12 oz. of "Fancy Crêpe" yarn or rayon and wool bouclé equivalent to 4-ply in thickness.

2 No. 10 needles (adjust size of needles, if necessary, to obtain given tension with the yarn used).

2 yds. of 36-in. satin for the lining.

N.B.—If pure wool is used 10 oz. 4-ply will be sufficient.

MEASUREMENTS

To fit a 34-in. bust loosely.
Length to shoulder seam, 19½ ins.
Sleeve seam, 16¼ ins.

TENSION

Work to produce 6¼ sts. to 1 in.

The Back.—Using No. 10 needles cast on 129 sts. and work in the following diagonal patt.:—

1st row.—* K. 1, p. 31; rep. from * to last st., k. 1.

2nd row.—K. 1, * p. 1, k. 29, p. 1, k. 1; rep. from * to end.

3rd row.—P. 2, * k. 1, p. 27, k. 1, p. 3; rep. from * to last 31 sts., k. 1, p. 27, k. 1, p. 2.

4th row.—K. 3, * p. 1, k. 25, p. 1, k. 5; rep. from * to last 30 sts., p. 1, k. 25, p. 1, k. 3.

5th row.—P. 4, * k. 1, p. 23, k. 1, p. 7; rep. from * to last 29 sts., k. 1, p. 23, k. 1, p. 4.

6th row.—K. 5, * p. 1, k. 21, p. 1, k. 9; rep. from * to last 28 sts., p. 1, k. 21, p. 1, k. 5.

7th row.—P. 6, * k. 1, p. 19, k. 1, p. 11; rep. from * to last 27 sts., k. 1, p. 19, k. 1, p. 6.

8th row.—K. 7, * p. 1, k. 17, p. 1, k. 13; rep. from * to last 26 sts., p. 1, k. 17, p. 1, k. 7.

9th row.—P. 8, * k. 1, p. 15, k. 1, p. 15; rep. from * to last 25 sts., k. 1, p. 15, k. 1, p. 8.

10th row.—K. 9, *p. 1, k.13, p. 1, k.17; rep. from * to last 24 sts., p. 1, k. 13, p. 1, k. 9.

11th row.—P. 10, * k. 1, p. 11, k. 1, p. 19; rep. from * to last 23 sts., k. 1, p. 11, k. 1, p. 10.

12th row.—K. 11, * p. 1, k. 9, p. 1, k. 21; rep. from * to last 22 sts., p. 1, k. 9, p. 1, k. 11.

13th row.—P. 12, * k. 1, p. 7, k. 1, p. 23; rep. from * to last 21 sts., k. 1, p. 7, k. 1, p. 12.

14th row.—K. 13, * p. 1, k. 5, p. 1, k. 25; rep. from * to last 20 sts., p. 1, k. 5, p. 1, k. 13.

15th row.—P. 14, * k. 1, p. 3, k. 1, p. 27; rep. from * to last 19 sts., k. 1, p. 3, k. 1, p. 14.

16th row.—K. 15, * p. 1, k. 1, p. 1, k. 29; rep. from * to last 18 sts., p. 1, k. 1, p. 1, k. 15.

17th row.—P. 16, * k. 1, p. 31; rep. from * to last 17 sts., k. 1, p. 16.

18th row.—As 16th row.

19th row.—As 15th row.

20th row.—As 14th row.

21st row.—As 13th row.

22nd row.—As 12th row.

23rd row.—As 11th row.

24th row.—As 10th row.

25th row.—As 9th row.
26th row.—As 8th row.
27th row.—As 7th row.
28th row.—As 6th row.
29th row.—As 5th row.
30th row.—As 4th row.
31st row.—As 3rd row.
32nd row.—As 2nd row.

These 32 rows form the patt.

Commence again at the 1st row and continue in patt. until the work measures $12\frac{1}{2}$ ins.

Shape Armholes thus: Continuing in patt., cast off 6 sts. at beginning of next 2 rows, then dec. 1 st. at each end of the next 10 rows (97 sts.).

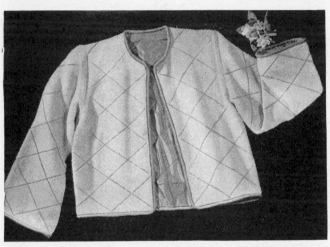

The bedjacket is knitted in diamond-patterned stocking-stitch. The lining, which is made of wool-back satin, is stitched along the lines of these diamonds to imitate quilting.

Continue in patt. on these sts. until the work measures $19\frac{1}{2}$ ins., ending with row on wrong side of work. (The right side is the purl side of the fabric.)

Shape Shoulders thus: Cast off 11 sts. at beginning of the next 6 rows.

Cast off remaining sts.

The Right Front.—Using No. 10 needles cast on 65 sts. and work in patt. as given for the back until the work measures $12\frac{1}{2}$ ins. You should end with a row on the right side of the work facing you.

Shape Armhole thus: Cast off 6 sts. at beginning of the next row, then dec. 1 st. at this same edge on the next 10 rows (49 sts.).

Continue in patt. until work measures 17 ins., ending at the straight front edge.

Shape Neck thus: Cast off 8 sts. at the beginning of the next row, then dec. 1 st. at this same edge on the next 8 rows (33 sts.).

Continue in patt. until work measures $19\frac{1}{2}$ ins., ending at armhole edge.

Shape Shoulder thus:—

Next row.—Cast off 11 sts., patt. to end.

Next row.—Patt. to end.

Rep. last 2 rows once.

Cast off remaining 11 sts.

The Left Front.—Using No. 10 needles cast on 65 sts. and work in patt. as given for the back until the work measures $12\frac{1}{2}$ ins., ending with row on wrong side of work.

Shape Armhole and complete the front as given for the right front.

The Sleeves.—Using No. 10 needles cast on 97 sts. and work in patt. as given for the back until the work measures $16\frac{1}{2}$ ins.

Shape Top thus: Dec. 1 st. at both ends of every alternate row until 85 sts. remain, then dec. at both ends of every row until 25 sts. remain. Cast off remaining sts.

Make-up.—Press work lightly on wrong side with hot iron over a damp cloth.

Join the side seams neatly, taking care to match the patt. correctly.

Place lining and knitted fabric together, wrong sides facing one another (purl side of knitted fabric is right side) and first tack, then machine stitch, all the diagonal lines, to give a quilted effect. "Quilt" the sleeve pieces in the same way. Cut off all surplus satin. Join seams and bind all edges with crossway strips over a piping cord. Alternatively this may be done before the quilting in the form of a piping. The hood (see below) can be attached to the neck of the bedjacket with press fasteners, so that it is handy to slip on.

Here is another idea for the bedjacket. In the middle of each diamond, embroider a flower or a motif. Finish by picot edging the jacket in a contrasting shade.

Quilted Hood

TO MATCH THE BEDJACKET

MATERIALS

3 oz. of the yarn used for the bedjacket.
2 No. 10 knitting needles.
$\frac{1}{2}$ yd. of the satin used for lining the bedjacket.

TENSION $6\frac{1}{2}$ sts. to 1 in.

Cast on 65 sts. and work in the diamond patt. as given for the bedjacket until work measures about 26 ins. Cast off.

Make-up.—Press work lightly on the wrong side (the purl side is the right side) under a damp cloth. Bind the long edges with crossway strips over a piping cord, then cut a piece of satin the same size as the knitted fabric, allowing small turnings and "quilt" to match the bedjacket, turning in and slip stitching the raw edges afterwards.

The hood may be worn separately or attached to the neck of the bedjacket with press fasteners.

The hood is very warm, and kind to hair rumpled by sleep.

Bedroom Slippers

IN RUG WOOL

It's fashionable now to make your own bedroom slippers. These are made in rug wool, with gay coloured cords.

MATERIALS

4 oz. of rug wool.

2 No. 4 knitting needles.

About 2 yds. of thick soft cord (or twisted cord made from odd knitting wool).

A pair of slipper soles.

MEASUREMENTS

To fit a 5 or 6 size sole.

TENSION   3 sts. to 1 in.

Cast on 66 sts. (using the two-needle method of casting on) and work 2 rows st.st. (1 row k., 1 row p.).

3rd row.—(K. 31, k. 2 tog.) twice, k. to end.

4th row.—(P. 30, p. 2 tog.) twice, p. to end.

5th row.—(K. 29, k. 2 tog.) twice, k. to end.

Continue thus dec. twice in the middle of every row until 52 sts. remain.

Next row.—(K. 1, k. 2 tog.) twice, k. 10, (k. 2 tog., k. 1) 6 times, k. 2 tog., k. 10, (k. 2 tog., k. 1) twice.

Cast off. Make another slipper in the same way.

Sew up the back seam. Lace the cord up the front of the slippers as far as the top edge, then continue to lace the two edges together so that the opening will just go over the foot to fit the ankle neatly. Leave ends to tie in a bow. Stitch the lower edges of slippers firmly to the soles.

Here are two more suggestions to set your imagination working. Embroider coloured flowers or stars all over the slippers or knit them in gay stripes.

Classic Cardigan

WITH POCKETS

MATERIALS

13 oz. 4-ply wool.
2 No. 8 and 2 No. 12 knitting needles.
9 buttons.

MEASUREMENTS

Length, 25 ins.   Chest, 38 ins.
Sleeve seam, 19 ins.

TENSION

6 sts. to 1 in.

The Back.—Using No. 8 needles cast on 124 sts. and work in following patt.:—

1st row.—* (K. 1, p. 1) 3 times, k. 7; rep. from * to last 7 sts., (k. 1, p. 1) 3 times, k. 1.

2nd row.—* (P. 1, k. 1) 3 times, p. 1, k. 6; rep. from * to last 7 sts. (p. 1, k. 1) 3 times, p. 1.

These 2 rows form the g.st. and rib patt. which is used throughout.

Continue in patt. until the work measures 17 ins., ending with row on wrong side of work.

Shape Armholes thus: Cast off 7 sts. at beg. of next 2 rows, then dec. 1 st. at both ends of the next 6 rows (98 sts. remain).

Continue in patt. without shaping until work measures 24½ ins. from lower edge, ending with row on wrong side of work.

Shape Shoulders thus: Cast off 10 sts. at beg. of the next 6 rows.

Cast off remaining 38 sts.

Pocket Linings.—Using No. 8 needles cast on 33 sts. and work in patt. for 4½ ins.,

ending with a row on the right side

Leave these sts. on a spare needle and work a second piece in the same way, leaving these sts. also on a spare needle.

The Right Front.—Using No. 8 needles cast on 59 sts. and work in patt. for 4¾ ins., ending with row on right side of work.

Next row.—Patt. 13 sts., k. 33 sts., patt. 13. Rep. this row twice more.

Next row.—Patt. 13 sts., cast off the next 33 sts., patt. to end.

Next row.—Patt. 13 sts., sl. 33 sts. for a pocket lining on to the left-hand needle with wrong side of work facing, and work in patt. to end of row.

Continue in patt. until the work measures 17 ins., ending with row on wrong side of work.

Shape Armhole and Front Edge thus:—

Next row.—K. 2 tog., patt. to end.

Next row.—Cast off 7 sts., patt. to end.

Next row.—K. 2 tog., patt. to last 2 sts., k. 2 tog.

Next row.—K. 2 tog., patt. to end.

Rep. last 2 rows twice.

This completes the armhole shaping, 42 sts. remain.

Continue in patt., dec. 1 st. at the front edge on every alternate row until 40 sts. remain, then dec. on every 4th row until 30 sts. remain.

Continue in patt. without shaping until work measures 25½ ins., ending at armhole edge.

Shape Shoulder thus:—

Next row.—Cast off 10 sts., patt. to end.

The cardigan is knitted in a wide rib of garter stitch and plain and purl.

Next row.—Patt. to end.

Rep. last 2 rows once.

Cast off remaining 10 sts.

The Left Front.—Using No. 8 needles cast on 59 sts. and work in patt., inserting the pocket lining as given for the right front, for 17 ins., ending with row on wrong side of work.

Shape Armhole and Front Edge thus:—

Next row.—Cast off 7 sts., patt. to last 2 sts., k. 2 tog.

Next row.—Patt. to end.

Next row.—K. 2 tog., patt. to last 2 sts., k. 2. tog.

Next row.—Patt. to last 2 sts., k. 2 tog.

Rep. last 2 rows twice.

This completes the armhole shaping, 42 sts. remain.

Continue in patt., shaping the front edge and shoulder exactly as given for the right front.

The Sleeves.—Using No. 12 needles cast on 66 sts. and work in patt. as follows:

1st row.—(P. 1, k. 1) twice, * k. 6, (k. 1, p. 1) 3 times, k. 1 ; rep. from * to last 10 sts., k. 6, (k. 1, p. 1) twice.

2nd row.—(K. 1, p. 1) twice, * k. 6, (p. 1, k. 1) 3 times, p. 1 ; rep. from * to last 10 sts., k. 6, (p. 1, k. 1) twice.

Rep. these 2 rows for 3 ins.

Change to No. 8 needles and continue in patt., inc. 1 st. at both ends of the 5th row and every following 6th row until there are 104 sts. on the needle, working the increased sts. into the patt.

Continue without shaping until the work measures 19 ins. from commencement.

Shape Top thus: Dec. 1 st. at both ends of next row and every alternate row until 92 sts. remain, then dec. at both ends of every row until 28 sts. remain.

Cast off remaining sts.

The Front Band.—Using No. 12 needles cast on 8 sts. and work ½ in. in g.st.

Next row.—K. 2, cast off 4 sts. for a buttonhole, k. to end.

Next row.—K. 2, cast on 4 sts., k. 2.

* Continue in g.st. until work measures 2 ins. from commencement of the previous buttonhole, then make another buttonhole in next 2 rows. Rep. from * 7 times.

Continue in g.st. until the band is the correct length to fit all round fronts and back of neck edges when slightly stretched.

Cast off loosely.

Make-up.—Press the work lightly on wrong side with a hot iron over a damp cloth.

Join side, shoulder and sleeve seams.

Stitch sleeves into armholes, matching seams with side seams.

Stitch all round pocket linings on wrong side of work.

Place the centre of front band to centre back of neck with the top buttonhole just below the commencement of the left front shaping and stitch the band neatly all round front and back of neck edges.

Sew buttons on to right front band matching with buttonholes.

Press the seams.

Taking things comfortably. His spade, his pipe, and above all, the right clothes must play their part in the programme. This well-fitting cardigan is his idea of comfort, with his favourite neckline and pockets in which to put things.

"Should be good." It is good—*only we mean your lumber jacket, not your photography. Actually it's the same design as the classic cardigan only it has a high round neckline and a deep welt instead of pockets.*

Ribbed Lumber Jacket

MATERIALS

11 oz. 4-ply wool.

2 No. 8 and 2 No. 12 knitting needles.

11 buttons.

MEASUREMENTS

Length, 23 ins.   Chest, 38 ins.

Sleeve seam, 19 ins.

TENSION

6 sts. to 1 in.

The Back.—Using No. 12 needles cast on 124 sts. and work 4 ins. in k. 1, p. 1 rib.

Change to No. 8 needles and the following patt.:—

1st row.—* (K. 1, p. 1) 3 times, k. 7; rep. from * to last 7 sts., (k. 1, p. 1) 3 times, k. 1.

2nd row.—* (P. 1, k. 1) 3 times, p. 1, k. 6; rep. from * to last 7 sts., (p. 1, k. 1) 3 times, p. 1.

These 2 rows form the patt. Continue in patt. until work measures 15 ins.

Shape Armholes thus : Cast off 7 sts. at beg. of next 2 rows, then dec. 1 st. at both ends of the next 6 rows (98 sts. remain).

Continue in patt. without shaping until work measures 23 ins. from lower edge, ending with row on wrong side of work.

Shape Neck and Shoulders thus:—

Next row.—Cast off 10 sts., there now being 1 st. on right-hand needle, patt. 23, k. 2 tog., turn.

Continue on 25 sts. for one shoulder thus:—

Next row.—Cast off 2 sts., patt. to end.

Next row.—Cast off 10 sts., patt. to last 2 sts., k. 2 tog.

Next row.—Cast off 2 sts., patt. to end. Cast off remaining sts.

Rejoin wool to needle point and cast off the centre 26 sts., work in patt. to end of row.

Continue for second shoulder thus :

Next row.—Cast off 10 sts., patt. to last 2 sts., k. 2 tog.

Next row.—Cast off 2 sts., patt. to end.

Rep. last 2 rows once.

Cast off remaining 10 sts.

The Right Front.—Using No. 12 needles cast on 58 sts. and work 4 ins. in k. 1, p. 1 rib, inc. 1 st. at end of last row (59 sts.).

Change to No. 8 needles and continue in patt. as given for back until work measures 15 ins. from lower edge, ending with row on right side of work at the side edge.

Shape Armhole thus: Cast off 7 sts. at beg. of next row, then dec. 1 st. at this same edge on the next 6 rows (46 sts. remain).

Continue without shaping until work measures 20½ ins. from lower edge, ending at straight front edge.

Shape Neck and Shoulder thus : Cast off 4 sts. at beg. of next row, then dec. 1 st. at neck edge on each of the next 12 rows (30 sts. remain).

Continue in patt. without shaping until work measures 23 ins. from lower edge, ending at armhole edge.

Next row.—Cast off 10 sts., patt. to end.

Next row.—Patt. to end.

Rep. last 2 rows once.

Cast off remaining 10 sts.

The Left Front.—Continue exactly as given for the right front until work

The lumber jacket is knitted to the same pattern as the cardigan, except for the high round neckline.

measures 15 ins. from lower edge, ending with row on wrong side of work at the side edge. Shape armhole and complete the front as given for right front.

The Sleeves.—Using No. 12 needles cast on 54 sts. and work 3 ins. in k. 1, p. 1 rib.

Next row.—Rib 4, * work twice into next st., rib 3; rep. from * to last 2 sts., rib 2 (66 sts.).

Change to No. 8 needles and continue in patt. as follows:—

1st row.—(P. 1, k. 1) twice, * k. 6, (k. 1, p. 1) 3 times, k. 1; rep. from * to last 10 sts., k. 6, (k. 1, p. 1) twice.

2nd row.—(K. 1, p. 1) twice, * k. 6, (p. 1, k. 1) 3 times, p. 1 ; rep. from * to last 10 sts., k. 6, (p. 1, k. 1) twice.

Rep. these 2 rows once.

Continue in patt., inc. 1 st. at both ends of next row and every following 6th row until there are 104 sts. on the needle.

Continue without shaping until work measures 19 ins. from commencement.

Shape Top thus : Dec. 1 st. at both ends of every alternative row until 92 sts. remain, then dec. at both ends of every row until 28 sts. remain. Cast off remaining sts.

Right Front Band.—Using No. 12 needles cast on 8 sts. and work in g.st. for 20½ ins.

Leave these sts. on the No. 12 needle.

Left Front Band.—Using No. 12 needles cast on 8 sts. and work in g.st. for ½ in.

Next row.—K. 2, cast off 4 sts. for a buttonhole, k. to end.

Next row.—K. 2, cast on 4 sts. k. 2.

* Continue in g.st. until work measures 2 ins. from the commencement of the previous buttonhole, then make another buttonhole in next 2 rows.

Rep. from * 8 times, then continue in g.st. until work measures 2 ins. from commencement of the last buttonhole. Leave these sts. on the No. 12 needle.

The Neck Band.—Join the shoulder seams.

With right side of the work towards you k. 8 sts. for right front band, then on to the same needle pick up and k. 32 sts. along neck edge to shoulder seam, 48 sts. along back of neck edge, 32 sts. along front neck edge, then k. 8 sts. for left front band.

Next row.—* K. 1, p. 1 ; rep. from * to end.

Next row.—* K. 1, p. 1 ; rep. from * to last 6 sts., cast off 4 sts., rib to end.

Next row.—Rib 2, cast on 4 sts., rib to end.

Continue in rib until work measures 1 in. from commencement of neck band.

Cast off loosely in rib.

Make-up.—Press the work lightly with a hot iron over a damp cloth. Join side and sleeve seams. Stitch sleeves into armholes, matching seams with side seams Stitch front bands neatly to the front edges. Sew buttons on to right front band, matching with buttonholes. Press the seams.

THE BEST KIND OF "SLIP-ON"

Sleeveless Pullover

WITH ROUND NECK

MATERIALS

6 oz. 4-ply wool.

2 No. 14, 2 No. 12 and 2 No. 8 needles.

MEASUREMENTS

Length, 21 ins.   Chest size, 40 ins.

TENSION

6 sts. to 1 in. on No. 8 needles, measured over the slightly stretched rib.

The Back.—Using No. 12 needles cast on 122 sts. and work in the following rib.

1st row.—* K. 2, p. 2; rep. from * to last 2 sts., k. 2.

2nd row.—* P. 2 k. 2; rep. from * to last 2 sts., p. 2.

This rib of k. 2, p. 2 is used throughout the pullover.

Rep. these 2 rows until work measures 3 ins. Change to No. 8 needles and keeping the rib correct, inc. 1 st. at both ends of the 10th and every following 6th row until there are 142 sts. on the needle

Continue without shaping until work measures 13 ins. from the beginning.

Shape Armholes thus: Cast off 8 sts. at beg. of each of the next 2 rows. Then, still keeping the rib correct, dec. 1 st. at both ends of every row until there are 110 sts. on the needle.

Continue without shaping until work measures 21 ins. from the beginning.

Shape Neck and Shoulders thus:—

1st row.—Cast off 8, rib 28, including st. already on the needle when the casting-off is completed, k. 2 tog., turn.

2nd row.—K. 2 tog., rib to the end.

3rd row.—Cast off 8, rib 18, k. 2 tog., turn.

4th row.—K. 2 tog., rib to the end.

5th row.—Cast off 8, rib 8, k. 2 tog., turn.

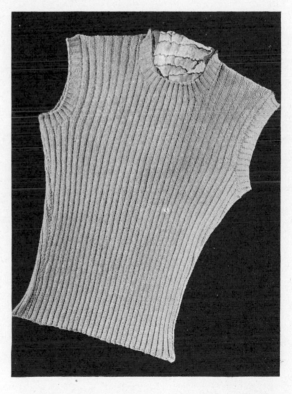

Utility garment reduced to simplest form. Knitted in plain rib, high round neck, no welt.

Battle dress for gardeners—or perhaps it should be "after the battle" dress. When a man finishes working he should slip on something to prevent a chill. Make it light and simple like this pullover.

6th row.—K. 2 tog., rib to the end.

Cast off remaining sts.

Place the centre 34 sts. on a spare needle for the neck and work on the second set of sts. in the same way, re-joining the wool at the needle point and ribbing 1 row to begin with in order to commence the shoulder shaping at the armhole edge.

The Front.—Work exactly as given for the back until the armhole shapings have been completed, and there are 110 sts. on the needle. Continue in rib without shaping until work measures 18 ins. from the beg.

Shape Neck and Shoulders thus:—

Next row.—Rib 41, turn.

Continue to work on these 41 sts., dec. 1 st. at the neck edge on every row until there are 32 sts. on the needle. Continue without shaping until work measures 21 ins. from the beg., ending with a row at the armhole edge.

Next row.—Cast off 8, rib to the end.

Next row.—Rib to the end.

Rep. these 2 rows twice more. Cast off remaining sts.

Place the centre 28 sts. on a spare needle and work on the second set of 41 sts. in the same way.

The Front Neck Band.—Starting at the neck edge of the left-hand shoulder, with the right side of the work facing, and using No. 14 needles, pick up and k. 36 sts. along the side of the neck, 28 sts. from the spare needle and 36 sts. along the right edge of the neck. There are now 100 sts. on the needle. Work on these 100 sts. in a rib of k. 2, p. 2 for 1 in. Cast off fairly loosely in rib.

The Back Neck Band.—Starting at the neck edge of the right-hand shoulder, with the right side of the work facing and using No. 14 needles, pick up and k. 10 sts. along the side of the neck, 34 sts. from the spare needle and 10 sts. from the left side of the neck. Work on these 54 sts. in a rib of k. 2, p. 2 for 1 in. Cast off fairly loosely in rib.

The Sleeve Bands.—Join the shoulder seams. With the right side of the work facing and using No. 14 needles, pick up and k. 156 sts. round the armhole edge. Work on these 156 sts. in a rib of k. 2, p. 2 for 1 in. Cast off fairly loosely in rib.

Make-up.—Press all knitting, with the exception of the waist ribbing, lightly on the wrong side, using a warm iron over a damp cloth. Join the side seams and press.

FURTHER TO THIS SUGGESTION, MAKE

Sleeved Ribbed Pullover

MATERIALS

11 oz. of 4-ply wool will be required.

MEASUREMENTS

Sleeve seam, 19 ins.

The Back.—This is worked exactly as given for the original back until the side shapings have been completed and there are 142 sts. on the needle. Now continue without shaping until work measures 13½ ins. from the beg.

Shape the armholes as given in the original instructions, and complete the neck and shoulders in the same way.

The Front.—Work as given for the instructions for the original back until the side shapings have been completed and there are 142 sts. on the needle. Continue without shaping until the work measures 13½ ins. from the beg.

Shape the armholes as given in the original instructions.

Divide for the Neck.—There are now 110 sts. on the needle.

Next row.—Rib 54, turn.

Next row.—K. 2 tog., rib to the end.

Next row.—Rib 53, turn.

Continue in this way, dec. 1 st. at the beg. of every alternate row at the neck edge until there are 32 sts. on the needle.

Continue without shaping until work measures 21 ins. from the beg., ending with a row at the armhole edge.

Shape Shoulders thus:—

Next row.—Cast off 8 sts., rib to end.

Next row.—Work to the end.

Rep. these 2 rows twice more. Cast off remaining sts.

Place the 2 centre sts. on a spare needle and leave for the present, and

The pullover has long sleeves and a V neck but is basically the same as the sleeveless slip-on.

work on the second set of 54 sts. in the same way for the other shoulder.

The Sleeves.—Using No. 12 needles cast on 60 sts. and work in a rib of k. 2, p. 2 for 3 ins. Change to No. 8 needles and continue in rib, inc. 1 st. at both ends of the next and every following 6th row until there are 90 sts. on the needle. Continue without shaping until work measures 19 ins. from the beg.

Shape Top thus : Dec. 1 st. at both ends of every alternate row until there are 56 sts. on the needle. Then dec. 1 st. at both ends of every row until there are 24 sts. on the needle. Cast off.

Back Neck Band.—This is worked as given for the back neck band in the original instructions.

Front Neck Band.—Beginning at the neck edge of the left shoulder, and with the right side of the work facing, and using No. 14 needles, pick up and k. 60 sts. along the neck edge, the 2 sts. from the spare needle and 60 sts. along the right side of the neck. There are now 122 sts. on the needle.

Work on these 122 sts. as follows:—

1st row.—* P. 2, k. 2 ; rep. from * to end.

2nd row.—Work 58 sts. in this rib, p. 2 tog., k. 2, p. 2 tog., rib to the end.

3rd row.—Work 57 sts. in rib, p. 2 tog., p. 2, p. 2 tog., rib to end.

Continue in this way, dec. 1 st. at each side of the centre 2 sts. until the neck ribbing measures 1 in. Cast off fairly loosely in rib.

Make-up.—Press all the knitting with the exception of the waist and wrist ribbing, on the wrong side, lightly, using a warm iron over a damp cloth. Join the side, shoulder and sleeve seams and stitch the sleeves into the armholes. Press all seams.

Week-end kit for week-end weather. But although the pullover is ideal for days off, it is also a safe bet for working days. It goes unobtrusively under whatever jacket or tunic has to be worn.

"*No, I shan't need a coat!*" *Not with this pullover. Actually it was designed for men who sometimes discard collar and tie too. The high straight neck needs no more than a scarf or handkerchief.*

FOR REAL CLOTHES ECONOMY

Straight Neck Pullover

IN TIGHT CABLE STITCH

MATERIALS

12 oz. of 4-ply wool.
2 No. 8 and 2 No. 12 knitting needles.
A short spare needle pointed at both ends.

MEASUREMENTS

Length, 21 ins.   Chest, 38 ins.
Sleeve seam, 19 ins.

TENSION

2 complete patterns (12 sts.) measure 1½ ins. unstretched.

Front and Back Both Alike.   Using No. 12 needles cast on 122 sts. and work in the following patt.:—

1st row.—* P. 2, k. 4; rep. from * to last 2 sts., p. 2.

2nd row.—*K. 2, p. 4; rep. from * to last 2 sts. k. 2.

3rd row.—* P. 2, sl. the next 2 sts. on to spare needle and leave at front of work, k. next 2 sts., then k. 2 sts. from spare needle; rep. from * to last 2 sts., p. 2.

4th row.—As 2nd row.

These 4 rows form the patt.

Continue in patt. until work measures 3½ ins., ending with row on wrong side of the work.

Change to No. 8 needles and continue in patt., inc. 1 st. at both ends of the 5th row and every following 4th row until there are 146 sts. on the needle, working increased sts. into the patt.

Continue in patt. without shaping until work measures 13½ ins. from lower edge.

Shape Armholes thus : Keeping continuity of the patt., cast off 6 sts. at the beg. of the next 2 rows, then dec. 1 st. at both ends of the next 12 rows (110 sts. remain).

Continue in patt. without shaping until the work measures 21 ins. from lower edge, ending with row on wrong side of work.

Shape Neck and Shoulders thus: Keeping

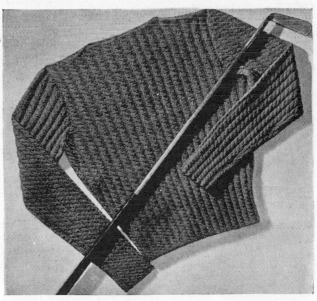

The pullover is knitted in a small tight cable which gives an interesting effect and a particularly firm fabric.

continuity of the patt., cast off 7 sts. at the beg. of the next 4 rows, then cast off 8 sts. at the beg. of the next 4 rows, but k. the last 2 of these 4 rows plain instead of in patt., thus forming a ridge of g.st. at the neck edge.

Cast off remaining 50 sts. loosely.

Work a second piece in the same way.

The Sleeves.—Using No. 12 needles cast on 74 sts. and work in patt. for 3 ins. Change to No. 8 needles and continue in patt., inc. 1 st. at both ends of the 5th row and every following 6th row until there are 98 sts. on the needle, then inc. at both ends of every 8th row until there are 110 sts. on the needle, working the increased sts. into the patt. Continue in patt. without shaping until the work measures 19 ins. from commencement.

Shape Top thus : Dec. 1 st. at both ends of every row until 30 sts. remain.

Cast off remaining sts.

Make-up.—Press work lightly on wrong side to the correct measurements, using a hot iron over a damp cloth.

Join side, shoulder and sleeve seams.

Stitch sleeves into armholes, matching seams with side seams. Press the seams.

ANOTHER EDITION IN CABLE

Sleeveless Pullover

MATERIALS

7 oz. of 4-ply wool.
2 No. 8 and 2 No. 12 knitting needles. A short spare needle pointed at both ends.

MEASUREMENTS

Length, 21 ins.   Chest, 38 ins.

TENSION

2 complete patterns (12 sts.) measure $1\frac{1}{2}$ ins. unstretched.

Front and Back Both Alike.—Using No. 12 needles cast on 122 sts. and work in following patt. :—

1st row.—* P. 2, k. 4; rep. from * to last 2 sts., p. 2.

2nd row.—* K. 2, p. 4; rep. from * to last 2 sts., k. 2.

3rd row.—* P. 2, sl. the next 2 sts. on to spare needle and leave at front of work, k. next 2 sts., then k. 2 sts. from spare needle; rep. from * to last 2 sts., p. 2.

4th row.—As 2nd row.

These 4 rows form the patt.

Continue in patt. until work measures $3\frac{1}{2}$ ins. ending with a row on wrong side of work.

Change to No. 8 needles and continue in patt., inc. 1 st. at both ends of the 5th row and every following 4th row until there are 146 sts. on the needle, working the increased sts. into the patt.

Continue in patt. until the work measures 13 ins., ending with row on right side of work.

Shape Armholes and Work Armhole Bands thus :—

1st row.—K. 12, patt. to last 12 sts., k. 12.

2nd row.—K. 12, patt. to last 12 sts., k. 12.

3rd to 4th rows.—Rep. last 2 rows once.

5th row.—Cast off 8 sts., there now being 1 st. on right-hand needle, k. 3, work in patt. to last 12 sts., k. 4, cast off remaining 8 sts. Rejoin wool at needle point.

"Gosh, what a beauty!" Well, he's studying aeroplanes but the
same remark goes for his pullover. It's the sleeveless version of the
cable rib jersey. The neckline is the same as the long-sleeved version.

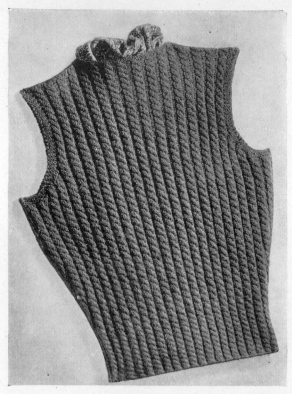

6th row.—K. 4, p. 2 tog., work in patt. to last 6 sts., p. 2 tog., k. 4.

7th row.—K. 4, k. 2 tog., work in patt. to last 6 sts., k. 2 tog., k. 4.

Rep. last 2 rows 4 times.

16th row.—As 6th row.

17th row.—K. 4, work in patt. to last 4 sts., k. 4.

Rep. last 2 rows twice.

This completes the armhole shaping and 104 sts. remain.

Continue in patt. with armhole bands in g.st. until the work measures 21 ins., ending with row on wrong side of work.

Shape Neck and Shoulders thus : Continuing in patt., cast off 7 sts. at the beg. of the next 8 rows.

Cast off remaining 48 sts. loosely.

Work a second piece in the same way.

Both versions of this pullover are designed with an eye to simplicity in making. There are no borders to sew on, and fine needles give the " welt " effect.

Make-up.—Press the work lightly on wrong side to correct measurements, using a hot iron over a damp cloth. Backstitch the shoulder seams. Join side seams, Press the seams.

Socks with Clocks

JUST A BIT DIFFERENT

MATERIALS

4 oz. of 3-ply wool.

4 No. 13 knitting needles.

MEASUREMENTS

Length of leg to bottom of heel, 15 ins.

Length of foot, 10 ins.

TENSION

$9\frac{1}{2}$ sts. to 1 in.

Cast on 84 sts., 28 sts. on each of 3 needles and work in rounds of k. 1, p. 1 rib for 3 ins.

Continue in smooth fabric (each round

knit) for a further 3 ins., finishing at the end of the round.

Next round.—K. 17, p. 3, k. 3, p. 3, k. 33, p. 3, k. 3, p. 3, k. 16.

Rep. the last round until the work measures 12 ins. from the commencement, finishing at the end of the round.

Divide for Heel:—

Next row.—K. 22 sts., turn.

Next row.—P. 43 sts., turn.

Leave the remaining 41 sts. on the 2 needles for the instep and continue in rows on the 43 heel sts. thus:—

1st row.—K. to end.

2nd row.—P. to end.

Rep. the last 2 rows 16 times.

Turn Heel:—

1st row.—K. 25, k. 2 tog., turn.

2nd row.—P. 8, p. 2 tog., turn.

3rd row.—K. 9, k. 2 tog., turn.

4th row.—P. 10, p. 2 tog., turn.

5th row.—K. 11, k. 2 tog., turn.

6th row.—P. 12, p. 2 tog., turn.

Continue in this way, working 1 more st. before the k. 2 tog. on every row until the sts. are all worked on to one needle.

Now slip the two sets of instep sts. on to one needle and work for the foot thus:

Next row.—K. 12 heel sts., now with a second needle, k. the remaining 13 heel sts., then pick up and k. 18 sts. down side of heel flap, now with a third needle, work across instep sts. thus:—

K. 1, sl. 1, k. 2 tog., p.s.s.o., k. to last 4 sts., sl. 1, k. 2 tog., p.s.s.o., k. 1 (37 sts.) now with a fourth needle k. up 18 sts. along second side of the heel flap, then k. the 12 heel sts. (This will be regarded as the end of the round.)

K. 1 round, then shape for instep thus:

Next row.—First needle: k. to last 3 sts., k. 2 tog., k. 1; second needle: k. to end; third needle: k. 1, sl. 1, k. 1, p.s.s.o., k. to end.

Next round.—K. to end.

Rep. the last 2 rounds until 74 sts. remain in the round (19 + 37 + 18 sts.).

Continue in smooth fabric without shaping until work measures 8 ins. from the back of the heel, finishing at the end of the round.

Shape Toe:—

1st round.—First needle: k. to last 3 sts., k. 2 tog., k. 1; second needle: k. 1, sl. 1, k. 1, p.s.s.o., k. to last 3 sts., k. 2 tog., k. 1; third needle: k. 1, sl. 1, k. 1, p.s.s.o., k. to end.

2nd round.—K. to end.

Rep. the last 2 rounds until 18 sts. remain.

Now k. the 5 sts. from the first needle on to the third needle and graft or cast off the two sets of sts. tog.

Work a second sock, in the same way.

Press work lightly with a hot iron and damp cloth.

A good pattern for socks is absolutely indispensable. These are the very best hand-knitted socks that can be designed. An unusual touch is the addition of ribbed clocks to take the place of decreasings in shaping the legs.

Man's Crochet Béret

MATERIALS

2 oz. 3-ply wool.
A steel crochet hook, No. 1½.

MEASUREMENTS

To fit an average size head.

TENSION

About 7 sts. and 8 rows to 1 in.

Commence with 8 ch. and form these into a ring with a sl.st.

Work 8 d.c. into this ring, then continue in d.c. as follows:—

(*N.B.*—It will be found advisable to mark the commencement of the round with a coloured thread.)

1st round.—2 d.c. into each d.c. of previous round.

2nd round.—1 d.c. into each d.c.

3rd round.—* 1 d.c. into each of next 3 d.c., 2 d.c. into next d.c.; rep. from * to end.

4th round.—* 1 d.c. into each of next 4 d.c., 2 d.c. into next d.c.; rep. from * to end.

5th round.—* 1 d.c. into each of next 5 d.c., 2 d.c. into next d.c.; rep. from * to end.

6th round.—1 d.c. into each d.c.

7th round.—* 1 d.c. into next d.c., 2 d.c. into next d.c.; rep. from * to end.

8th round.—1 d.c. into each d.c.

9th round.—As 7th round.

10th to 13th rounds.—Rep. the 8th round 4 times.

14th round.—* 1 d.c. into each of next 6 d.c., 2 d.c. into next d.c.; rep. from * to end.

15th to 17th rounds.—Rep. the 8th round 3 times.

18th round.—As 7th round.

19th to 21st rounds.—Rep. the 8th round 3 times.

22nd round.—* 1 d.c. into each of next 5 d.c., 2 d.c. into next d.c.; rep. from * to end.

23rd round.—1 d.c. into each d.c.

24th round.—* 2 d.c. into next d.c., 1 d.c. into each of next 4 d.c.; rep. from * to last st., 2 d.c. into next d.c.

25th to 26th rounds.—Rep. the 23rd round twice.

27th round.—(1 d.c. into each of next 8 d.c., 2 d.c. into next d.c.) twice, 1 d.c. into each of next 40 d.c., (2 d.c. into next d.c., 1 d.c. into each of next 8 d.c.) 4 times, 1 d.c. into each of next 40 d.c., (2 d.c. into next d.c., 1 d.c. into each of next 8 d.c.) twice.

28th to 30th rounds.—Rep. the 23rd round 3 times.

31st round.—* 1 d.c. into each of next 9 d.c., 2 d.c. into next d.c.; rep. from * to end.

32nd to 34th rounds.—Rep. the 23rd round 3 times.

35th round.—* 1 d.c. into each of next 10 d.c., 2 d.c. into next d.c.; rep. from * to end.

36th to 38th rounds.—Rep. the 23rd round 3 times.

39th round.—* 1 d.c. into each of the next 11 d.c., 2 d.c. into next d.c.; rep. from * to end.

40th round.—1 d.c. into each d.c.

41st round.—* 1 d.c. into each of next 12 d.c., 2 d.c. into next d.c.; rep. from * to end.

42nd round.—* 1 d.c. into each of next 13 d.c., 2 d.c. into next d.c.; rep. from * to end.

43rd round.—1 d.c. into each d.c.

Rep. the 43rd round for 1 in.

Dec. as follows:—

1st round.—* 1 d.c. into each of next 14 d.c., miss next d.c.; rep. from * to end.

"*Sure, we're going out walks!*" *When the dog sees the béret and the scarf
he knows it's going to be country and rabbits. The béret is plain crochet.
The scarf* (p. *150) is in triangles of plain and purl with garter-st. edges.*

2nd round.—* 1 d.c. into each of next 13 d.c., miss next d.c.; rep. from * to end.

3rd round.—* 1 d.c. into each of next 12 d.c., miss next d.c.; rep. from * to end.

4th round.—* 1 d.c. into each of next 11 d.c., miss next d.c.; rep. from * to end.

5th round.—* 1 d.c. into each of next 10 d.c., miss next d.c.; rep. from * to end.

6th round.—1 d.c. into each d.c.

Rep. the last round for 1 in.

Break off the wool and fasten off.

Make-up.—Press work lightly with a hot iron over a damp cloth, then turn the béret inside out and turn up and press ½ in. at the edge. This may be slip-stitched if desired, or a narrow strip of leather stitched to the extreme edge of the crochet work to fold inside in wear.

Man's Sports Scarf

MATERIALS

5 oz. 4-ply wool.

2 No. 7 knitting needles.

MEASUREMENTS

Length, 54 ins. Width, 12 ins.

TENSION

5½ sts. to 1 in.

Cast on 65 sts. and work in g.st. (each row k.) for 1½ ins.

Continue in patt. with g.st. borders:—

1st row.—K. 4, * k. 1, p. 7; rep. from * to last 5 sts., k. 5.

2nd row.—K. 4, * p. 1, k. 7; rep. from * to last 5 sts., p. 1, k. 4.

3rd row.—K. 4, * k. 2, p. 5, k. 1; rep. from * to last 5 sts., k. 5.

4th row.—K. 4, p. 2, * k. 5, p. 3; rep. from * to last 11 sts., k. 5, p. 2, k. 4.

Detail of the pattern of the scarf.

5th row.—K. 7, * p. 3, k. 5; rep. from * to last 10 sts., p. 3, k. 7.

6th row.—K. 4, p. 3, * k. 3, p. 5; rep. from * to last 10 sts., k. 3, p. 3, k. 4.

7th row.—K. 8, * p. 1, k. 7; rep. from * to last 9 sts., p. 1, k. 8.

8th row.—K. 4, p. 4, * k. 1, p. 7; rep. from * to last 9 sts., k. 1, p. 4, k. 4.

9th to 12th rows.—Work 4 rows in g.st.

13th row.—K. 4, p. 4, * k. 1, p. 7; rep. from * to last 9 sts., k. 1, p. 4, k. 4.

14th row.—K. 8, * p. 1, k. 7; rep. from * to last 9 sts., p. 1, k. 8.

15th row.—K. 4, p. 3, * k. 3, p. 5; rep. from * to last 10 sts., k. 3, p. 3, k. 4.

16th row.—K. 7, * p. 3, k. 5; rep. from * to last 10 sts., p. 3, k. 7.

17th row.—K. 4, p. 2, * k. 5, p. 3; rep. from * to last 11 sts., k. 5, p. 3, k. 4.

18th row.—K. 6, * p. 5, k. 3; rep. from * to last 3 sts., k. 3.

19th row.—K. 4, * p. 1, k. 7; rep. from * to last 5 sts., p. 1, k. 4.

20th row.—K. 4, * k. 1, p. 7; rep. from * to last 5 sts., k. 5.

21st to 24th rows.—Work 4 rows in g.st.

These 24 rows form the patt.

Continue in patt. until work measures 52½ ins. from commencement, ending with an 8th or 20th patt. row.

Work 1½ ins. in g.st. Cast off loosely.

Press work lightly with hot iron over a damp cloth on wrong side.

Plain Ribbed Gloves

KNITTED IN FOUR-PLY WOOL

MATERIALS

2 oz. 4-ply wool.

2 No. 12 knitting needles.

TENSION

About 10 sts. to 1 in., measured over the unstretched rib.

The Right-hand Glove.—Cast on 53 sts. and work in rib thus:—

1st row.—* K. 1, p. 1; rep. from * to last st., k. 1.

2nd row.—* P. 1, k. 1; rep. from * to last st., p. 1.

Rep. these 2 rows for 3 ins., ending with 2nd row of the rib.

Shape Thumb Gusset:—

1st row.—Rib 26, k. 1 st. into right-hand loop of the next st. in row below, k. the st., then k. 1 st. into left-hand loop of this same st. (this will be referred to as k. 3 times into next st.), rib 26.

2nd row.—Rib 26, p. 3, rib 26.

3rd row.—Rib 26, k. 3, rib 26.

4th row.—As 2nd row.

5th row.—Rib 27, k. 3 times into next st., rib 27.

6th to 8th rows.—Work 3 rows in rib.

9th row.—Rib 28, k. 3 times into next st., rib 28.

10th row.—Rib 28, p. 3, rib 28.

11th row.—Rib 28, k. 3, rib 28.

12th row.—As 10th row.

13th row.—Rib 29, k. 3 times into next st., rib 29.

14th to 16th rows.—Work 3 rows in rib.

17th row.—Rib 30, k. 3 times into next st., rib 30.

18th row.—Rib 30, p. 3, rib 30.

19th row.—Rib 30, k. 3, rib 30.

20th row.—As 18th row.

21st row.—Rib 31, k. 3 times into next st., rib 31.

22nd to 24th rows.—Work 3 rows in rib.

25th row.—Rib 32, k. 3 times into next st., rib 32.

26th row.—Rib 32, p. 3, rib 32.

27th row.—Rib 32, k. 3, rib 32.

28th row.—As 26th row.

29th row.—Rib 33, k. 3 times into next st., rib 33.

30th to 32nd rows.—Work 3 rows in rib.

33rd row.—Rib 34, k. 3 times into next st., rib 34.

34th row.—Rib 34, p. 3, rib 34.

35th row.—Rib 34, k. 3, rib 34.

36th row.—As 34th row.

37th row.—Rib 35, k. 3 times into next st., rib 35.

38th row.—Rib to end.

39th row.—Rib 47, turn, cast on 1 st.

40th row.—Rib 22 sts., turn and cast on 1 st.

Work 2½ ins. in rib on these 23 sts. for the thumb, ending with row on wrong side of work.

Next row.—(Rib 3, work 3 tog.) 3 times, rib 2, work 3 tog.

Next row.—Rib to end.

Next row.—(K. 2 tog.) 7 times, k. 1.

Break off the wool, leaving a fairly long piece to be slipped through the remaining sts. and fasten off, then join the thumb seam.

Now with the right-hand needle, k. up 3 sts. through the base of the thumb, work in rib to end (55 sts.).

Continue in rib for 2 ins., ending with row on wrong side of work, then commence the fingers thus:—

The First Finger:—

Next row.—Rib across 36 sts., turn and cast on 1 st.

Next row.—Rib 18 sts., turn and cast on 1 st.

Work 3 ins. in rib on these 19 sts., ending with row on wrong side of work.

Plain, serviceable, hardwearing, these are the sort of gloves that no man can have enough of, come wintry weather

Next row.—(Rib 3, work 3 tog.) 3 times, rib 1.

Next row.—Rib to end.

Next row.—(K. 2 tog.) 6 times, k. 1.

Break off the wool and complete to match the thumb.

The Second Finger.—Now with the right-hand needle, k. up 3 sts. at base of the first finger, rib across 7 sts., turn, cast on 1 st.

Next row.—Rib 18 sts., turn, cast on 1 st.

Work 3¼ ins. in rib on these 19 sts., ending with row on wrong side of work.

Shape top and complete as given for first finger.

The Third Finger.—Now with the right-hand needle, k. up 3 sts. at base of the second finger, rib across 6 sts., turn cast on 1 st.

Next row.—Rib 16 sts., turn, cast on 1 st.

Work 3 ins. in rib on these 17 sts., ending with row on wrong side of work.

Next row.—(Rib 3, work 3 tog.) twice, rib 3, work 2 tog.

Next row.—Rib to end.

Next row.—(K. 2 tog.) 6 times.

Break off the wool and complete to match the thumb.

The Fourth Finger.—Now with the right-hand needle, k. up 3 sts. at base of the third finger, rib next 6 sts.

Work 2½ ins. in rib on these 15 sts., ending with row on wrong side of work.

Next row.—(Rib 3, work 3 tog.) twice, rib 3.

Next row.—Rib to end.

Next row.—(K. 2 tog.) 5 times, k. 1.

Break off the wool, leaving a fairly long piece as before to be slipped through remaining sts. and fasten off, then join finger and side of hand seam.

The Left-hand Glove.—Work exactly as given for the right-hand glove.

Press work lightly with hot iron over a damp cloth.

Ribbed Waistcoat

IN TWO COLOURS

MATERIALS

4 oz. 3-ply wool in light grey.
1 oz. 3-ply wool in dark grey.
2 No. 10 and 2 No. 12 knitting needles.
6 buttons.

MEASUREMENTS

Length from neck edge to lower edge of back, 18 ins.
Width all round at under-arm, 37 ins.

TENSION

$7\frac{1}{2}$ sts. to 1 in.

Pocket Linings (Two Pieces).—Using No. 10 needles and light grey wool cast on 26 sts. and work in following patt.:—

1st row.—P. to end.

2nd row.—* K. 1, p. 1; rep. from * to end.

Rep. these 2 rows until work measures 3 ins., ending with a p. row.

Leave sts. on a spare needle and work a second piece in the same way, leaving these sts. also on a spare needle.

Right Front.—Using No. 10 needles and light grey wool cast on 2 sts.

Work in patt., shaping as follows:—

1st row.—P. twice into each st. (4 sts.).

2nd row.—Cast on 2 sts., * k. 1, p. 1; rep. from * to end.

3rd row.—P. twice into first st., p. to last st., p. twice into next st.

4th row.—Cast on 2 sts., * p. 1, k. 1; rep. from * to end.

5th row.—P. twice into first st., p. to last st., p. twice into next st.

6th row.—Cast on 2 sts.; * k. 1, p. 1; rep. from * to end.

Rep. the last 4 rows, that is, 3rd to 6th rows inclusive, 6 times (62 sts.).

Work 8 rows in patt. without shaping, thus ending at the front edge.

Continue in patt., inc. 1 st. at the side edge on next row and on every following 8th row until the work measures $2\frac{1}{2}$ ins. at the straight front edge, ending with row on wrong side of work.

Next row.—P. 18, cast off the next 26 sts., p. to end.

Next row.—Patt. to the last 18 sts., then slip 26 sts. for a pocket lining on to the left-hand needle, work in patt. across these sts. to end of row.

Continue in patt., inc. at the side edge as before on every 8th row until there are 68 sts. on the needle. Proceed without shaping until work measures 8 ins. at the straight front edge, ending at the front edge.

Shape Front Edge and Armhole thus:—

1st row.—P. 2 tog., p. to end.

2nd to 4th rows.—Work 3 rows in patt.

5th row.—As 1st row.

6th row.—Cast off 8 sts., patt. to end.

7th row.—Work to last 2 sts., p. 2 tog.

8th row.—P. 2 tog., patt. to end.

9th row.—P. 2 tog., p. to last 2 sts., p. 2 tog.

10th row.—As 8th row.

Rep. last 4 rows once.

15th row.—As 7th row.

16th row.—Patt. to end.

17th row.—As 9th row.

18th row.—As 16th row.

Rep. last 4 rows 5 times.

This completes the armhole shaping.

A question of etiquette. To all earnest enquirers! it is perfectly correct to sit in shirt sleeves when wearing this smart tailored waistcoat, knitted in a simple rib with contrasting borders in knit 1, purl 1 rib.

Continue in patt., working the armhole edge straight and continuing to dec. at the front edge on every 6th row until 25 sts. remain. Proceed without shaping until work measures 17½ ins. from the commencement of the straight front edge, ending at armhole edge.

Shape Shoulder thus:—

Next row.—Cast off 8 sts., patt. to end.

last 2 sts., p. twice into next st., p. 1.

4th row.—* P. 1, k. 1; rep. from * to end, cast on 2 sts.

5th row.—As 3rd row.

6th row.—* K. 1, p. 1; rep. from * to end, cast on 2 sts.

Rep. the last 4 rows 6 times (62 sts.).

Work 8 rows in patt. without shaping, thus ending at the side edge.

The waistcoat borders are knitted separately and sewn on.

Next row.—Patt. to end.

Rep. last 2 rows once.

Cast off remaining sts.

The Left Front.—Using No. 10 needles and light grey wool cast on 2 sts. and work in patt., shaping to match the right front as follows:—

1st row.—P. twice into each st. (4 sts.).

2nd row.—(K. 1, p. 1) twice, cast on 2 sts.

3rd row.—P. twice into first st., p. to

Continue in patt., inc. 1 st. at the side edge on next row and on every following 8th row until the work measures 2½ ins. at the straight front edge, ending with row on wrong side of work.

Next row.—P. to the last 44 sts., cast off next 26 sts., p. to end.

Next row.—Patt. across 18 sts., slip 26 sts. for a pocket lining on to the left-hand needle, work in patt. across these sts. to end of row.

Continue in patt., inc. 1 st. at the side edge as before on every 8th row until there are 68 sts. on the needle. Proceed without shaping until work measures 8 ins. at the straight front edge, ending at the front edge.

Now keeping the patt. correct, shape front edge and armhole and complete this front exactly as given for the right front.

The Back.—Using No. 10 needles and light grey wool cast on 130 sts. and work 8 rows in patt.

Continue in patt., inc. 1 st. at each end of the next row and every following 8th row until there are 142 sts. on the needle. Proceed without shaping until work measures 8½ ins. from lower edge.

Shape Armholes thus: Continuing in patt., cast off 8 sts. at beg. of the next 2 rows, then dec. 1 st. at each end of the next 8 rows. Now dec. at each end of every alternate row until 86 sts. remain. Proceed without shaping until work measures 17 ins. from lower edge, ending with row on wrong side of work.

Shape Shoulders thus: Cast off 8 sts. at beg. of the next 4 rows, then cast off 9 sts. at beg. of the next 2 rows.

Cast off remaining sts.

The Front Border.—Using No. 12 needles and dark grey wool cast on 2 sts.

Work in k. 1, p. 1 rib, and inc. 1 st. at the same edge on every row until there are 8 sts. on the needle. Work straight in the rib for 3½ ins., then make a buttonhole in the next 2 rows thus:—

Next row.—Rib 2, cast off 4 sts., rib to end.

Next row.—Rib 2, cast on 4 sts., rib 2.

* Continue in rib for 1½ ins., measured from centre of previous buttonhole, then make another buttonhole in the next 2 rows. Rep. from * 4 times.

Continue in rib until the short edge is the correct length to go all round front and back of neck edges, finishing at the point on the right front. Stretch rib

slightly while measuring. Now dec. 1 st. at the shortest edge on every row until 2 sts. remain.

K. 2 tog. and fasten off.

The Lower Edge Border.—Using No. 12 needles and dark grey wool cast on 2 sts.

Work in k. 1, p. 1 rib, inc. 1 st. at the same edge on every row until there are 8 sts. on the needle.

Continue in rib without shaping for 29 ins., then dec. 1 st. at the shaped or shortest edge on every row until 2 sts. remain. K. 2 tog. and fasten off.

The Armhole Borders.—Using No. 12 needles and dark grey wool cast on 8 sts. Work in k. 1, p. 1 rib without shaping until the band is the correct length to fit all round armhole edge when slightly stretched. Cast off.

Work a second border in the same way.

The Pocket Borders.—Using No. 12 needles and dark grey wool cast on 8 sts. and work in k. 1, p. 1 rib for 3 ins.

Cast off in rib.

Work a second border in the same way.

Make-up.—Press work, excepting the ribbing, lightly on wrong side with a hot iron over a damp cloth.

Join side and shoulder seams.

Pin centre of the front border to centre back of neck, arranging the top buttonhole just below the commencement of the left front shaping and the cast-on and cast-off edges to the front points.

Stitch the shortest edge neatly all round front and back of neck edges.

Now stitch the shortest edge of the lower edge border along lower edge, matching the points with front border points and joining neatly.

Stitch armhole borders round armhole edges, matching joins to the side seams.

Stitch a pocket border along the cast-off edge of each pocket. Stitch round pocket linings on wrong side of work.

Sew buttons on to right front to match with buttonholes. Press the seams.

Tailored Sports Shirt

KNITTED IN TWO-PLY WOOL

MATERIALS

7 oz. 2-ply knitting wool.
2 No. 11 knitting needles.
3 buttons.

MEASUREMENTS

Length, 27 ins.
Chest, 40 ins.
Sleeve seam, 6 ins.

TENSION

9 sts. to 1 in.

The Pocket Lining.—Cast on 37 sts. and work in following patt:—

1st row.—P. 1, * k. 8, p. 1; rep. from * to end.

2nd row.—P. to end.

Rep. these 2 rows for 3½ ins., ending with a 1st patt. row. Break off wool and leave sts. on a spare needle.

The Front.—Cast on 180 sts. and work 1 in. in k. 1, p. 1 rib.

Continue in patt. thus:—

1st row.—K. 4, p. 1, * k. 8, p. 1; rep. from * to last 4 sts., k. 4.

2nd row.—P. to end.

Rep. these 2 rows until work measures 19½ ins. from lower edge, ending with a p. row.

Shape Armholes and divide for Front Opening thus:—

Next row.—Cast off 8 sts., patt. to end.

Next row.—Cast off 8 sts., p. 87 sts., counting st. already on right-hand needle after casting off, turn, leaving remaining 77 sts. on a spare needle.

Work on this set of sts. thus:—

Next row.—K. 2, patt. to last 2 sts., k. 2 tog.

Next row.—K. 2 tog., patt. to last 2 sts., k. 2.

Rep. last 2 rows twice.

Continue in patt. with g.st. front border, dec. 1 st. at armhole edge on every alternate row until 73 sts. remain.

Continue without shaping until work measures 25 ins. from lower edge, ending at front opening edge.

Shape Neck and Shoulder thus.—Continuing in patt., cast off 13 sts. at beg. of the next row, then dec. 1 st. at neck edge on every row until 45 sts. remain.

Continue without shaping until work measures 27 ins. from lower edge, ending at armhole edge.

Next row.—Cast off 11 sts., patt. to end.

Next row.—Patt. to end.

Rep. last 2 rows twice.

Cast off remaining sts.

Rejoin wool to second set of sts. at front edge and work thus:—

Next row.—Work in patt. to end.

Continue in patt., dec. 1 st. at armhole edge on each of next 6 rows, then dec. 1 st. at this same edge on every alternate row until 68 sts. remain, ending at armhole edge.

Next row.—K. 2 tog., patt. across 12 sts., cast off next 37 sts., patt. to end.

Next row.—P. to last 13 sts., slip sts. for pocket lining on to left-hand needle, p. across these sts., p. to end.

Continue in patt., dec. 1 st. at armhole edge on every alternate row until 63 sts. remain, then proceed without shaping

Two models like this were designed for the women's section, do you remember?
For the first time on record, the male section of the community approved,
saying they wouldn't mind that themselves. Well, what do your menfolk think?

until work measures 25 ins. from lower edge, ending at front opening edge.

Shape Neck thus.—Continuing in patt., cast off 3 sts. at beg. of next row, then dec. 1 st. at neck edge on every row until 45 sts. remain.

Proceed without shaping until work measures 27 ins. from lower edge, ending at armhole edge.

Shape shoulder as given for first shoulder.

The Back.—Work exactly as given for front until armhole shaping is reached and work measures 19½ ins. from lower edge.

Shape Armholes thus: Continuing in patt., cast off 8 sts. at beg. of next 2 rows, then dec. 1 st. at each end of the next 6 rows. Now dec. 1 st. at each end of every alternate row until 136 sts. remain.

Proceed without shaping until work measures 27 ins. from lower edge, ending with a p. row.

Shape Neck and Shoulders thus:

Next row.—Cast off 11 sts., patt. 39 sts., counting st. already on right-hand needle after casting off, k. 2 tog., cast off next 34 sts., patt. to end.

Work on last set of sts. thus:

Next row.—Cast off 11 sts., patt. to last 2 sts., k. 2 tog.

Next row.—K. 2 tog., patt. to end.

Rep. last 2 rows twice.

Cast off remaining sts.

Rejoin wool to second set of sts. at needle point and work thus:—

1st row.—K. 2 tog., patt. to end.

2nd row.—Cast off 11 sts., patt. to last 2 sts., k. 2 tog.

3rd row.—As 1st row.

Rep. last 2 rows once.

Cast off remaining sts.

The Sleeves.—Using No. 11 needles cast on 134 sts. and work 1 in. in k. 1, p. 1 rib, inc. 1 st. at end of last row.

Continue in patt. as given for front, until work measures 6 ins. from commencement.

Shape Top thus.—Continuing in patt., dec. 1 st. at each end of next 5 rows, then work 1 row without shaping.

Rep. last 6 rows until 45 sts. remain.

Cast off remaining sts.

The Collar.—Using No. 11 needles cast on 179 sts.

1st row.—K. 2, * k. 1, p. 1; rep. from * to last 3 sts., k. 3.

The shirt is knitted in a wide rib and made in 2-ply wool. Only 7 oz. is needed for the whole garment.

2nd row.—K. 2, * p. 1, k. 1; rep. from * to last 3 sts., p. 1, k. 2.

3rd row.—K. 2, k. 2 tog., work in rib to last 4 sts., k. 2 tog., k. 2.

4th row.—K. 2, rib to last 2 sts., k. 2.

Rep. last 2 rows until work measures 2½ ins. from commencement, then shape top edge thus:—

Continuing in rib, cast off 34 sts. at beg. of next 2 rows, then cast off 6 sts. at beg. of next 4 rows.

Cast off remaining sts. in rib.

The Front Over-wrap.—With right side of work facing and using No. 11 needles, pick up and k. 50 sts. evenly along left front edge.

Work $\frac{1}{2}$ in. in k. 1, p. 1 rib, ending at neck edge.

Next row.—Rib 3, * cast off 3 sts., rib 17 sts., counting st. already on right-hand needle after casting off, rep. from * once, cast off 3 sts., rib to end.

Next row.—Rib 4, * cast on 3 sts., rib 17 sts.; rep. from * once, cast on 3 sts. rib 3.

Work $\frac{1}{2}$ in. in rib.

Cast off loosely in rib.

Pocket Borders (Two Pieces).—Cast on 44 sts. and work $\frac{1}{2}$ in. in k. 1, p. 1 rib. Cast off loosely in rib.

Make-up.—Press the work, excepting ribbing, lightly on wrong side with a hot iron over a damp cloth.

Join side, shoulder and sleeve seams. Stitch sleeves into armholes, matching seams with side seams.

Stitch lower edge of ribbed over-wrap across the under-wrap.

Stitch cast-off edge of collar round neck edge, beginning and ending about $\frac{1}{2}$ in. from each front edge.

Sew on buttons to match buttonholes.

Stitch cast-on edge of pocket border along cast-off edge of the pocket, stitching the border down at each side. Now stitch all round pocket lining on wrong side of work.

Press all seams.

Helmet with Ear Flaps

COMFORTABLE AND PRACTICABLE

MATERIALS

3 oz. 4-ply wool.

2 No. 10 and 2 No. 12 knitting needles.

TENSION

7 sts. to 1 in.

Using No. 12 needles cast on 150 sts. and work in k. 2, p. 2 rib for 1 in., beginning and ending the 1st row with k. 2.

Next row.—Rib 22 sts., sl. these sts. on to a safety pin, work in rib to last 22 sts., sl. the remaining 22 sts. on to a second safety pin.

Change to No. 10 needles and continue in st.st. (1 row k., 1 row p.) for $2\frac{1}{2}$ ins. ending with a p. row. (Work measures $3\frac{1}{2}$ ins. from commencement.)

Commence Ear Flaps thus:—

Next row.—K. 27 sts., turn.

Next row.—K. 22 sts., turn.

Work 2 ins. in g.st. (each row k.) on these 22 sts. Cast off.

Rejoin wool to main set of sts. and k. across the next 52 sts.

Now work 2 ins. in g.st. on the next 22 sts. Cast off.

Rejoin wool to remaining 5 sts., k. to end of row.

Next row.—P. 5, cast on 22 sts., p. 52, cast on 22 sts., p. 5.

Next row.—K. to end.

Next row.—P. 5, k. 22, p. 52, k. 22, p. 5.

Rep. last 2 rows once.

Continue in st.st. until work measures 7 ins. from commencement, ending with a p. row.

Cast off 34 sts. at the beg. of the next 2 rows, then continue in st.st. on remaining 38 sts. for $5\frac{1}{2}$ ins. ending with a p. row.

Break off the wool.

Stitch the two sets of 34 cast-off sts. along each side of the back piece.

Now with the No. 12 needles and with

Believe it or not, he can keep his head warm and hear at the same time when he's on duty. The helmet has adjustable ear flaps which tuck in when he's not got to be listening too.

right side of work towards you, work in rib across 22 sts. from a safety-pin, k. up 38 sts. along lower edge, k. 38 sts. from No. 10 needle, k. up 38 sts. along lower edge, work in rib across 22 sts. from safety-pin (158 sts.).

Work 3 ins. in k. 2, p. 2 rib.

Change to No. 10 needles and continue in rib until work measures $4\frac{1}{2}$ ins. from commencement of the ribbed band.

Cast off loosely in rib.

Make-up.—Press work, excepting the ribbing, lightly on wrong side using a hot iron over a damp cloth. Join the front seam by backstitching the two end ribs tog. neatly to form one k. 2 rib.

IN CABLE AND MOSS STITCH

Polo-neck Classic

IN FOUR-PLY WOOL

MATERIALS

11 oz. 4-ply wool.
2 No. 8, 2 No. 10 and a set of 4 No. 10 and No. 12 knitting needles.

MEASUREMENTS

Length, 24 ins.
Chest size, 38 ins.
Sleeve seam, 20 ins.

TENSION

. 6 sts. to 1 in.

The Front.—Using No. 10 needles cast on 122 sts. and work in the following rib:—

1st row.—* K. 2, p. 2; rep. from * to last 2 sts., k. 2.

2nd row.—* P. 2, k. 2; rep. from * to last 2 sts., p. 2.

Rep. these 2 rows until the work measures 2 ins. Change to No. 8 needles and continue in cable and moss st. as follows:—

1st row.—(P. 1, k. 1) 5 times, p. 1, * k. 8, (p. 1, k. 1) 7 times, p. 1; rep. from * to last 19 sts., k. 8, (p. 1, k. 1) 5 times, p. 1.

2nd row.—Moss st. 11, * p. 8, moss st. 15; rep. from * to last 19 sts., p. 8, moss st. 11.

Rep. these 2 rows once more.

5th row.—Moss st. 11, * cable the next 8 sts. thus: slip the next 4 sts. on to a spare needle and leave at the front of the work, k. the next 4 sts., then k. the 4 sts. from the spare needle, moss st. 15; rep. from * to last 19 sts., cable 8, moss st. 11.

Now rep. 2nd row once; then rep. 1st and 2nd rows 3 times more.

13th row.—Rep. 5th row.

Continue in this way, working a cable on every 8th row until the work measures 15½ ins. from the beg., ending with a cable row.

Shape Underarm thus:—

Next row.—Place the first 9 sts. on a spare needle and leave for the present, moss st. 2, * p. 8, moss st. 15; rep. from * to the last 19 sts., p. 8, moss st. 11.

Next row.—Place the first 9 sts. on to a spare needle and leave for the present, moss st. 2, * k. 8, moss st. 15; rep. from * to last 10 sts., k. 8, moss st. 2.

There are now 104 sts. on the needle. Continue working on these sts., keeping the moss st. panels correct until another cable row has been worked.

Next row.—Moss st. 2, * p. 3, p. 2 tog., p. 3, moss st. 15; rep. from * to last 10 sts., p. 3, p. 2 tog., p. 3, moss st. 2 (99 sts. on needle).

Next row.—Moss st. 2, * k. 7, moss st. 15; rep. from * to last 9 sts., k. 7, moss st. 2.

Next row.—Moss st. 2, * p. 7, moss st. 15; rep. from * to last 9 sts., p. 7, moss st. 2.

Rep. these 2 rows once more.

Begin Yoke thus:—

1st row.—P. 1, * k. 9, moss st. 13; rep. from * to last 10 sts., k. 9, p. 1.

2nd row.—* P. 5, k. 1, p. 5, moss st. 11; rep. from * to last 11 sts., p. 5, k. 1, p. 5.

3rd row.—K. 4, * p. 1, k. 1, p. 1, k. 5,

"Getting what you want?" Well he usually does: Look at his polo-neck jersey for instance. It's a grand piece of work. It's knitted in a fairly soft 4-ply wool and in an interesting combination of stitches. The main part of the jersey is knitted in moss stitch varied with a broad cable rib. The yoke is knitted in a combination of wavy stripes of moss stitch and stocking stitch, with ribbed polo collar.

The yoke of the jersey is knitted in a combination of moss stitch and stocking stitch wavy rib and a reversed stocking stitch straight rib. The rest of the jersey is in cable and moss stitch.

moss st. 9, k. 5; rep. from * to the last 7 sts., p. 1, k. 1, p. 1, k. 4.

4th row.—P. 3, * moss st. 5, p. 5, moss st. 7, p. 5; rep. from * to last 8 sts., moss st. 5, p. 3.

5th row.—K. 2, * moss st. 7, k. 5, moss st. 5, k. 5; rep. from * to last 9 sts., moss st. 7, k. 2.

6th row.—P. 1, * moss st. 9, p. 5, moss st. 3, p. 5; rep. from * to last 10 sts., moss st. 9, p. 1.

7th row.—* Moss st. 11, k. 5, p. 1, k. 5; rep. from * to last 11 sts., moss st. 11.

8th row.—Moss st. 12, * p. 9, moss st. 13; rep. from * to last 21 sts., p. 9, moss st. 12.

9th row.—Moss st. 5, * k. 1, moss st. 7, k. 7, moss st. 7; rep. from * to last 6 sts., k. 1, moss st. 5.

10th row.—Moss st. 4, * p. 3, moss st. 7, p. 5, moss st. 7; rep. from * to last 7 sts., p. 3, moss st. 4.

11th row.—Moss st. 3, * k. 5, moss st.

7, k. 3, moss st. 7; rep. from * to last 8 sts., k. 5, moss st. 3.

12th row.—Moss st. 2, * p. 7, moss st. 7, p. 1, moss st. 7; rep. from * to last 9 sts., p. 7, moss st. 2.

13th row.—P. 1, * k. 9, moss st. 13; rep. from * to last 10 sts., k. 9, p. 1.

14th row.—* P. 11, moss st. 11; rep. from * to last 11 sts., p. 11.

15th row.—K. 12, * moss st. 9, k. 13; rep. from * to last 21 sts., moss st. 9, k. 12.

16th row.—P. 13, * moss st. 7, p. 15; rep. from * to last 20 sts., moss st. 7, p. 13.

17th row.—K. 14, * moss st. 5, k. 17; rep. from * to last 19 sts., moss st. 5, k. 14.

18th row.—P. 15, * moss st. 3, p. 19; rep. from * to last 18 sts., moss st. 3, p. 15.

19th row.—K. 16, * p. 1, k. 21; rep. from * to last 17 sts., p. 1, k. 15.

20th row.—K.

21st row.—P.

22nd row.—K.

23rd row.—P.

24th row.—K.

25th row.—K. 5, * p. 1, k. 21; rep. from * to last 6 sts., p. 1, k. 5.

26th row.—P. 4, * k. 1, p. 1, k. 1, p. 19; rep. from * to last 7 sts., k. 1, p. 1, k. 1, p. 4.

27th row.—K. 3, * moss st. 5, k. 17; rep. from * to last 8 sts., moss st. 5, k. 3.

28th row.—P. 2, * moss st. 7, p. 15; rep. from * to last 9 sts., moss st. 7, p. 2.

29th row.—K. 1, * moss st. 9, k. 13; rep. from * to last 10 sts., moss st. 9, k. 1.

30th row.—* Moss st. 11, p. 11; rep. from * to last 11 sts., moss st. 11.

31st row.—Moss st. 12, * k. 9, moss st. 13; rep. from * to last 21 sts., k. 9, moss st. 12.

32nd row.—Moss st. 5, * p. 1, moss st. 7, p. 7, moss st. 7; rep. from * to last 6 sts., p. 1, moss st. 5.

33rd row.—Moss st. 4, * k. 3, moss st. 7, k. 5, moss st. 7; rep. from * to last 7 sts., k. 3, moss st. 4.

34th row.—Moss st. 3, * p. 5, moss st. 7, p. 3, moss st. 7; rep. from * to last 8 sts., p. 5, moss st. 3.

35th row.—Moss st. 2, * k. 7, moss st. 7, k. 1, moss st. 7; rep. from * to last 9 sts., k. 7, moss st. 2.

36th row.—K. 1, * p. 9, moss st. 13; rep. from * to last 10 sts., p. 9, k. 1.

37th row.—* K. 11, moss st. 11; rep. from * to last 11 sts., k. 11.

38th row.—P. 12, * moss st. 9, p. 13; rep. from * to last 21 sts., moss st. 9, p. 12.

39th row.—K. 13, * moss st. 7, k. 15; rep. from * to last 20 sts., moss st. 7, k. 13.

40th row.—P. 14, * moss st. 5, p. 17; rep. from * to last 19 sts., moss st. 5, p. 14.

41st row.—K. 15, * moss st. 3, k. 19; rep. from * to last 18 sts., moss st. 3, k. 15.

42nd row.—P. 16, * k. 1, p. 21; rep. from * to last 17 sts., k. 1, p. 16.

43rd row.—P.

44th row.—K.

45th row.—P.

46th row.—K.

47th row.—P.

48th row.—P. 5, * k. 1, p. 21; rep. from * to last 6 sts., k. 1, p. 5.

Divide for Neck:—

49th row.—K. 4, moss st. 3, k. 19, moss st. 3, k. 11, turn.

50th row.—P. 2 tog., p. 18, moss st. 5, p. 17, moss st. 5, p. 3.

51st row.—K. 2, moss st. 7, k. 15, moss st. 7, k. 6, k. 2 tog.

52nd row.—P. 2 tog., p. 4, moss st. 9, p. 13, moss st. 9, p. 1.

53rd row.—Moss st. 11, k. 11, moss st. 11, k. 2, k. 2 tog.

54th row.—P. 2 tog., moss st. 13, p. 9, moss st. 12.

55th row.—Moss st. 5, k. 1, moss st. 7, k. 7, moss st. 7, k. 1, moss st. 5, k. 2 tog.

56th row.—K. 2 tog., moss st. 3, p. 3. moss st. 7, p. 5, moss st. 7, p. 3, moss st. 4.

57th row.—Moss st. 3, k. 5, moss st. 7, k. 3, moss st. 7, k. 5, p. 1, k. 2 tog.

58th row.—P. 2 tog., p. 6, moss st. 7, p. 1, moss st. 7, p. 7, k. 1, p. 1.

59th row.—P. 1, k. 9, moss st. 13, k. 6, k. 2 tog.

60th row.—P. 2 tog., p. 6, moss st. 11, p. 11.

61st row.—K. 12, moss st. 9, k. 6, k. 2 tog.

62nd row.—P. 8, moss st. 7, p. 13.

63rd row.—K. 14, moss st. 5, k. 9.

64th row.—P. 10, k. 1, p. 1, k. 1, p. 15.

65th row.—K. 16, p. 1, k. 11.

66th row.—K.

67th row.—P.

68th row.—K.

69th row.—P.   Cast off.

Place the centre 18 sts. on a spare needle and leave for the present and work on the second set of sts. for the right shoulder as follows:—

1st row.—K. 12, moss st. 3, k. 19, moss st. 3, k. 4.

2nd row.—P. 3, moss st. 5, p. 17, moss st. 5, p. 9, p. 2 tog.

3rd row.—K. 2 tog., k. 7, moss st. 7, k. 15, moss st. 7, k. 2.

4th row.—P. 1, moss st. 9, p. 13, moss st. 9, p. 5, p. 2 tog.

5th row.—K. 2 tog., k. 3, moss st. 11, k. 11, moss st. 11.

6th row.—Moss st. 12, p. 9, moss st. 13, p. 1, p. 2 tog.

7th row.—P. 2 tog., moss st. 6, k. 1, moss st. 7, k. 7, moss st. 7, k. 1, moss st. 5.

8th row.—Moss st. 4, p. 3, moss st. 7, p. 5, moss st. 7, p. 3, moss st. 4, k. 2 tog.

9th row.—K. 2 tog., moss st. 2, k. 5, moss st. 7, k. 3, moss st. 7, k. 5, moss st. 3.

10th row.—P. 1, k. 1, p. 7, moss st. 7, p. 1, moss st. 7, p. 7, p. 2 tog.

11th row.—K. 2 tog., k. 7, moss st. 13, k. 9, p. 1.

12th row.—P. 11, moss st. 11, p. 7, p. 2 tog.

13th row.—K. 2 tog., k. 7, moss st. 9, k. 12.

14th row.—P. 13, moss st. 7, p. 9.

15th row.—K. 10, moss st. 5, k. 14.

16th row.—P. 15, k. 1, p. 1, k. 1, p. 11.

17th row.—K. 12, p. 1, k. 16.

18th row.—K.

19th row.—P.

20th row.—K.

21st row.—P.

Cast off.

The Back.—Work exactly as given for the front until the 48th row of the yoke pattern has been worked, then continue as follows:—

49th row.—K. 4, * p. 1, k. 1, p. 1, k. 19; rep. from * to last 7 sts., p. 1, k. 1, p. 1, k. 4.

50th row.—P. 3, * moss st. 5, p. 17; rep. from * to last 8 sts., moss st. 5, p. 3.

51st row.—K. 2, * moss st. 7, k. 15; rep. from * to last 9 sts., moss st. 7, k. 2.

52nd row.—P. 1, * moss st. 9, p. 13; rep. from * to last 10 sts., moss st. 9, p. 1.

53rd row.—* Moss st. 11, k. 11; rep. from * to last 11 sts., moss st. 11.

54th row.—Moss st. 12, * p. 9, moss st. 13; rep. from * to last 21 sts., p. 9, moss st. 12.

55th row.—Moss st. 5, * k. 1, moss st. 7, k. 7, moss st. 7; rep. from * to last 6 sts., k. 1, moss st. 5.

56th row.—Moss st. 4, * p. 3, moss st. 7, p. 5, moss st. 7; rep. from * to last 7 sts., p. 3, moss st. 4.

57th row.—Moss st. 3, * k. 5, moss st. 7, k. 3, moss st. 7; rep. from * to last 8 sts., k. 5, moss st. 3.

58th row.—Moss st. 2, * p. 7, moss st. 7, p. 1, moss st. 7; rep. from * to last 9 sts., p. 7, moss st. 2.

59th row.—P. 1, * k. 9, moss st. 13; rep. from * to last 10 sts., k. 9, p. 1.

60th row.—* P. 11, moss st. 11; rep. from * to last 11 sts., p. 11.

61st row.—K. 12, * moss st. 9, k. 13; rep. from * to last 21 sts., moss st. 9, k. 12.

62nd row.—P. 13, * moss st. 7, p. 15; rep. from * to last 20 sts., moss st. 7, p. 13.

63rd row.—K. 14, * moss st. 5, k. 17; rep. from * to last 19 sts., moss st. 5, k. 14.

64th row.—P. 15, * moss st. 3, p. 19; rep. from * to last 18 sts., moss st. 3, p. 15.

65th row.—K. 16, * p. 1, k. 21; rep. from * to last 17 sts., p. 1, k. 16.

This illustration shows the arrangement of stitches in the polo-neck jersey. Moss stitch, stocking stitch, reverse stocking stitch and cable stitch are all used.

66th row.—K.

67th row.—P.

68th row.—K.

69th row.—P.

70th row.—Cast off 28 sts. Place the next 43 sts. on a spare needle, rejoin the wool and cast off the remaining 28 sts.

The Sleeves.—Join the shoulder seams, and with the right side of the work facing and using No. 8 needles take the 9 sts. left on the spare needle for the left front armhole, then pick up and k. 116 sts. evenly along the front and back armhole and finally the 9 sts. from the spare needle for the left back armhole. There are now 134 sts. on the needle. Work on these sts. as follows:—

1st row.—Moss st. 9, p. 2 tog., moss st. 5, * p. 8, moss st. 15; rep. from * to last 24 sts., p. 8, moss st. 5, p. 2 tog., moss st. 9.

2nd row.—Moss st. 9, k. 2 tog., moss st. 3, * k. 8, moss st. 15; rep. from * to last 22 sts., k. 8, moss st. 3, k. 2 tog., moss st. 9.

Continue in this way, dec. 1 st. at both ends of every row until there are 116 sts. on the needle, working in the cable on the 5th and then on every 8th row as given for the front.

Continue without shaping on the 116 sts. until the sleeve measures 4 ins. from the picked up edge. Now dec. 1 st. at both ends of the next and every following 6th row until there are 78 sts. on the needle, working in the cable on every 8th row as before.

Continue without shaping until the sleeve measures 17 ins. from the picked-up edge. Change to No. 10 needles and work 3 ins. in a rib of k. 2, p. 2. Cast off loosely in rib.

Pick up and work the right sleeve in the same way.

The Collar.—With the right side of the work facing and using 4 No. 12 needles begin at the left shoulder seam and pick up and k. 33 sts. along the neck edge, 18 sts. from the spare needle, 34 sts. along the neck edge to the right shoulder and 43 sts. from the spare needle. There should now be 128 sts. on the needles. Arrange them evenly on the three needles and work in a rib of k. 2, p. 2 for 2½ ins. Change to No. 10 needles and continue in rib for a further 3½ ins. When the total depth of the collar is 6 ins. cast off loosely in rib.

Make-up.—Press all the knitting, with the exception of the ribbing, with a warm iron over a damp cloth. Join the side and sleeve seams. Press all seams.

New Stitches to Choose From

POINTED RIB

This stitch requires a number of stitches divisible by 8, plus 1 st.

1st row.—P. 1, * k. 1, p. 2, k. 1, p. 2, k. 1, p. 1; rep. from * to end.

2nd row.—K. 1, * p. 1, k. 2, p. 1, k. 2, p. 1, k. 1; rep. from * to end.

3rd row.—As 1st row.

4th row.—As 2nd row.

5th row.—P. 1, * m. 1, sl. 1, k. 1, p.s.s.o., p. 1, k. 1, p. 1, k. 2 tog., m. 1, k. 1; rep. from * to end.

6th row.—P. 1, * k. into back of loop, p. 1, k. 1, p. 1, k. 1, p. 1, k. into back of loop, p. 1; rep. from * to end.

7th row.—K. 1, * p. 1, m. 1, sl. 1, k. 1, p.s.s.o., k. 1, k. 2 tog., m. 1, p. 1, k. 1; rep. from * to end.

8th row.—P. 1, * k. 1, k. into back of loop, p. 3, k. into back of loop, k. 1, p. 1; rep. from * to end.

9th row.—K. 1, * p. 2, m. 1, sl. 1, k. 2 tog., p.s.s.o., m. 1, p. 2, k. 1; rep. from * to end.

10th row.—P. 1, * k. 2, p. into back of loop, p. 1, p. into back of loop, k. 2, p. 1; rep. from * to end.

11th row.—K. 1, * p. 2, k. 1, p. 1, k. 1, p. 2, k. 1; rep. from * to end.

12th row.—P. 1, * k. 2, p. 1, k. 1, p. 1, k. 2, p. 1; rep. from * to end.

13th row.—As 11th row.

14th row.—As 12th row.

15th row.—K. 1, * p. 1, k. 2 tog., m. 1, k. 1, m. 1, sl. 1, k, 1, p.s.s.o., p. 1, k. 1; rep. from * to end.

16th row.—K. 1, * k. 1, p. 1, k. into back of loop, p. 1, k. into back of loop, p. 1, k. 1, p. 1; rep. from * to end.

17th row.—K. 1, * k. 2 tog., m. 1, p. 1, k. 1, p. 1, m. 1, sl. 1, k.1, p.s.s.o., k. 1; rep. from *to end.

18th row.—K. 1, * p. 1, k. into back of loop, k. 1, p. 1, k. 1, k. into back of loop, p. 2; rep. from * to end.

19th row.—K. 2 tog., * m. 1, p. 2, k. 1, p. 2, m. 1, sl. 1, k. 2 tog., p.s.s.o.; rep. from * to end, ending last rep. with sl. 1, k. 1, p.s.s.o., instead of sl. 1, k. 2 tog., p.s.s.o.

20th row.—K. 1, * p. into back of loop, k. 2, p. 1, k. 2, p. into back of loop, k. 1; rep. from * to end.

Rep. these 20 rows.

Zigzag cable pattern, can be used for cardigans, etc.

ZIGZAG CABLE PATTERN

This stitch requires a number of stitches divisible by 8, plus 1 st.

1st row.—K. 1, * slip next 2 sts. on to a spare needle and leave at front of work, k. next 2 sts., k. 2 sts. from spare needle, k. 4; rep. from * to end.

2nd and each alternate row.—P.

3rd row.—* K. 3, slip next 2 sts. on to spare needle and leave at front of work, k. next 2 sts., k. 2 sts. from spare needle, k. 1; rep. from * to last st., k. 1.

5th row.—* K. 3, slip next 2 sts. on to spare needle and leave at back of work, k. next 2 sts., k. 2 sts. from spare needle, k. 1; rep. from * to last st., k. 1.

7th row.—K. 1, * slip next 2 sts. on to spare needle and leave at back of work, k. next 2 sts., k. 2 sts. from spare needle, k. 4; rep. from * to end.

8th row.—P.

These 8 rows form the pattern.

Detail of pointed rib stitch and a suggestion for using it.

CABLE RIB

This stitch requires a number of stitches divisible by 9, plus 1 st.

1st row.—* K. 1, p. 2, k. 4, p. 2; rep. from * to last st., k. 1.

2nd row.—P. 1, * k. 2, p. 4, k. 2, p. 1; rep. from * to end.

3rd and 4th rows.—Rep. 1st and 2nd rows once.

5th row.—* K. 1, p. 2, slip next 2 sts. on to a spare needle and leave at front of work, k. next 2 sts., then k. 2 sts. from spare needle, p. 2; rep. from * to last st., k. 1.

6th row.—As 2nd row. Rep. these 6 rows.

HONEYCOMB PATTERN

This stitch requires a number of stitches divisible by 4, plus 2 sts.

1st row.—K. to end.

2nd row.—P. to end.

3rd row.—K. 1, * sl. 2, k. 2; rep. from * to last st., k. 1.

4th row.—K. 1, * p. 2, sl. 2; rep. from * to last st., k. 1.

5th row.—K. to end.

6th row.—P. to end.

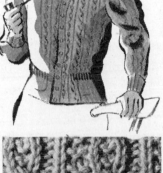

Cable rib pattern and a suggestion of how it would look

7th row.—K. 1, * k. 2, sl. 2; rep. from * to last st., k. 1.

8th row.—K. 1, * sl. 2, p. 2; rep. from * to last st., k. 1. Rep. these 8 rows.

FEATHER RIB

This stitch requires a number of stitches divisible by 8.

1st row.—* P. 4, k. 4; rep. from * to end.

2nd row.—P. 3, * k. 4, p. 4; rep. from * to last 5 sts., k. 4, p. 1.

3rd row.—K. 2, * p. 4, k. 4; rep. from * to last 6 sts., p. 4, k. 2.

4th row.—P. 1, * k. 4, p. 4; rep. from * to last 7 sts., k. 4, p. 3. Rep. these 4 rows.

LOZENGE CABLE

This stitch requires a number of stitches divisible by 18, plus 1 st.

1st row.—K. 1, * p. 6, k. 2, p. 1, k. 2, p. 6, k. 1; rep. from * to end.

2nd row.—P. 1, * k. 6, p. 2, k. 1, p. 2, k. 6, p. 1; rep. from * to end.

3rd row.—K. 1, p. 4, * k. the 3rd and 4th sts. on left-hand needle, then p. the first and 2nd sts. and slip

Feather rib is an excellent stitch to use for a man's garment.

all 4 sts. off the needle tog. (this will be referred to as "cross next 4 sts. in front of work"), p. 1, cross next 4 sts. at back of work (that is, by dropping the first and 2nd sts. on left-hand needle off the needle and leaving at front of work, p. next 2 sts., then k. the 2 dropped sts.), p. 9; rep. from * to end, ending last rep. with p. 4, k. 1 instead of p. 9.

4th row.—K. 5, * p. 2, k. 5, p. 2, k. 9; rep. from * to end, ending last rep. with k. 5 instead of k. 9.

5th row.—K. 1, p. 2, * cross next 4 sts. in front of work, p. 5, cross next 4 sts. at back of work, p. 5; rep. from * to end, ending last rep. with p. 2, k. 1 instead of p. 5.

6th row.—K. 3, * p. 2, k. 9, p. 2, k. 5; rep. from * to end, ending last rep. with k. 3 instead of k. 5.

7th row.—K. 1, * cross next 4 sts. in front of work, p. 4, k. 1, p. 4, cross next 4 sts. at back of work, p. 1; rep. from * to end.

8th row.—K. 1, * p. 2, k. 6, p. 1, k. 6, p. 2, k. 1; rep. from * to end.

9th row.—K. 3, * p. 6, k. 1, p. 6, k. 2, p. 1, k. 2; rep. from * to end, ending last rep. with k. 3 instead of k. 2, p. 1, k. 2.

10th row.—As 8th row.

11th to 20th rows.—Rep. 9th and 10th rows 5 times.

21st row.—K. 1, * cross next 4 sts. at back

of work, p. 9, cross next 4 sts. in front of work, p. 1; rep. from * to end.

22nd row.—K. 3, * p. 2, k. 9, p. 2, k. 5; rep. from * to end, ending last rep. with k. 3 instead of k. 5.

23rd row.—K. 1, * p. 2, cross next 4 sts. at back of work, p. 5, cross next 4 sts. in front of work, p. 3; rep. from * to end.

24th row.—K. 5, * p. 2, k. 5, p. 2, k. 9; rep. from * to end, ending last rep. with k. 5 instead of k. 9.

25th row.—K. 1, * p. 4, cross next 4 sts. at back of work, p. 1, cross next 4 sts. in front of work, p. 4, k. 1; rep. from * to end.

26th row.—K. 7, * p. 2, k. 1, p. 2, k. 6, p. 1, k. 6; rep. from * to last 12 sts., p. 2, k. 1, p. 2, k. 7.

27th row.—K. 1, * p. 6, k. 2, p. 1, k. 2, p. 6, k. 1; rep. from * to end.

28th row.—P. 1, * k. 6, p. 2, k. 1, p. 2, k. 6, p. 1; rep. from * to end.

29th to 38th rows.—Rep. the 27th and 28th rows 5 times.

Rep. the last 36 rows (that is, the 3rd to 38th rows inclusive).

Generally speaking it is best to use a bold pattern, like cable, for fairly heavy sports garments. Anything that is designed to be worn under a jacket, such as a waistcoat or sleeveless pullover, should be knitted in a fairly small pattern.

If you like a neat "all-over" pattern try honeycomb stitch.

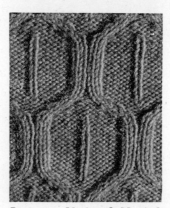

Lozenge cable is a bold stitch to use for sports garments.

Simple Ribbed Vests

FOR A FIRST-SIZE BABY

MATERIALS

1 oz. 2-ply wool for short sleeves. 1½ oz. for long sleeves.
2 No. 9 and 2 No. 11 knitting needles.
3 small buttons.
A fine crochet hook.
1 yd. narrow ribbon.

MEASUREMENTS

Length, 10½ ins.
Chest, 16 ins. slightly stretched.
Sleeve seam (long), 5½ ins.; (short) 1½ ins.

TENSION

Using No. 9 needles, 7½ sts. to 1 in. measured with rib stretched.

The Back.—Using No. 9 needles cast on 60 sts. loosely and work in k. 2, p. 2, rib as follows:—

1st row.—K. 1, * k. 2, p 2; rep. from * to last 3 sts., k. 3.

2nd row.—K. 1, * p. 2, k. 2; rep. from * to last 3 sts., p. 2, k. 1.

Rep. these 2 rows until work measures 7½ ins. from lower edge.

Shape for Armholes thus:—

Next row.—Rib the first 6 sts., then sl. these sts. on to a safety-pin, continue in rib to the last 6 sts., then sl. these sts. on to a second safety-pin (48 sts.).

Continue in rib without shaping until work measures 10½ ins. from lower edge.

Cast off loosely in rib.

The Front.—Proceed exactly as given for the back until work measures 6½ ins. from lower edge, ending with row on right side of work.

Divide for the Front Opening thus:—

Next row.—Rib across 28 sts., k. next 4 sts. for the overwrap, turn, leave remaining sts. on a spare needle.

Continue in rib with the 4 overwrap sts. in g.st. on these 32 sts. for right side of the front for 4 rows, thus ending at the front edge.

Make a buttonhole in next row thus: K. 2, w.fd., k. 2 tog. for the buttonhole, work in rib to end.

Continue in rib and g.st. until work measures 7½ ins. from lower edge, ending at the side edge.

Shape the Armhole thus:—

Next row.—Rib 6 sts., sl. these 6 sts. on to a safety-pin, work in rib to last 4 sts., k. 4.

Continue as before in rib and g.st., making two more buttonholes in the overwrap each 1 in. above the preceding buttonhole, until work measures 9 ins. from lower edge, ending at the front edge just after completing the third buttonhole.

Shape for Neck and Shoulder thus: Continuing in rib, cast off 7 sts. at beg. of next row, then dec. 1 st. at neck edge on every row until 11 sts. remain.

"This is what I call comfort." Carol lies kicking contentedly in her vest and pilch. The vest is simple ribbing. The pilch is the very latest "envelope" shape.

Continue without shaping until work measures 10½ ins. from lower edge.

Cast off loosely in rib.

Sl. the second set of sts. for left side of the front on to a No. 9 needle with point to inner edge and cast on 4 sts. for the underwrap.

Next row.—K. the 4 underwrap sts., work in rib to end.

Continue in rib and g.st. underwrap until the work measures 7½ ins. from lower edge, ending at the side edge.

Shape for the armhole as given for right side of the front, then continue without shaping until work measures 9 ins. from lower edge, ending at the front edge.

Shape neck and complete the shoulder as given for right side of front.

The Sleeves (Long).—Join the shoulder seams.

Using No. 9 needles and with right side of work facing, work in rib across 6 sts.

from a safety-pin, k. up 24 sts. along armhole edge to shoulder seam, 24 sts. along armhole edge to underarm sts., work in rib across 6 sts. from second safety-pin (60 sts.).

Continue in rib shaping as follows:—

1st row.—Work in rib to end.

2nd row.—Rib 6, work 2 tog., work in rib to last 8 sts., work 2 tog., rib 6.

3rd row.—Work in rib to end.

Rep. last 2 rows 7 times (44 sts.).

Continue in rib, dec. 1 st. at both ends of the 5th row and every following 8th row until 38 sts. remain. Continue without shaping until work measures 5 ins. from the picked up sts. along the armhole.

Change to No. 11 needles and continue in rib until work measures 6 ins. from the picked up sts. along the armhole, ending with row on wrong side of work.

Cast off loosely in rib, using the No. 9 needle.

Alternative Short Sleeves.—Proceed exactly as given for the long sleeve, dec. until 44 sts. remain.

Change to No. 11 needles and continue in rib until work measures 2 ins. from the picked up armhole sts., ending with row on wrong side of work.

Cast off loosely in rib, using a No. 9 needle.

Make-up.—Press work lightly with a hot iron over a damp cloth, taking care not to stretch the fabric.

Join side and sleeve seams. Stitch lower edge of underwrap along back of the overwrap.

Work a row of ribbon holes round neck edge thus: Commence at right front edge, 4 ch. into first st., miss next 2 sts., 1 tr. into next st., * 2 ch., miss about 2 sts., 1 tr. into next st.; rep. from * to end.

Thread ribbon through holes at neck and sew buttons on to underwrap to match with buttonholes. Press the seams.

A Jersey for a Real Boy

To make the vest into a first-size jersey, use 3-ply wool instead of 2-ply for a slightly bigger garment and a slightly thicker fabric. Substitute a crochet cord for the ribbon round the neck, or pick up and k. the sts. round the neck and work about $\frac{1}{2}$ in. of k. 1, p. 1 rib, making another buttonhole at the front edge before casting off.

For knickers to match the jersey, use the instructions given for the knickers of the "Boy's First Suit," (*see* page 176), but make waist to crutch measurement $7\frac{1}{2}$ ins. instead of 8 ins., by working 1 in. of rib instead of $1\frac{1}{2}$ ins. at the waist. Omit the straps and substitute a row of holes for crochet cord or elastic after working $\frac{1}{2}$ in. of the waist ribbing.

The jersey may be decorated by working simple smocking or herring-bone st. on the ribbing at yoke and cuffs.

The vest can have long or short sleeves. If possible, get rubber buttons that won't come to grief in washing, or dig into the child.

New Design Pilch

SHAPED LIKE AN ENVELOPE

MATERIALS

1 oz. 3-ply wool.
2 No. 9 and 2 No. 12 knitting needles.
A fine crochet hook.
¾ yd. narrow elastic.

MEASUREMENTS

Waist to crutch, 8 ins.
Width all round at widest part, 20 ins.

TENSION

7 sts. to 1 in.

Using No. 12 needles cast on 140 sts. and work ½ in. in k. 2, p. 2 rib.

Next row.—* Rib 2, m. 1, p. 2 tog.; rep. from * to end.

Continue in rib for 1 in. (Work measures 1½ ins. from commencement.)

Change to No. 9 needles and work 2½ ins. in st.st. (1 row k., 1 row p.), ending with a p. row. (Work measures 4 ins. from commencement.)

Next row.—K. 1, k. 2 tog., k. to last 3 sts., k. 2 tog., k. 1.

Next row.—P. 1, p. 2 tog., p. to last 3 sts., p. 2 tog., p. 1.

Rep. the last 2 rows until 4 sts. remain.

Next row.—K. 1, k. 2 tog., k. 1.

Next row.—P. 3 tog., and fasten off.

Make-up.—Press work lightly on wrong side with a hot iron over a damp cloth.

Join the two side edges, thus forming the centre seam, then stitch the cast-off point at lower edge to the lower edge of the centre front seam and about 1 in. along the shaped edge on each side.

Now work a row of d.c. all round leg edge loosely, then work the following picot edging into the d.c.: Commence with 1 s.c. into first st., * 3 ch., 1 d.c. into the first of these ch., miss next st., 1 s.c. into next st.; rep. from * all round.

Thread elastic through holes at the waist.

Press the seams.

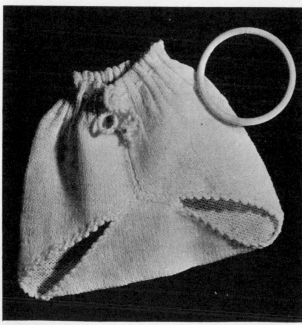

The pilch, made in stocking stitch and picot edged, is designed to be easy to make and use.

Carrying Shawl

IN A SIMPLE LACE STITCH

MATERIALS

6 oz. 3-ply baby wool.
2 No. 6 knitting needles.
A medium size crochet hook.

MEASUREMENTS

36-in. square.

TENSION

Approximately 5½ sts. to 1 in.

Cast on 189 sts. and work in moss st. and lace st. squares thus:—

1st row.—* (K. 1, m. 1, k. 2 tog.) 7 times, (p. 1, k. 1) 10 times, p. 1; rep. from * to last 21 sts., (k. 1, m. 1, k. 2 tog.) 7 times.

2nd row.—As 1st row.

3rd row. * K. 1, p. 1; rep. from * to last st., k. 1.

4th row.—As 3rd row.

Rep. these 4 rows until work measures 4 in. from commencement, ending with a 4th patt. row.

Next row.—(K. 1, p. 1) 10 times, k. 1, * k. 1, m. 1, k. 2 tog.; rep. from * to last 21 sts., (k. 1, p. 1) 10 times, k. 1.

Next row.—(K. 1, p. 1) 10 times, k. 1, * k. 1, m. 1, k. 2 tog.; rep. from * to last 21 sts., (k. 1, p. 1) 10 times, k. 1.

Next row.—* K. 1, p. 1; rep. from * to last st., k. 1.

Next row.—K. 1, * p. 1, k. 1; rep. from * to end.

Rep. last 4 rows until work measures 8 ins. from commencement, ending with a 4th row.

** **Next row.**—(K. 1, m. 1, k. 2 tog.) 14 times, * (k. 1, p. 1) 10 times, k. 1, (k. 1, m. 1, k. 2 tog.) 7 times; rep. from

Detail of the stitch of the shawl

* to last 21 sts., (k. 1, m. 1, k. 2 tog.) 7 times.

Next row.—As previous row.

Next row.—K. 1, * p. 1, k. 1; rep. from * to end.

Next row.—As previous row.

Rep. last 4 rows until work measures 12 ins. from commencement, ending with a 4th row.***

Next row.—* (K. 1, p. 1) 10 times, k. 1, (k. 1, m. 1, k. 2 tog.) 7 times; rep. from * to last 21 sts., (k. 1, p. 1) 10 times, k. 1.

Next row.—As previous row.

Next row.—* K. 1, p. 1; rep. from * to last st., k. 1.

Next row.—As previous row.

Rep. these 4 rows until work measures 16 ins. from commencement, ending with a 4th row.**

Rep. from ** to ** once, then rep. from ** to *** once more.

Next row.—(K. 1, p. 1) 10 times, k. 1, * k. 1, m. 1, k. 2 tog.; rep. from * to last 21 sts., (k. 1, p. 1) 10 times, k. 1.

Next row.—As previous row.

Next row.—* K. 1, p. 1; rep. from * to last st., k. 1.

Next row.—As previous row.

Rep. these 4 rows until work measures 32 ins. from commencement, ending with a 2nd row.

Next row.—* (K. 1, m. 1, k. 2 tog.) 7 times, (p. 1, k. 1) 10 times, p. 1; rep. from * to last 21 sts., (k. 1, m. 1, k. 2 tog.) 7 times.

Next row.—As previous row.

Next row.—* K. 1, p. 1; rep. from * to last st., k. 1.

Next row.—As previous row.

Rep. these 4 rows until work measures 36 ins. from commencement, ending with a 2nd row.

Cast off loosely to match cast-on edge (36 ins. in length).

Press work to correct measurements.

Work a row of picot edge all round outer edges thus: Commence with 1 s.c. into first st., * 3 ch., 1 d.c. into first of these ch., miss next st., 1 s.c. into next st.; rep. from * all round.

A 44-in. Square Shawl

8 oz. 3-ply baby wool.

Cast on 231 sts. instead of 189 sts. and work exactly as given until work measures 16 ins. from commencement, ending with a 4th patt. row.

Now rep. from ** to ** twice instead of once, then rep. from ** to *** once more.

Now continue as given, rep. the next 4 patt. rows until work measures 40 ins. instead of 32 ins. from commencement, ending with a 4th row, then rep. the next 4 rows until work measures 44 ins. instead of 36 ins. from commencement, ending with a 2nd row.

Cast off loosely to match cast-on edge. 44 ins. in length. Complete with edging as given for the 36-in. square.

Jersey and Knickers

FOR THE SIX TO TWELVE MONTHS OLD

MATERIALS

2 oz. 3-ply wool in white.
2 oz. 3-ply wool in blue (or 3 oz. if one colour only is used).
2 No. 9 and 2 No. 12 knitting needles.
A fine crochet hook.
6 small buttons.

MEASUREMENTS

Jersey: Length, 10½ ins.
Chest, 19 ins.
Sleeve seam, 7 ins.
Knickers: Waist to crutch, 8 ins.
Width all round at widest part, 22 ins.

TENSION

7 sts. to 1 in.

THE JERSEY

Front.—Using No. 12 needles and the blue wool cast on 66 sts. and work 1 row in k. 1, p. 1 rib.

Change to the white wool and continue in rib for 1½ ins., inc. 1 st. at end of last row (67 sts.).

Change to No. 9 needles and following patt.:—

1st row.—* P. 3, k. 5; rep. from * to last 3 sts., p. 3.

2nd row.—* K. 1, m. 1, k. 2 tog., p. 5; rep. from * to last 3 sts., k. 1, m. 1, k. 2 tog.

3rd row.—As the 1st row.

4th row.—P. to end.

5th row.—K. 4, * p. 3, k. 5; rep. from * to last 7 sts., p. 3, k. 4.

6th row.—P. 4, * k. 1, m. 1, k. 2 tog., p. 5; rep. from * to last 7 sts., k. 1, m. 1, k. 2 tog., p. 4.

7th row.—As 5th row.

8th row.—P. to end. These 8 rows form the patt.

Continue in patt. until work measures 7 ins. from lower edge, ending with row on wrong side of work.

Shape Armholes: Keeping continuity of the patt., cast off 4 sts. at beg. of the next 2 rows, then dec. 1 st. at each end of every row until 53 sts. remain.

Continue without shaping until work measures 9¼ ins. from lower edge, ending with row on wrong side of work.

Shape Neck thus:—

Next row.—Patt. across 19 sts., turn.

Work in patt. on these 19 sts., dec. 1 st. at neck edge on every row until 15 sts. remain, then continue without shaping until work measures 10½ ins. from lower edge, ending at armhole edge.

Shape Shoulders thus:—

Next row.—Cast off 5 sts., patt. to end.

Next row.—Patt. to end.

Rep. last 2 rows once.

Cast off remaining sts.

With right side of work facing, slip the centre 15 sts. on to a spare needle, rejoin

The knickers are in blue, in stocking stitch with ribbed bands. The jersey is in white, edged with blue, in a very simple but effective fancy stitch.

wool to remaining 19 sts. and work to match the first side.

Front Neck Band.—With right side of work facing and using No. 12 needles and white wool, k. up 13 sts. along neck edge, 15 sts. from spare needle, 13 sts. along neck edge (41 sts.). Work ½ in. in k. 1, p. 1 rib, ending with row on wrong side of work. Change to blue wool and work 1 row in rib. Cast off loosely in rib.

The Back.—Work exactly as given for the front until armhole shapings are completed and 53 sts. remain.

Continue in patt. without shaping until work measures 10½ ins. from lower edge, ending with row on wrong side of work.

Shape Neck and Shoulders thus:—

Next row.—Cast off 5 sts., patt. across 12 sts., counting st. already on right-hand needle after casting off, k. 2 tog., turn.

"*I'm a pretty big fellow now:*" *So he seems in his first real suit, which is both boyish and pretty. Crossed straps keep his "trousers" suspended; and the whole suit is designed for comfort and utility.*

Work on these 13 sts. for one shoulder:

Next row.—K. 2 tog., patt. to end.

Next row.—Cast off 5 sts., patt. to last 2 sts., k. 2 tog.

Next row.—K. 2 tog., patt. to end.

Cast off remaining 5 sts.

Slip the centre 15 sts. on to a spare needle, rejoin white wool to remaining 19 sts., and work 1 row to armhole edge.

Next row.—Cast off 5 sts., patt. to last 2 sts., k. 2 tog.

Next row.—K. 2 tog., patt. to end.

Rep. last 2 rows once.

Cast off remaining sts.

Back Neck Band.—With right side of work facing and using No. 12 needles and white wool, k. up 8 sts. along neck edge, 15 sts. from spare needle, 8 sts. along neck edge (31 sts.).

Work as given for the front neck band.

The Sleeves.—Using No. 12 needles and blue wool cast on 34 sts. and work 1 row in k. 1, p. 1 rib.

Change to the white wool and continue in rib for 1 in., inc. 1 st. at end of last row.

Change to No. 9 needles and continue in patt. as given for the front, inc. 1 st. at each end of the 5th row and every following 6th row until there are 51 sts. on the needle, working these extra sts. into the patt.

Continue without shaping until work measures 7 ins. from lower edge, ending with row on wrong side of work.

Shape Top thus: Continuing in patt., dec. 1 st. at each end of every row until 15 sts. remain.

Cast off remaining sts.

THE KNICKERS

The Front:—

Right Leg: Using No. 12 needles and blue wool cast on 38 sts. and work in k. 1, p. 1 rib for ¾ in.

Leave these sts. on a spare needle.

Left Leg: Work as given for right leg, then join the two legs thus:—

Using No. 9 needles k. 38 sts. for left leg, cast on 15 sts. for gusset, k. 38 sts. for right leg (91 sts.).

Next row.—P. to end.

Continue in st.st. shaping the gusset thus:—

1st row.—K. 38, k. 2 tog., k. to last 40 sts., k. 2 tog., k. 38.

2nd row.—P. to end.

Rep. last 2 rows 5 times.

Stitch of the jersey of the boy's suit.

Next row.—K. 38, k. 3 tog., k. 38 (77 sts.).

Work 5 rows in st.st. then shape as follows:—

Next row.—K. 36, k. 2 tog., k. 1, k. 2 tog., k. 36.

Work 3 rows in st.st.

Next row.—K. 35, k. 2 tog., k. 1, k. 2 tog., k. 35.

Work 3 rows in st.st.

Continue thus, dec. 1 st. at each side of the centre st. on next row and on every following 4th row until 59 sts. remain.

Continue without shaping until work measures 7 ins. from the cast-on gusset sts., ending with a p. row.

Change to No. 12 needles and work 1½ ins. in k. 1, p. 1 rib, ending with row on wrong side of work.

Next row.—Cast off 12 sts. loosely in rib, work in rib across 8 sts., counting st. already on right-hand needle after casting off, cast off next 21 sts. loosely in rib, work in rib across 8 sts. counting st.

The boy's suit can be knitted in a variety of stitches. Here it is in stocking stitch, decorated with a little simple embroidery.

already on right-hand needle after casting off, cast off remaining 12 sts.

Now, using the blue wool and No. 12 needles, work in rib on one set of 8 sts. for 14 ins. Cast off in rib, then work the second strap to match.

The Back.—Proceed exactly as given for the front until work measures 7 ins. from the cast-on gusset sts., ending with a p. row.

Shape Back thus:—

1st row.—K. 38, turn.
2nd row.—P. 17, turn.
3rd row.—K. 23, turn.
4th row.—P. 29, turn.
5th row.—K. 34, turn.
6th row.—P. 39, turn.

Continue in this way, taking up 5 sts. more on every row until sts. are all worked on to one needle.

Change to No. 12 needles and work 1½ ins. in k. 1, p. 1 rib.

Cast off loosely in rib.

Make-up.—Press work, excepting the ribbing, lightly on wrong side, using a hot iron over a damp cloth.

The Jersey.—Join shoulder seams for about ½ in. at armhole edges.

Join side and sleeve seams. Stitch sleeves into armholes, matching seams with side seams.

Work 2 rows of d.c. along each shoulder edge, using the white wool and making 3 small chain button loops at regular intervals on each front shoulder in the 2nd row.

Sew on buttons to match with loops.

The Knickers.—Join side, leg and gusset seams.

Cross the ribbed straps at the back and stitch to the back waist ribbing in required position.

Stitch the two straps tog. where they cross at centre back.

Press the seams.

For an "Everyday" Suit

If you would like to make the suit very plain, knit the jersey in stocking stitch instead of in the pattern, or choose one of the simple alternative stitches shown on page 217.

First-size Frock

WITH LACE STITCH BORDERS

MATERIALS

2½ oz. 2-ply wool. (4 oz. will make dress and matinée coat to match.)
2 No. 9 and 2 No. 12 knitting needles.
A fine crochet hook.
6 small buttons. 1 yd. of narrow ribbon.

MEASUREMENTS

Length, 16 ins. Chest, 16 ins.
Sleeve seam: (short) 1½ ins.; (long), 5½ ins.

TENSION

7½ sts. to 1 in.

The Front and Back (Both Alike).—
Using No. 9 needles cast on 143 sts. and work in moss st. thus:—

1st row.— * K. 1, p. 1; rep. from * to last st., k. 1.

Rep. this row for 1 in.

Continue in patt. thus:—

1st row.—K. 2, * w.fd., sl. 1, k. 1, p.s.s.o., k. 5, k. 2 tog., w.fd., k. 1; rep. from * to last st., k. 1.

2nd and each alternate row.—P. to end.

3rd row.—K. 3, * w.fd., sl. 1, k. 1, p.s.s.o., k. 3, k. 2 tog., w.fd., k. 3; rep. from * to end.

5th row.—K. 4, * w.fd., sl. 1, k. 1, p.s.s.o., k. 1, k. 2 tog., w.fd., k. 5; rep. from * to end, ending last rep. with k. 4 instead of k. 5.

7th row.—K. 5, * w.fd., sl. 1, k. 2 tog., p.s.s.o., w.fd., k. 7; rep. from * to end, ending last rep. with k. 5 instead of k. 7.

9th row.—K. 2, * w.fd., sl. 1, k. 1, p.s.s.o., k. 2 tog., w.fd., k. 1; rep. from * to last st., k. 1.

10th row.—As 2nd row.

11th to 18th rows.—Rep. 9th and 10th rows 4 times.

19th row.—K. 3, * w.fd., sl. 1, k. 1, p.s.s.o., k. 3, k. 2 tog., w.fd., k. 3; rep. from * to end.

21st row.—K. 4, * w.fd., sl. 1, k. 1, p.s.s.o., k. 1, k. 2 tog., w.fd., k. 5; rep. from * to end, ending last rep. with k. 4 instead of k. 5.

23rd row.—K. 5, * w.fd., sl. 1, k. 2 tog., p.s.s.o., w.fd., k. 7; rep. from * to end, ending last rep. with k. 5 instead of k. 7.

24th row.—P. to end.

Work 3 rows in moss st.

Next row.—P. to end.

Next row.—K. to end.

Continue in st.st. until work measures 12 ins. from lower edge, ending with a p. row.

Change to No. 12 needles and dec. for the waist thus:—

Next row.— * K. 3 tog., k. 2 tog., k. 2 tog.; rep. from * to last 3 sts., k. 3 tog. (61 sts.).

Detail of the lace stitch border.

Next row.—* P. 1, k. 1; rep. from * to last st., p. 1.

Next row.—* K. 1, p. 1; rep. from * to last st., k. 1.

Rep. former row once more.

Next row.—* Rib 2, m. 1, p. 2 tog.; rep. from * to last st., k. 1.

Work 3 more rows in k. 1, p. 1 rib, thus ending with row on wrong side of work.

Change back to No. 9 needles and work 2 rows in moss st.

Shape Armholes thus: Cast off 3 sts. at beg. of the next 2 rows, then dec. 1 st. at each end of the next 4 rows (47 sts.).

Now rep. 1st to 24th rows inclusive as given for the patterned border at lower edge, once, beginning and ending the 1st and each alternate row with k. 2.

Shape Neck thus:—

Next row.—(K. 1, p. 1) 8 times, k. 1, cast off next 13 sts., (k. 1, p. 1) 8 times, counting st. already on right-hand needle after casting off, k. 1.

"It does suit me, doesn't it?" Carol seems to know that she's wearing a particularly smart frock. The matching matinée jacket lies beside her. The shawl she is lying on is the carrying shawl (page 175).

Frock and matinée coat in stocking stitch with fancy borders.

Work 4 rows in moss st. on the last set of 17 sts., dec. 1 st. at neck edge on each row. Work 1 row without shaping.

Cast off in moss st.

Rejoin wool to second set of 17 sts. at needle point and work to match the first side. Work a second piece in the same way.

The Short Sleeves.—Using No. 12 needles cast on 42 sts. and work ¾ in. in k. 1, p. 1 rib.

Next row.—* Rib. 4, work twice into next st.; rep. from * to last 2 sts., rib 2 (50 sts.).

Change to No. 9 needles and work 1 in. in st.st., ending with a p. row.

Shape Top thus: Dec. 1 st. at both ends of every row until 18 sts. remain.

Cast off remaining sts.

The Long Sleeve.—Using No. 12 needles cast on 36 sts. and work in k. 1, p. 1 rib for ¾ in.

Change to No. 9 needles and continue in st.st. inc. 1 st. at each end of the 3rd row and every following 6th row until there are 50 sts. on the needle.

Continue without shaping until work measures 5½ ins. from commencement, ending with a p. row.

Shape Top as given for the short sleeve.

Make-up.—Press work lightly on wrong side using a hot iron over a damp cloth.

Join shoulder seams for about ½ in. at armhole edges. Join side and sleeve seams.

Stitch sleeves into armholes, matching seams with side seams and gathering any extra fullness to top of sleeve.

Now work 2 rows of d.c. along each shoulder edge, making 3 small ch. button loops at regular intervals on each front shoulder in the 2nd row, the first one being at the neck edge.

Now work a row of picot edging all round back and front neck edge thus: Commence with 1 s.c. into first st., * 3 ch., 1 d.c. into the first of these ch., miss next st., 1 s.c. into next st; rep. from * to end.

Sew buttons on to back shoulders to match with loops. Press the seams. Thread ribbon through holes in waist ribbing.

First-size Matinée Coat

TO MATCH THE FROCK

MATERIALS

1½ oz. 2-ply wool (4 oz. will make matinée coat and dress to match).
2 No. 9 and 2 No. 12 knitting needles.
A fine crochet hook.
¾ yd. narrow ribbon.

MEASUREMENTS

Length, 9½ ins.
Chest, 20 ins. all round at under-arm.
Sleeve seam, 6 ins.

TENSION

7½ sts. to 1 in.

Using No. 9 needles commence at lower edge and cast on 147 sts.

Work in moss st. thus:—

1st row.—* K. 1, p. 1; rep. from * to last st., k. 1.

Rep. this row for 1 in.

Continue in patt. with moss-st. borders thus:—

1st row.—Moss st. 7 sts., k. 2, * w.fd., sl. 1, k. 1, p.s.s.o., k. 5, k. 2 tog., w.fd., k. 1; rep. from * to last 8 sts., k. 1, moss st. 7.

2nd and each alternate row.—Moss st. 7, p. to last 7 sts., moss st. 7.

3rd row.—Moss st. 7, k. 3, * w.fd., sl. 1, k. 1, p.s.s.o., k. 3, k. 2 tog., w.fd., k. 3; rep. from * to last 7 sts., moss st. 7.

5th row.—Moss st. 7, k. 4, * w.fd., sl. 1, k. 1, p.s.s.o., k. 1, k. 2 tog., w.fd., k. 5; rep. from * to last 16 sts., w.fd., sl. 1, k. 1, p.s.s.o., k. 1, k. 2 tog., w.fd., k. 4, moss st. 7.

7th row.—Moss st. 7, k. 5, * w.fd., sl. 1, k. 2 tog., p.s.s.o., w.fd., k. 7; rep. from * to last 15 sts., w.fd., sl. 1, k. 2 tog., p.s.s.o., w.fd., k. 5, moss st. 7.

9th row.—Moss st. 7, k. 2, * w.fd., sl. 1, k. 1, p.s.s.o., k. 2 tog., w.fd., k. 1; rep. from * to last 8 sts., k. 1, moss st. 7.

10th row.—As 2nd row.

11th to 18th rows.—Rep. 9th and 10th rows 4 times.

19th row.—Moss st. 7, k .3, * w.fd., sl. 1, k. 1, p.s.s.o., k. 3, k. 2 tog., w.fd., k. 3; rep. from * to last 7 sts., moss st. 7.

21st row.—Moss st. 7, k. 4, * w.fd., sl. 1, k. 1, p.s.s.o., k. 1, k. 2 tog., w.fd., k. 5; rep. from * to last 16 sts., w.fd., sl. 1, k. 1, p.s.s.o., k. 1, k. 2 tog., w.fd., k. 4, moss st. 7.

23rd row.—Moss st. 7, k. 5, * w.fd., sl. 1, k. 2 tog., p.s.s.o., w.fd., k. 7; rep. from * to last 15 sts., w.fd., sl. 1, k. 2 tog., p.s.s.o., w.fd., k. 5 moss st. 7.

24th row.—As 2nd row.

Work 3 rows in moss st. across all sts.

Next row.—Moss st. 7, p. to last 7 sts., moss st. 7.

Next row.—Moss st. 7, k. to last 7 sts., moss st. 7.

Continue thus, working in st.st. with moss-st. borders until work measures 6 ins. from lower edge, ending with row on wrong side of work.

Shape Armholes and divide work into back and fronts thus:—

Next row.—Moss st. 7, k. 26 sts., cast off next 8 sts., k. 65 sts. counting st. already on right-hand needle after casting off, cast off next 8 sts., k. to last 7 sts., moss st. 7.

Continue in st.st. with moss-st. border on last set of 33 sts., dec. 1 st. at armhole edge on each of the next 3 rows (30 sts.).

Continue without shaping until work measures 8½ ins. from lower edge, ending at the front edge.

Change to No. 12 needles and work in moss st. across all sts. for ½ in., ending at front edge.

Shape Neck and Shoulder thus: Continuing in moss st., cast off 10 sts. at beg. of next row, then dec. 1 st. at neck edge on every row until 16 sts. remain. Continue without shaping until work measures $9\frac{1}{2}$ ins. from lower edge, ending at armhole edge.

Next row.—Cast off 5 sts., moss st. to end.
Next row.—Moss st. to end.
Rep. last 2 rows once.
Cast off remaining sts.

With wrong side of work facing, rejoin wool to 65 sts. for the back and work in st.st. dec. 1 st. at each end of every row until 59 sts. remain.

Continue without shaping until work measures $8\frac{1}{2}$ ins. from lower edge.

Change to No. 12 needles and continue in moss st. for 1 in., until work measures $9\frac{1}{2}$ ins. from lower edge, ending with row on wrong side of work.

Shape Neck and Shoulders thus: Cast off 5 sts. at beg. of the next 4 rows, then cast off 6 sts. at beg. of the next 2 rows.

Cast off remaining sts.

With wrong side of work facing, rejoin wool to 33 sts. for the second side of the front and work to match the first side.

The Sleeves.—Using No. 9 needles cast on 41 sts. and work in moss st. for $\frac{1}{2}$ in., inc. 1 st. at each end of the last row (43 sts.).

Now rep. patt. rows 1st to 24th inclusive as given for border at lower edge, once, omitting the moss st. 7 at each end of every row.

Now continue in st.st. inc. 1 st. at each end of next row and every following 4th row until there are 55 sts. on the needle.

Continue without shaping until work measures 6 ins. from lower edge, ending with a p. row.

Shape the Top thus: Dec. 1 st. at each end of every row until 19 sts. remain.
Cast off remaining sts.

Make-up.—Press work lightly on the wrong side using a hot iron over a damp cloth.

Join shoulder and sleeve seams.

Stitch sleeves into armholes with the underarm seam to the centre of the cast-off armhole sts. and with any extra fullness arranged at top of sleeve.

Make the set different by omitting to knit the lacy borders and using embroidery for decoration.

Work a row of ribbon holes round neck edge thus: Commence with 4 ch. into 1st st. at right front edge, miss next st., 1 d.c. into next st., * 2 ch., miss next st., 1 d.c. into next st.; rep. from * to end.

Next row.—1 s.c. into 1st st., * 3 ch., 1 d.c. into the first of these ch., miss next st., 1 s.c. into next st.; rep. from * to end.

Now make 3 small chain button loops down the right front edge, the first at the neck edge, and the others at 1 in. intervals.

Sew on buttons to match with loops.
Press the seams.

Thread ribbon through holes at neck.

Coat and Leggings Suit

IN TWO SIZES

For Girl or Boy, 6 to 12 months, with alternative instructions for smaller size.

MATERIALS

4 oz. 3-ply baby wool.

2 No. 9 and 2 No. 12 knitting needles.

A fine crochet hook.

6 buttons. 6 press studs. ¾ yd. elastic.

MEASUREMENTS

The Coat: Length, 10 ins.

Chest, 22 ins.

Sleeve seam, 6½ ins.

The Leggings: Length of front seam, 8 ins.

Width round at widest part, 22 ins.

TENSION

7 sts. to 1 in.

THE COAT FOR GIRL

Commence at the left front edge and cast on 64 sts.

Work in g.st. (each row k.) for ½ in.

Continue in st.st. with g.st. stripes thus:

1st row.—K. to end.

2nd row.—P. to last 2 sts., k. 2.

3rd to 5th rows.—Rep. 1st and 2nd rows once, then rep. 1st row once more.

6th row.—K. to end.

7th and 8th rows.—Rep. 1st and 2nd rows once.

9th row.—K. to last 2 sts., k. twice into next st., k. 1.

10th row.—As 2nd row.

11th row.—As 1st row.

12th row.—As 6th row.

13th row.—As 9th row.

14th row.—As 2nd row.

15th and 16th rows.—Rep. 1st and 2nd rows once.

17th row.—As 9th row.

18th row.—As 6th row.

19th and 20th rows.—Rep. 1st and 2nd rows once.

21st row.—As 9th row.

22nd row.—As 2nd row.

23rd row.—K. to end.

24th row.—Cast on 4 sts., k. to end (72 sts.). (Work should measure about 3 ins. from commencement.)

25th row.—K. to end.

26th row.—K. 14, p. to last 2 sts., k. 2.

27th and 28th rows.—Rep. 25th and 26th rows once.

29th row.—As 25th row.

30th row.—K. to end.

31st row.—K. to last 14 sts., turn.

32nd row.—P. to last 2 sts., k. 2.

33rd row.—As 25th row.

34th row.—As 26th row.

35th row.—As 25th row.

36th row.—As 30th row.

Rep. last 12 rows, i.e. 25th to 36th rows inclusive, twice more, ending the last rep. at the 35th row instead of the 36th row.

Next row.—Cast off 26 sts. for armhole, k. to end (46 sts.). (Work should measure about 2½ ins. from the 4 cast-on sts.)

Work 5 rows in st.st. with 2 sts. at lower edge in g.st.

Next row.—Cast on 26 sts., k. to end (72 sts.).

Work for back thus:—

1st row.—K. to end.

2nd row.—K. 14, p. to last 2 sts., k. 2.

3rd and 4th rows.—Rep. 1st and 2nd rows once.

5th row.—As 1st row.

6th row.—K. to end.

7th to 12th rows.—Rep. 1st to 6th rows inclusive once.

13th row.—As 1st row.

14th row.—As 2nd row.

15th row.—K. to last 14 sts., turn.

16th row.—P. to last 2 sts., k. 2.

17th row.—As 1st row.

18th row.—K. to end.

Rep. 1st to 18th rows inclusive 4 times, then rep. 1st to 11th rows inclusive once more.

Next row.—Cast off 26 sts., k. to end (46 sts.). (Work should now measure about 8 ins. at the top edge from 26 cast-on sts.)

Work 5 rows in st.st. with 2 sts. at lower edge in g.st.

Next row.—Cast on 26 sts., k. to end (72 sts.).

Work for right front thus:—

1st row.—K. to end.

2nd row.—K. 14, p. to last 2 sts., k. 2.

3rd row.—K. to last 14 sts., turn.

4th row.—P. to last 2 sts., k. 2.

5th row.—As 1st row.

6th row. K. to end.

7th to 10th rows.—Rep. 1st and 2nd rows twice.

11th row.—As 1st row.

12th row.—K. to end.

Rep. last 12 rows once, then rep. 1st to 11th rows once more.

Next row.—Cast off 4 sts., k. to end.

37th row.—K. to end.

38th row.—P. to last 2 sts., k. 2.

39th row.—K. to last 2 sts., k. 2 tog.

40th row.—As 38th row.

41st row.—As 37th row.

42nd row.—K. to end.

43rd row.—As 39th row.

44th row.—As 38th row.

45th to 46th rows.—Rep. 37th to 38th rows once.

47th row.—As 39th row.

48th row.—K. to end.

49th row.—As 37th row.

50th row.—As 38th row.

51st row.—As 39th row (64 sts.).

52nd row.—As 38th row.

53rd row.—As 37th row.

54th row.—K. to end.

Work 5 rows in st.st. with 2 sts. in g.st. at lower edge.

Work ½ in. in g.st. Cast off loosely.

The Sleeves.—Commence at the side edge and cast on 46 sts.

Continue in st.st. and g.st. as follows:—

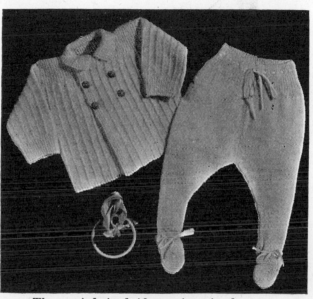

The coat is knitted sideways in a simple garter-stitch rib. The leggings are in stocking stitch.

1st row.—K. to end.

2nd row.—K. 10, p. to end.

3rd to 5th rows.—Rep. 1st and 2nd rows once, then rep. 1st row once more.

6th row.—K. to end.

7th to 8th rows.—Rep. 1st and 2nd rows once.

9th row.—K. to last 10 sts., turn.

10th row.—P. to end.

11th row.—As 1st row.

12th row.—K. to end.

Rep. last 12 rows 5 times.

Rep. 1st and 2nd rows twice, then rep. 1st row once more. Cast off.

"*Give a chap a hand up, and I'll show you how well my leggings fit.*" *Well,*
we can get the general effect, thanks, Michael. This is the larger size in the
suit. The coat is all severe and boyish, blue buttons are its only decoration.

Work a second sleeve in the same way.

The Collar.—Cast on 10 sts. and work in g.st. thus:—

Work 10 rows in g.st.

Next row.—K. to last 3 sts., turn.

Next row.—K. to end.

Work 10 rows in g.st.

Rep. the last 12 rows until the shortest edge of work measures 7½ ins. from commencement.

Cast off.

Make-up.—Press work lightly with a hot iron over a damp cloth on wrong side of the work.

Join shoulder and sleeve seams.

Stitch sleeves into armholes, with underarm seam to the centre of the straight ½ in.

The garter-stitch rib of the coat.

in between the cast-on and cast-off armhole stitches.

Stitch the shortest edge of the collar round neck edge, beginning and ending about 1½ ins. from each front edge.

Stitch on press fasteners for fastening, wrapping the right front over the left front, the first pair at neck edge, then others at intervals of about 2 ins.

Stitch buttons on to right front on top of the press fasteners.

Work the following picot edge round edge of the collar, sleeve edges, then down right front edge and round lower edge, also along the 4th g.st. ridge counting from the front border:—

Commence with 1 s.c. into first st., * 3 ch., 1 d.c. into the first of these ch., miss next st., 1 s.c. into next st.; rep. from * to end. Press the seams.

THE BOY'S COAT

Work exactly as given for the girl's coat but when making up, wrap the left front over the right front instead of vice versa to fasten and omit the picot edging.

THE LEGGINGS

Right Leg.—Using No. 12 needles cast on 72 sts. and work ½ in. in k. 1, p. 1 rib.

Next row.—Make elastic holes thus: * Rib 2, m. 1, p. 2 tog.; rep. from * to end.

Continue in rib until work measures 2 ins. from commencement, changing to No. 9 needles for the last row of rib.

Shape for Back thus:—

1st row.—K. 9, turn.

2nd and each alternate row.—P. to end.

3rd row.—K. 18, turn.

5th row.—K. 27, turn.

7th row.—K. 36, turn.

9th row.—K. 45, turn.

11th row.—K. to end.

12th row.—P. to end.

Continue in st.st. inc. 1 st. at beg. of the next row and of every following 6th row until there are 78 sts. on the needle.

Proceed without shaping until work measures 8 ins. from commencement at the short front edge, ending with a p. row.

Shape Leg thus:—

Next row.—K. 1, k. 2 tog., k. to last 3 sts., k. 2 tog., k. 1.

Next row.—P. to end.

Rep. last 2 rows until 36 sts. remain.

Continue in st.st. without shaping until the inside leg edge measures 8 ins., ending with a p. row (or length required).

Shape Foot thus:—

Next row.—Make ribbon holes: * K. 2, m. 1, k. 2 tog.; rep. from * to end.

Next row.—K. 15 sts., turn.

Next row.—Sl. 1, k. 9, turn.

Rep. the last row 22 times.

Next row.—K. 10, then on to this same needle k. up 12 sts. along side of instep flap, k. across remaining 21 sts.

Next row.—K. 43, then k. up 12 sts. along second side of instep flap, k. next

The smaller size in the coat and legging suit.
Meant for a girl, it is finished with picot edging.

5 sts. (60 sts.). Work 10 rows in g.st.

Dec. for foot thus:—

1st row.—K. 16, k. 2 tog., k. 8, k. 2 tog., k. 22, (k. 2 tog.) twice, k. 6.

2nd row.—K. 5, (k. 2 tog.) twice, k. 20, k. 2 tog., k. 8, k. 2 tog., k. to end.

3rd row.—K. 15, k. 2 tog., k. 6, k. 2 tog., k. to last 8 sts., (k. 2 tog.) twice, k. 4.

4th row.—K. 3, (k. 2 tog.) twice, k. 17, k. 2 tog., k. 6, k. 2 tog., k. to end.

Cast off.

Left Leg.—Work as given for right leg to the end of the waist ribbing.

Shape Back thus:—

1st row.—P. 9, turn.

2nd and each alternate row.—K. to end.

3rd row.—P. 18, turn.

5th row.—P. 27, turn.

7th row.—P. 36, turn.

9th row.—P. 45, turn.

11th row.—P. to end.

Continue in st.st. inc. 1 st. at the end of the next row and of every following 6th

row until there are 78 sts. on the needle.

Proceed without shaping until work measures 8 ins. at the short front edge, ending with a p. row.

Shape leg as given for right leg, ending with the row of ribbon holes at the commencement of the foot shaping.

K. 1 row across all sts., then shape foot as given for right foot.

Make-up. — Press work lightly on wrong side with a hot iron over a damp cloth.

Join foot and leg seams, then join back and front seams.

Thread elastic through holes at the waist and ribbon through holes at the ankles. If preferred, a crochet cord made in chain with double wool can be threaded through holes at waist and ankles.

Press the seams.

For the Smaller Size

Coat: Length, 9½ ins.

Chest, 20 ins.

Sleeve, 6 ins.

Leggings: Front seam, 7½ ins.

Width round at widest part, 20 ins.

Use No. 10 needles where No. 9 are stated, producing a tension of 7½ sts. to 1 in. This will give the measurement stated above for the coat.

For the leggings make the following additional alterations:—

Shape the leg when work measures 7½ ins. instead of 8 ins. from commencement and shape the foot when leg edge measures 7½ ins. instead of 8 ins.

Little Girl's Vest

IN RIB AND MOSS STITCH

TWO TO FOUR YEARS OLD

MATERIALS

3 oz. 3-ply wool.
2 No. 9 knitting needles.
A fine crochet hook.
1 yd. narrow ribbon.

MEASUREMENTS

Chest, 18 ins. unstretched (stretching to fit 21 in. to 23 in.). Length, 17 ins.

TENSION

About 7 sts. to 1 in.

Using No. 9 needles cast on 69 sts. and work in k. 3, p. 1 rib thus:—

1st row.—P. 1, * k. 3, p. 1; rep. from * to end.

2nd row.—* K. 1, p. 3; rep. from * to last st., k. 1.

Rep. these 2 rows until work measures 13 ins. from commencement.

Commence moss st. yoke thus:—

Next row.—* K. 1, p. 1; rep. from * to last st., k. 1. Rep. this row for 1½ ins., ending with row on wrong side of work.

Shape Neck thus:—

Next row.—Moss st. 29, cast off the next 11 sts., moss st. to end.

Continue in moss st. on first set of 29 sts., dec. 1 st. at neck edge on each of the next 8 rows.

Continue in moss st. on 21 sts. until work measures 17 ins. from lower edge, ending at armhole edge.

Shape Shoulders thus:—

Next row.—Cast off 7 sts., moss st. to end.

Next row.—Moss st. to end.

Rep. last 2 rows once.

Cast off remaining 7 sts.

Rejoin wool to second set of 29 sts. at neck edge and work as given for the first side.

The Back.—Work exactly as given for the front, continuing in moss st. for 3½ ins., ending with row on wrong side of work. (Work measures 16½ ins. from lower edge.)

Shape Neck and Shoulders thus:—

Next row.—Moss st. 25, cast off next 19 sts., moss st. to end.

Work 4 rows in moss st. on last set of 25 sts., dec. 1 st. at neck edge on each row.

Next row.—Cast off 7 sts., moss st. to end.

Next row.—Moss st. to end.

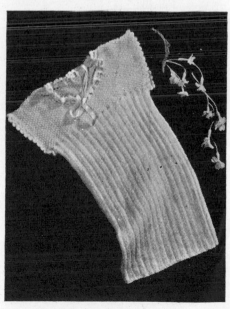

The vest is knitted in rib with moss stitch yoke, and finished with picot edging.

Rep. last 2 rows once.

Cast off remaining 7 sts.

Rejoin wool to second set of 29 sts. at neck edge and work 4 rows in moss st., dec. 1 st. at neck edge on each row.

Work 1 row without shaping to armhole edge, then shape shoulder as given for first shoulder.

Make-up.—Press work very lightly on wrong side with a hot iron over a damp cloth, taking care not to stretch the rib.

Join shoulder seams, then join the side seams to the commencement of the moss st. yoke.

Work a row of ribbon holes round neck edge thus: Commence at a shoulder seam with right side of work facing, 3 ch. into the seam, miss about $\frac{1}{4}$ in. neck edge, 1 tr. into next st., * 2 ch., miss about $\frac{1}{4}$ in. neck edge, 1 tr. into next st; rep. from * all round; join with a sl.st. Now work a row of picot edge into this row of holes thus: 1 s.c. into first st., * 3 ch., 1 d.c. into the first of these ch., miss next st., 1 s.c. into next st.; rep. from * to end.

Work a row of picot edge all round each armhole edge.

Thread ribbon through holes at neck and tie at centre front.

Press the seams lightly.

Striped Sun Suit

PLAY CLOTHES FOR THE UNDER SIX

MATERIALS

3 oz. 3-ply wool in white.

2 oz. 3-ply wool in cyclamen (or other contrast).

2 No. 12 and 2 No. 14 knitting needles.

A medium-size bone crochet hook.

MEASUREMENTS

Shoulder to crutch, 17 ins. to 18 ins.

Waist to crutch, $9\frac{1}{2}$ ins.

Width round waist below ribbing, 23 ins.

TENSION

$8\frac{1}{2}$ sts. and 14 rows to 1 in measured over the patt.

The Left Leg. *N.B.*—1 ball each of cyclamen and white wool will be required; do not break off colour not in use but carry neatly up side of work to avoid ends.

Commence working at the back seam with No. 12 needles and white wool. Cast on 7 sts.

1st row (wrong side of work) P. to end.

2nd row.—Using cyclamen wool, k. to end.

3rd row.—As 2nd row.

4th row.—Using white wool, k., inc. 1 st. at beg. of row.

5th row.—Using white wool, p., inc. 1 st. at end of row.

6th row.—Using cyclamen wool, k., inc. 1 st. at beg. of row.

7th row.—Using cyclamen wool, k., inc. 1 st. at end of row.

Rep. 4th to 7th rows inclusive 5 times, then rep. 4th and 5th rows once more (33 sts.).

30th row.—Using cyclamen wool, cast on 12 sts., k. to end.

31st row.—Using cyclamen wool, k. to end.

32nd row.—Using white wool, cast on 12 sts., k. to end.

33rd row.—Using white wool, p. to end.

34th to 35th rows.—Rep. 30th and 31st rows once.

"Just finish the story, please." Waiting to be dressed, young Mary
sits in her vest and knickers looking at pictures. Still it's a grand
vest, isn't it? Dainty, yet warm and serviceable as you please.

36th row.—Using white wool, cast on 7 sts., k. to end.

37th row.—Using white wool, p. to end.

38th row.—As 30th row.

39th row.—As 31st row (88 sts.).

Continue in patt. without shaping for 1½ ins., ending with row on wrong side of work.

Continuing in patt., dec. 1 st. at beg. of the next row and every following 14th row until 80 sts. remain.

The striped sun suit is knitted in a rib that makes a particularly "tough" fabric.

Continue without shaping until shortest edge of work (measuring from the 12 cast-on sts. at end of the back seam shaping) measures 11½ ins., ending at the shaped edge.

Shape for Front Edge as follows:—

1st row.—Cast off 16 sts., patt. to end.

2nd row.—Patt. to end.

3rd row.—Cast off 8 sts., patt. to end.

4th row.—Patt. to end.

Rep. 3rd and 4th rows 3 times.

Continue in patt., dec. 1 st. at shaped edge on every row until 7 sts. remain.

Work 3 rows without shaping.

Cast off remaining sts.

The Waist Ribbing.—With right side of work facing and using No. 14 needles and white wool, k. up 102 sts. along the shaped top edge (side edge of work).

Work ½ in. in k. 1, p. 1 rib, ending with row on wrong side of work.

Next row.—Make cord holes thus: * Rib 2, w.r.n., p. 2 tog., rib 2; rep. from * to end.

Work ½ in. in rib. Cast off loosely in rib.

The Right Leg.—With No. 12 needles and white wool cast on 7 sts.

1st row (wrong side of work).—P. to end.

2nd row.—Using cyclamen wool, k. to end.

3rd row.—As 2nd row.

4th row.—Using white wool, k., inc. 1 st. at end of row.

5th row.—Using white wool, p., inc. 1 st. at beg. of row.

6th row.—Using cyclamen wool, k., inc. 1 st. at end of row.

7th row.—Using cyclamen wool, k., inc. 1 st. at beg. of row.

Rep. 4th to 7th rows inclusive 5 times, then rep. 4th and 5th rows once more.

30th row.—Using cyclamen wool, k. to end.

31st row.—Using cyclamen wool, cast on 12 sts., k. to end.

32nd row.—Using white wool, k. to end.

33rd row.—Using white wool, cast on 12 sts., p. to end.

34th row.—As 30th row.

35th and 36th rows.—Rep. 31st and 32nd rows once.

37th row.—Using white wool, cast on 7 sts., p. to end.

38th row.—Using cyclamen wool, k. to end.

39th row.—As 31st row.

40th row.—Using white wool, k. to end (88 sts.).

Continue in patt. without shaping for 1½ ins., ending with row on right side of work. Now work shapings and complete

"They'll never find us here." Playing hide and seek in her sun suit, Mary thinks she and bear have escaped all eyes—but the camera found her. The sun suit is finished with a gay cord. The straps cross behind her back.

this leg exactly as given for the left leg, including the waist ribbing.

The Leg Bands (two pieces).—Using No. 14 needles and white wool cast on 10 sts.

Work in k. 1, p. 1 rib for 16 ins., measured when slightly stretched.

Cast off in rib.

The Shoulder Straps (two pieces).—Using No. 14 needles and white wool cast on 12 sts.

Work in k. 1, p. 1 rib for 16 ins.

Cast off in rib.

Make-up.—Press work, excepting the ribbing, lightly on wrong side with a hot iron and damp cloth.

Stitch leg bands round lower edge of legs, slightly stretching band while sewing.

Join leg seams and back and front seams, making narrow seams for neatness.

Stitch shoulder straps to waist ribbing, each strap about 2 ins. from centre front and in a corresponding position at the back. Cross the straps at the back before fixing into position.

Using double wool make a crochet cord and thread through holes at waist, finishing off the ends with tassels. Press seams.

Boys Wear Shorts

Little girls can wear sun suits, but real tough boys prefer shorts. They can be made from the same instructions as the sun suit, with just these few differences.

MATERIALS

3 oz. 3-ply wool.
2 No. 12 and 2 No. 14 knitting needles.
A medium-size crochet hook.
¾ yd. elastic.

MEASUREMENTS

Waist to crutch, 9½ ins.
Width round waist below ribbing, 23 ins.

The Left Leg.—Using No. 12 needles cast on 7 sts. Work in the patt. of 2 rows st.st., 2 rows g.st., shaping exactly as given but using only the one shade of wool.

The Waist Ribbing.—With right side of work facing and using No. 14 needles, k. up 102 sts. along the shaped top edge (side edge of work).

Work 1 in. in k. 1, p. 1 rib, ending with row on wrong side of work.

Cast off loosely in rib.

The Right Leg.—Using No. 12 needles cast on 7 sts. Work in patt., shaping exactly as given, but using only the one shade of wool. Work the waist ribbing as given for the left leg.

The Leg Bands.—Work exactly as given.

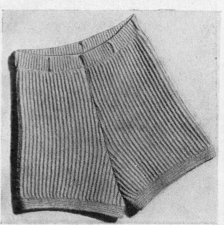

Real boys wear shorts. They are made from the same instructions as the sun suit.

Make-up.—Proceed exactly as given, but omit the stitching on of shoulder straps and crochet cord. Make 6 crochet slots to take a belt (1 at each side seam, 2 at front and 2 at back), or work elastic casing round waist thus: Using the crochet hook and with wrong side of work facing, commence at a seam with 1 s.c. into the top edge of the waist ribbing, * 5 ch., 1 d.c. into the ribbing about ¾ in. down and about ½ in. along, 5 ch., 1 d.c. into top edge of the ribbing about ½ in. along; rep. from * to end, ending with 1 s.c. into the first s.c. Thread elastic through the casing thus formed.

"*Do you dare me?*" *John's mischievous grin indicates we'd best hurry up and take his photograph before he dashes away, so look at his natty shorts quickly—they are the tough boy's equivalent of the sun suit.*

Lace or Plain Socks

FOR THE FOUR- TO SIX-YEAR-OLD

MATERIALS

2 oz. 3-ply wool.
2 No. 13 knitting needles.

MEASUREMENTS

Length of leg, 6½ ins.
Length of foot, 7 ins. (adjustable).

TENSION

9½ sts. to 1 in.

Cast on 54 sts. and work 2½ ins. in k. 1, p. 1 rib, inc. 1 st. at end of the last row (55 sts.).

Continue in patt. as follows:—

1st row.—K. 1, p. 1, * k. 1, m. 1, k. 2 tog., p. 1, k. 1, p. 1; rep. from * to last 5 sts., k. 1, m. 1, k. 2 tog., p. 1, k. 1.

Rep. this row until work measures 5 ins. from commencement, ending with a row on wrong side of work.

Divide for Foot thus:—

Next row.—Work in patt. across 42 sts., turn.

Lace and plain socks. To save wool they are made without turnovers. For bigger sizes see page 199.

Next row.—Work in patt. across 29 sts., turn.

Continue in patt. on these 29 sts. for the instep for 5 ins. for a 7-in. foot, ending with a row on wrong side of work. (If necessary, work more or less inches at this point.)

Shape Toe thus:—

1st row.—K. 1, sl. 1, k. 1, p.s.s.o., k. to last 3 sts., k. 2 tog., k. 1.

2nd row.—P. to end.

Rep. last 2 rows 8 times. Leave remaining 11 sts. on a spare needle.

Now sl. the two sets of heel sts. on to one needle with the side edges to the centre to form the back seam.

With right side of work facing, work in st.st. (1 row k., 1 row p.) for 24 rows, ending with a p. row, then turn the heel as follows:—

1st row.—K. 18, k. 2 tog., turn.

2nd row.—P. 11, p. 2 tog., turn.

3rd row.—K. 11, k. 2 tog., turn.

Rep. the 2nd and 3rd rows 5 times, then rep. the 2nd row once more (12 sts.).

Next row.—K. 12, then on to this same needle, k. up 12 sts. along side of heel flap.

Next row.—P. to end then on to this same needle, pick up and p. 12 sts. along second side of heel flap.

Continue in st.st. on 36 sts. shaping the instep as follows:—

Next row.—K. 1, sl.

1, k. 1, p.s.s.o., k. to last 3 sts., k. 2 tog., k. 1.

Next row.—P. to end.

Rep. last 2 rows twice (30 sts.).

Continue without shaping until work measures the same as the top part of the foot to the commencement of the toe shaping, ending with a row on wrong side of work and dec. 1 st. at end of the last row.

Shape the toe as given for the top part of the foot, then graft or cast off the two sets of stitches together.

Work a second sock in the same way.

Make-up.—Press the work lightly on wrong side using a hot iron over a damp cloth.

Join foot and leg seams neatly.

Press the seams.

For the Plain Sock

Cast on 54 sts. and work 2½ ins. in k. 1, p. 1 rib, inc. 1 st. at end of the last row.

Continue in st.st. (1 row k., 1 row p.) until work measures 5 ins. from commencement, ending with a p. row.

Divide for Foot thus:—

Next row.—K. 42 sts., turn.

Next row.—P. 29 sts., turn.

Continue in st.st. instead of patt. on these 29 sts. for the instep and shape the toe exactly as given for the lace sock.

Now work on the two sets of heel stitches and complete the foot exactly as given.

For Still Bigger Sizes

use needles one or two sizes larger and make the legs and feet longer by working extra length before dividing for the heel and before shaping the toe.

Make the plain socks in narrow stripes to use up odd quantities of wool. Or make tops in one colour, legs and feet in a second colour and toes in a third colour, thus making use of three odd balls of less than ½ oz. each. When using up oddments it is a good idea to work both socks at the same time, either on separate short needles or on one longer needle. In this way you will avoid running out of a certain colour when working the second sock.

Three-Quarter Socks

FOR THE EIGHT- TO TEN-YEAR-OLD

MATERIALS

3 oz. 4-ply wool in brown.

¼ oz. 4-ply wool in green.

¼ oz. 4-ply wool in scarlet.

2 No. 12 knitting needles.

MEASUREMENTS

Length of leg, 15 ins.

Length of foot, 8 ins.

TENSION

8 sts. to 1 in.

Using the brown wool cast on 60 sts. and work in rib thus:—

Change to green wool and work 2 rows in k. 1, p. 1 rib.

Change to brown wool and work 2 rows in k. 1, p. 1 rib.

Change to scarlet wool and work 2 rows in k. 1, p. 1 rib.

Change to brown wool, and work 2 rows in st.st. (1 row k., 1 row p.), inc. 1 st. at the end of the last row (61 sts.).

Continue in following patt.:—

Join in green wool. (*N.B.*—When using the two shades of wool carry colour not in use loosely across back of work to retain elasticity.)

1st row.—K. 1 green, * k. 1 brown, k. 3

The three-quarter socks have turnovers for boys and not for girls. The fancy tops are attractive and save wool.

green, k. 1 brown, k. 1 green; rep. from * to end.

2nd row.—P. 1 green, * p. 1 brown, p. 3 green, p. 1 brown, p. 1 green; rep. from * to end.

3rd row.—K. 2 brown, * k. 3 green, k. 3 brown; rep. from * to end, ending last rep. with k. 2 instead of k. 3 brown.

4th row.—P. 1 brown, * p. 2 green, p. 1 brown; rep. from * to end.

5th row.—Using green wool, k to end.

6th row.—As 4th row.

7th row.—As 3rd row.

8th row.—As 2nd row.

9th row.—As 1st row.

10th row.—Using brown wool, p. to end.

11th row.—Using brown wool, k. to end.

Break off the green wool and join in the scarlet wool.

12th row.—P. 2 scarlet, * p. 1 brown, p. 1 scarlet, p. 1 brown, p. 3 scarlet; rep. from * to end, ending last rep. with p. 2, instead of p. 3, scarlet.

13th row.—K. 2 scarlet, * k. 1 brown, k. 1 scarlet, k. 1 brown, k. 3 scarlet; rep. from * to end, ending last rep. with k. 2, instead of k. 3, scarlet.

14th row.—P. 2 scarlet, * p. 3 brown, p. 3 scarlet; rep. from * to end, ending last rep. with 2 instead of p. 3 scarlet.

15th row. — K. 1 brown, * k. 2 scarlet, k. 1 brown; rep. from * to end.

16th row. — Using scarlet wool, p. to end.

17th row.—As 15th row.

18th row.—As 14th row.

19th row.—As 13th row.

20th row.—As 12th row.

Break off the scarlet wool.

Using brown wool work 2 rows in st.st., inc. 1 st. at end of the last row (62 sts.).

Using green wool, work 2 rows in k. 1, p. 1 rib.

Using brown wool work 2 rows in k. 1, p. 1 rib.

Using scarlet wool, work 2 rows in k. 1, p. 1 rib.

Break off green and scarlet wool.

Using brown wool continue in st.st. until work measures 7½ ins. from commencement, ending with a p. row. (If necessary, work more or less ins. at this point.)

Shape Leg thus:—

Next row.—K. 1, k. 2 tog., k. to last 3 sts., k. 2 tog., k. 1.

Work 5 rows in st.st.

Rep. the last 6 rows 5 times (50 sts.).

Continue in st.st. without shaping until work measures 12 ins. from commencement, ending with a p. row.

Divide for Heel and Foot thus:—

Next row.—K. 38 sts., turn.

Next row.—P. 26 sts., turn.

Continue in st.st. on these 26 sts. for the top part of foot for 6 ins., ending with a p. row. (If necessary work more or less ins. at this point.)

Shape Toe thus:—

Next row.—K. 1, sl. 1, k. 1, p.s.s.o., k. to last 3 sts., k. 2 tog., k. 1.

Next row.—P. to end.

Rep. last 2 rows until 10 sts. remain. Leave these sts. on a spare needle.

Now slip the remaining sts. on to one needle with side edges to the centre forming the back seam and with right side of work facing continue for the heel thus:—

Next row.—* Sl. 1, k. 1; rep. from * to end.

Next row.—P. to end.

Rep. last 2 rows 16 times, then turn the heel as follows:—

Next row.—K. 16, k. 2 tog., turn.

Next row.—P. 9, p. 2 tog., turn.

Next row.—K. 9, k. 2 tog., turn.

Rep. the last 2 rows until all side sts. are worked off and 10 sts. remain at the end of a p. row.

Next row.—K. to end, then k. up 14 sts. along side of heel flap, leaving the remaining edge free to form part of the leg.

Next row.—P. to end, then pick up and p. 14 sts. along second side of heel flap, leaving a corresponding edge free to match the first side.

Shape Instep thus:—

1st row.—K. 1, sl. 1, k. 1, p.s.s.o., k. to last 3 sts., k. 2 tog., k. 1.

2nd row.—P. to end.

Rep. last 2 rows 5 times (26 sts.).

Continue in st.st. without shaping until work measures the same as the top part of the foot to the commencement of the toe shaping, ending with a p. row. Shape toe as given for top part of foot, then graft or cast off the two sets of sts. tog.

Make-up.—Press work lightly on wrong side with a hot iron over a damp cloth.

Join foot seams, then join the back seam with a very narrow back st. seam, carefully matching the patt. in the border. Press the seams.

Thread fine elastic through the back of the ribbing at top edge, or make a zigzag crochet casing to take wider elastic.

TEN TO TWELVE YEARS OLD

MATERIALS

4 oz. 4-ply wool in dark grey.

½ oz. 4-ply wool in light grey.

2 No. 12 knitting needles.

MEASUREMENTS

Length of leg, 16 ins. (with top turned down).

Length of foot, 8½ ins. (adjustable).

TENSION

8 sts. to 1 in. measured over st.st.

Using dark grey wool cast on 72 sts. and work in rib thus:—

1st row.—*K. 3, p. 3; rep. from * to end.

Rep. this row 3 times.

Continue in following patt.: Join in the light wool.

1st row.—* K. 3 dark, k. 3 light; rep. from * to end. (Take the colour not in use loosely along back of work to retain elasticity and catch the dark wool in the back of the last st.)

2nd row and each alternate row.—P. to end, matching the colours of the preceding row.

3rd row.—K. 2 dark, * k. 3 light, k. 3 dark; rep. from * to last 4 sts., k. 3 light, k. 1 dark.

5th row.—K. 1 dark, * k. 3 light, k. 3 dark; rep. from * to last 5 sts., k. 3 light, k. 2 dark.

7th row.—* K. 3 light, k. 3 dark; rep. from * to end.

9th row.—K. 2 light, * k. 3 dark, k. 3 light; rep. from * to last 4 sts., k. 3 dark, k. 1 light.

11th row.—K. 1 light, * k. 3 dark, k. 3 light; rep. from * to last 5 sts., k. 3 dark, k. 2 light.

12th row.—As 2nd row.

Rep. the last 12 rows twice more.

Break off the light wool.

Next row.—Using dark wool, k. to end.

Work 1½ ins. in k. 1, p. 1 rib, ending with a row on the right side of the patterned border. This will now be regarded as the wrong side of the work to reverse the border for the turn-over top.

Continue in k. 2, p. 2 rib thus:—

Next row.—P. 1, * k. 2, p. 2; rep. from * to last 3 sts., k. 2, p. 1.

Next row.—K. 1, * p. 2, k. 2; rep. from * to last 3 sts., p. 2, k. 1.

Rep. these 2 rows for 5 ins., ending with row on wrong side of work. (If necessary work more or less ins. at this point.)

Shape Leg thus:—

1st row.—P. 1, k. 2 tog., work in rib to the last 3 sts., k. 2 tog., p. 1.

2nd row.—K. 1, p. 1, work in rib to last 2 sts., p. 1, k. 1.

3rd row.—P. 1, k. 1, work in rib to last 2 sts., k. 1, p. 1. Rep. last 2 rows once, then rep. 2nd row once more.

7th row.—P. 1, k. 2 tog., p. 1, work in rib to last 4 sts., p. 1, k. 2 tog., p. 1.

8th row.—K. 1, p. 1, k. 1, work in rib to last 3 sts., k. 1, p. 1, k. 1.

9th row.—P. 1, k. 1, p. 1, work in rib to last 3 sts., p. 1, k. 1, p. 1. Rep. last 2 rows once, then rep. 8th row once more.

13th row.—P. 1, k. 2 tog., work in rib to last 3 sts., k. 2 tog., p. 1.

14th row.—K. 1, p. 1, work in rib to last 2 sts., p. 1, k. 1.

15th row.—P. 1, k. 1, work in rib to last 2 sts., k. 1, p. 1. Rep. last 2 rows once, then rep. 14th row once more.

19th row.—P. 1, k. 2 tog., k. 1, work in rib to last 4 sts., k. 1, k. 2 tog., p. 1.

Work 5 rows in rib.

Rep. last 24 rows once more (56 sts.).

Continue in rib until work measures 13 ins. from the commencement of the k. 2, p. 2 rib, ending with row on wrong side of work.

Commence Foot thus:—

Next row.—Work in rib across 44 sts., turn.

Next row.—Rib across 32 sts., turn.

Continue in rib on these 32 sts. for the instep for 6 ins., ending with row on wrong side of work. (This is for an 8½-in.

foot, for an 8-in. foot work for only 5½ ins., for a 9-in. foot work for 6½-ins.).

Shape Toe thus:—

Next row.—K. 1, sl. 1, k. 1, p.s.s.o., k. to last 3 sts., k. 2 tog., k. 1.

Next row.—P. to end. Rep. last 2 rows. until 10 sts. remain, ending with a p. row.

Leave these sts. on a spare needle.

Now slip the two sets of sts. for the heel on to one needle with side edges in the centre forming the back seam and with right side of work facing work for the heel thus:—

Next row.—K. to end.

Next row.—P. to end.

Rep. last 2 rows 11 times.

Turn Heel thus:—

1st row.—K. 14, k. 2 tog., turn.

2nd row.—P. 5, p. 2 tog., turn.

3rd row.—K. 6, k. 2 tog., turn.

4th row.—P. 7, p. 2 tog., turn.

5th row.—K. 8, k. 2 tog., turn.

6th row.—P. 9, p. 2 tog., turn.

Continue thus, working 1 st. extra before the dec. on every row until the sts. are all worked on to one needle and 14 sts. remain.

Next row.—K. to end, then k. up 12 sts. along side of heel flap, turn.

Next row.—P. to end, then pick up and p. 12 sts. along second side of heel flap (38 sts.).

Shape Instep thus:—

Next row.—K. 1, sl. 1, k. 1, p.s.s.o., k. to last 3 sts., k. 2 tog., k. 1.

Next row.—P. to end.

Rep. last 2 rows twice (32 sts.).

Continue in st.st. without shaping until work measures the same as the top part of the foot to the commencement of the toe shaping, ending with a p. row.

Shape toe as given for top part of foot, then graft or cast off the two sets of sts. tog. Work a second sock in the same way.

Make-up.—Press work lightly with hot iron and damp cloth. Join foot and leg seams. Stitching border seam on reverse side of work, then turn over.

Wrist or Gauntlet Gloves

FOR EIGHT- TO TEN- YEAR-OLDS

MATERIALS

    2 oz. 4-ply wool.
    2 No. 12 knitting needles.

TENSION

    8 sts. to 1 in.

    The Right-hand Glove.—Using No. 12 needles cast on 44 sts. and work in k. 1, p. 1 rib for 2½ ins.

    Continue in patt. as follows:—

    1st row.—* K. 1, p. 1; rep. from * to end.

    2nd row.—K. to end.

    These 2 rows form the patt. Continue in patt. shaping for thumb gusset:—

    3rd row.—(K. 1, p. 1) 12 times, k. twice into next st., (p. 1, k. 1) into next st., (k. 1, p. 1) 9 times.

    4th row.—K. to end.

    5th row.—(K. 1, p. 1) 12 times, k. 2, p. 1, k. 1, (k. 1, p. 1) 9 times.

    6th row.—As 4th row.

    7th row.—(K. 1, p. 1) 12 times, (k. 1, p. 1) into next st., k. 1, p. 1, (k. 1, p. 1) into next st., (k. 1, p. 1) 9 times.

    8th to 10th rows.—Work 3 rows in patt.

    11th row.—(K. 1, p. 1) 12 times, k. twice into next st., (p. 1, k. 1) twice, (p. 1, k. 1) into next st., (k. 1, p. 1) 9 times.

    12th row.—K. to end.

    13th row.—(K. 1, p. 1) 12 times, k. 2, (p. 1, k. 1) 3 times, (k. 1, p. 1) 9 times.

    14th row.—As 12th row.

    15th row.—(K. 1, p. 1) 12 times, (k. 1, p. 1) into next st., (k. 1, p. 1) 3 times, (k. 1, p. 1) into next st., (k. 1, p. 1) 9 times.

    16th to 18th rows.—Work 3 rows in patt.

    19th row.—(K. 1, p. 1) 12 times, k. twice into next st., (p. 1, k. 1) 4 times, (p. 1, k. 1) into next st., (k. 1, p. 1) 9 times.

    20th row.—K. to end.

    21st row.—(K. 1, p. 1) 12 times, k. 2, (p. 1, k. 1) 5 times, (k. 1, p. 1) 9 times.

    22nd row.—As 20th row.

    23rd row.—(K. 1, p. 1) 12 times, (k. 1, p. 1) into next st., (k. 1, p. 1) 5 times, (k. 1, p. 1) into next st., (k. 1, p. 1) 9 times (56 sts.).

    24th row.—K. to end.

    25th row.—(K. 1, p. 1) 19 times, turn, cast on 1 st.

    26th row.—K. 15 sts., turn, cast on 1 st.

    Continue in patt. on 16 sts. for 1½ ins. for the thumb, ending with row on wrong side of work.

    Next row.—(K. 2 tog.) 8 times.

    Next row.—K. to end.

    Next row.—(K. 2 tog.) 4 times.

    Break off the wool leaving a fairly long end. Thread this through the remaining sts. and fasten off, then stitch down side edges to base of thumb. With right side of work facing rejoin wool to point of right-hand needle and k. up 4 sts. at base of thumb, work in patt. to end.

    Continue in patt. on 46 sts. for 1¼ ins. ending with row on wrong side of work.

    Commence Fingers thus:—

    The First Finger: Next row.—Patt. across 29 sts., turn and cast on 1 st.

    Next row.—K. 13 sts., turn; cast on 1 st.

    Continue in patt. on 14 sts. for 2¼ ins., ending with row on wrong side of work.

    Next row.—P. 1, (k. 2 tog.) 6 times, p. 1.

    Next row.—K. to end.

    Next row.—(K. 2 tog.) 4 times.

    Break off the wool and complete as given for the thumb.

    The Second Finger: With right side of work facing rejoin wool to right-hand needle and k. up 2 sts. at base of first finger, patt. across next 6 sts., turn and cast on 1 st.

    Next row.—K. 15, turn and cast on 1 st.

    Continue in patt. on 16 sts. for 2½ ins.,

ending with row on wrong side of work.

Next row.—(K. 2 tog.) 8 times.

Next row.—K. to end.

Next row.—(K. 2 tog.) 4 times.

Break off the wool and complete as given for the thumb.

The Third Finger: With right side of work facing, rejoin wool to right-hand needle and k. up 2 sts. at base of second finger, patt. across next 6 sts., turn and cast on 1 st.

Next row.—K. 15, turn and cast on 1 st.

Continue in patt. on 16 sts. for 2¼ ins., ending with row on wrong side of work, then shape the top and complete as given for second finger.

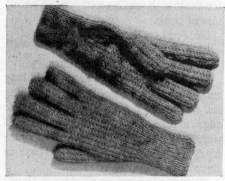

The gloves are knitted in a firm rib.

The Fourth Finger: With right side of work facing, rejoin wool to right-hand needle and k. up 2 sts. at base of third finger, work in patt. to end.

Continue in patt. on 12 sts. for 1¾ ins. ending with row on wrong side of work.

Next row.—(K. 1, k. 2 tog.) 4 times.

Next row.—K. to end.

Next row.—(K. 2 tog.) 4 times.

Break off the wool and complete as given for the thumb, stitching down side of hand to wrist edge.

The Left-hand Glove.—Proceed exactly as given for right-hand glove to the commencement of the thumb shaping. Work this as follows:—

1st row.—(K. 1, p. 1) 9 times, k. twice into next st., (p. 1, k. 1) into next st., (k. 1,

p. 1) 12 times. **2nd row.**—K. to end.

3rd row.—(K. 1, p. 1) 9 times, k. 2, p. 1, k. 1, (k. 1, p. 1) 12 times.

4th row.—As 2nd row.

5th row.—(K. 1, p. 1) 9 times, (k. 1, p. 1) into next st., k. 1, p. 1, (k. 1, p. 1) into next st., (k. 1, p. 1) 12 times.

6th to 8th rows.—Work 3 rows in patt.

Continue in this way, working the increasings exactly as given for the right-hand glove, but working only 18 sts. instead of 24 sts. in patt. before commencing the increasings and 24 sts. instead of only 18 sts. in patt. after the increasings until thumb gusset is complete and there are 56 sts. on the needle.

K. 1 row after the last inc. row.

Next row.—(K. 1, p. 1) 16 times, turn and cast on 1 st.

Next row.—K. 15 sts., turn, cast on 1 st.

Continue in patt. on 16 sts. for the thumb as given for thumb of right-hand glove, then complete the hand and fingers exactly as given for right-hand glove.

The Gauntlet Gloves

MATERIALS

2 oz. 4-ply wool.

2 No. 12 and 2 No. 10 knitting needles.

The Right-hand Glove.—Using No. 10 needles and with double wool cast on 44 sts. and work in k. 1, p. 1 rib for 3 ins.

Break off 1 ball of wool.

Change to No. 12 needles and continue in k. 1, p. 1 rib for ¾ in.

Continue in patt. as follows:—

1st row.—* K. 1, p. 1; rep. from * to end.

2nd row.—P. to end.

Now continue in patt. exactly as given for the short glove, but reversing the patt. by substituting a p. row for the k. row when following the instructions.

The Left-hand Glove.—Work the gauntlet as given above, then continue as given for the short glove, in patt. to match right-hand glove.

Boy's Plain Vest

FOR AN EIGHT- TO TEN-YEAR-OLD

MATERIALS

4 oz. 3-ply wool.
2 No. 9 and 2 No. 12 knitting needles.

MEASUREMENTS

Length, 22 ins.
Chest, 24 ins. unstretched (stretching to 26-in. to 28-in. chest)

TENSION

7 sts. to 1 in.

The Front.—Using No. 9 needles cast on 84 sts. and work 1 in. in k. 1, p. 1 rib.

Continue in st.st. (1 row k., 1 row p.) until work measures 16 ins. from lower edge, ending with a p. row.

Divide for Neck and Shape Armholes thus:—

Next row.—K. 40 sts., k. 2 tog., turn, leave remaining sts. on a spare needle.

Continue in st.st. on 41 sts., dec. 1 st. at neck edge on every alternate row until work measures 16½ ins. from lower edge, ending at the side edge.

Cast off 7 sts. at beg. of the next row, then dec. 1 st. at each end of every alternate row 9 times.

This completes the armhole shaping.

Now continue to dec. at neck edge only on every 4th row until 10 sts. remain. Continue without shaping until work measures 22 ins. from lower edge, ending with a p. row. Cast off.

Rejoin wool to second set of stitches at neck edge, k. 2 tog., k. to end of row.

Now work on these stitches to match the first side.

The Back.—Work as given for the front, continuing in st.st. until work measures 16½ ins. from lower edge, ending with a p. row.

Shape Armholes thus: Cast off 7 sts. at beg. of the next 2 rows, then dec. 1 st. at each end of every alternate row 9 times (52 sts.).

Continue without shaping until work measures 21 ins. from lower edge, ending with a p. row.

Shape Neck thus:—

Next row.—K. 15, cast off next 22 sts., k. to end.

Work 5 rows in st.st. on last set of 15 sts., dec. 1 st. at neck edge on every row.

Continue on 10 sts. until work measures 22 ins. from lower edge, ending with a p. row. Cast off.

Rejoin wool to remaining 15 sts. at neck edge and work to match the first side.

The Neck Border.—Using No. 12 needles cast on 6 sts. and work in k. 1, p. 1 rib for about 17 ins. or the correct length to fit all round neck edge.

Cast off in rib.

The Armhole Borders.—Using No. 12 needles cast on 6 sts. and work in k. 1, p. 1 rib for 12 ins. Cast off in rib.

Work a second border in the same way.

Make-up.—Press work lightly on wrong side using a hot iron over a damp cloth.

Join side and shoulder seams.

Pin the centre of the neck border to centre back of neck and stitch the border all round neck edge, overlapping the ends in the centre front and stitching the cast-on and cast-off edges along the shaped neck edges.

Stitch a border round each armhole, with the join to the side seam.

Press the seams.

Getting ready for school! Even an eight-year-old needs some supervision when dressing. Still he doesn't object to his vest, it's a real man's shape like daddy's, and it's warm, comfortable to wear and easy to make.

Best Lacy Jumper

KNITTED IN TWO-PLY WOOL

MATERIALS

3 oz. 2-ply wool.
2 No. 9 and 2 No. 12 knitting needles.
5 Buttons.

MEASUREMENTS

Length, 15½ ins.   Chest, 29 ins.
Sleeve seam, 2½ ins.

TENSION

7½ sts. to 1 in.

The Front.—Using No. 12 needles cast on 108 sts. and work 2½ ins. in k. 1, p. 1, rib, inc. 1 st. at end of the last row (109 sts.).

Change to No. 9 needles and the following patt.:—

1st row.—K. to end.

2nd and each alternate row.—P. to end.

3rd row. K. 5, * m. 1, sl. 1, k. 2 tog., p.s.s.o., m. 1, k. 9; rep. from * to last 8 sts., m. 1, sl. 1, k. 2 tog., p.s.s.o., m. 1, k. 5.

5th row.—K. 3, * k. 2 tog., m. 1, k. 3, m. 1, sl. 1, k. 1, p.s.s.o., k. 5; rep. from * to last 10 sts., k. 2 tog., m. 1, k. 3, m. 1, sl. 1, k. 1, p.s.s.o., k. 3.

7th row.—As the 3rd row.

9th row.—K. to end.

11th row.—K. 2 tog., m. 1, * k. 9, m. 1, sl. 1, k. 2 tog., p.s.s.o., m. 1; rep. from * to last 11 sts., k. 9, m. 1, sl. 1, k. 1, p.s.s.o.

13th row.—K. 2, m. 1, sl. 1, k. 1, p.s.s.o., * k. 5, k. 2 tog., m. 1, k. 3, m. 1, sl. 1, k. 1, p.s.s.o.; rep. from * to last 9 sts., k. 5, k. 2 tog., m. 1, k. 2.

15th row.—As the 11th row.

16th row.—P. to end.

These 16 rows form the patt.

Continue in patt. until work measures 10 ins. from lower edge, ending with an 8th or a 16th patt. row.

Divide for Front Opening and Shape Armholes thus:—

Next row.—Patt. 46 sts., (k. 1, p. 1) 4 times, turn, cast on 3 sts. for underwrap.

Work on these 57 sts. for left side of the front thus:—

Next row.—(K. 1, p. 1) 5 times, k. 1, p. to end.

Next row.—Patt. 46 sts., (k. 1, p. 1) 5 times, k. 1.

Rep. these 2 rows until work measures 10½ ins. from lower edge, ending at the side edge. Keeping continuity of the patt. and moss-st. border, cast off 6 sts. at beg. of next row, then dec. 1 st. at the side edge on the next 8 rows (43 sts.).

Continue without shaping until work measures 14½ ins. from lower edge, ending at the front edge.

Shape Neck thus: Cast off 10 sts. at beg. of the next row, then dec. 1 st. at neck edge on every row until 26 sts. remain.

Continue without shaping until work measures 15½ ins. from lower edge, ending at armhole edge.

Shape Shoulder thus:—

Next row.—Cast off 9 sts., patt. to end.

Next row.—Patt. to end.

Rep. last 2 rows once.

Cast off remaining 8 sts.

Rejoin wool to remaining 55 sts. at the front edge and work in patt. with moss-st. border thus:—

1st row.—(K. 1, p. 1) 4 times, patt. to end.

2nd row.—Patt. to last 8 sts., (p. 1, k. 1) 4 times.

"Ready for tea, dear?" Her hair is all brushed, her face is shining, she is dressed in her best and most treasured jumper. It is knitted in a charming open-work stitch. Like all good wear for children the style is simple.

Continue in patt. and moss st. until work measures 10½ ins. from lower edge, ending at the side edge.

Shape armhole as given for left side of the front, then continue on 41 sts. without shaping until work measures 14½ ins. from lower edge, ending at front edge.

Shape Neck thus: Cast off 8 sts. at beg. of the next row, then dec. 1 st. at neck edge on every row until 26 sts. remain.

Continue without shaping until work measures 15½ ins. from lower edge, ending at armhole edge. Shape shoulder as given for left shoulder.

The Back.—Work exactly as given for the front, continuing in patt. until work measures 10½ ins. from lower edge, ending with a p. row.

Shape Armholes thus: Keeping continuity of the patt., cast off 6 sts. at beg. of the next 2 rows, then dec. 1 st. at each end of the next 8 rows (81 sts.).

Continue in patt. without shaping until work measures 15½ ins. from lower edge, ending with a p. row.

Shape Neck and Shoulders thus:—

Next row.—Cast off 9 sts., there now being 1 st. on right-hand needle, patt. across 18 sts., k. 2 tog., turn.

Work on these stitches for first shoulder thus:—

Next row.—P. 2 tog., patt. to end.

Next row.—Cast off 9 sts., patt. to last 2 sts., K. 2 tog.

Next row.—P. 2 tog., patt. to end. Cast off remaining 8 sts.

Rejoin wool at needle point and work thus: Cast off 21 sts., patt. to end.

Next row.—Cast off 9 sts., patt. to last 2 sts., p. 2 tog.

Next row.—K. 2 tog., patt. to end. Rep. last 2 rows once. Cast off remaining 8 sts.

The Sleeves.—Using No. 12 needles cast on 61 sts., and work in moss st. thus:—

1st row.—* K. 1, p. 1; rep. from * to last st., k. 1.

Rep. this row for 1 in.

Next row.—* Moss st. 2, k. twice into next st., moss st. 2; rep. from * to last st., k. 1 (73 sts.).

Change to No. 9 needles and continue in patt. as given for the front until work measures 2½ ins., ending with a p. row.

Shape Top thus: Keeping continuity of the patt., dec. 1 st. at each end of every alternate row until 43 sts. remain, then dec. at each end of every row until 15 sts. remain. Cast off remaining sts.

The Collar.—Using No. 12 needles cast on 15 sts. and work 10 rows in moss st.

Next row.—Moss st. 10, turn.

Next row.—Moss st. to end.

Work 10 rows in moss st.

Rep. the last 12 rows until shortest edge of work measures 11 ins. Cast off.

The stitch of the girl's afternoon jumper.

Make-up.—Press work lightly on wrong side with a hot iron over a damp cloth.

Join side, shoulder and sleeve seams.

Stitch sleeves into armholes, matching seams with side seams and gathering the extra fullness to top of sleeve.

Stitch underwrap along lower edge at the back of the right front border.

Pin the centre of the shortest edge of the collar to centre back of neck and stitch the collar round neck edge, ending at right front edge, and at the beginning of the underwrap on left front. Make 5 small button loops down right front edge, the first at neck edge, the other 4 at regular intervals. Sew buttons on to underwrap, matching with button loops. Press seams.

Round-necked Jersey

THE "ALL OCCASIONS" CLASSIC

TWELVE TO FOURTEEN YEARS OLD

MATERIALS

4 oz. 3-ply wool.
2 No. 9 and 2 No. 12 knitting needles.
2 buttons.

MEASUREMENTS

Length, 16½ ins. Bust size, 30 ins.
Sleeve seam, 3½ ins.

TENSION

7 sts. to 1 in.

The Front.—Using No. 12 needles cast on 90 sts. and work 3 ins. in k. 1, p. 1 rib.

Change to No. 9 needles and continue in st.st. inc. 1 st. at each end of the 5th row and every following 6th row until there are 106 sts. on the needle. Continue without shaping until work measures 11 ins. from lower edge ending with a p. row.

Shape Armholes thus: Cast off 5 sts. at beg. of the next 2 rows, then dec. 1 st. at each end of the next 7 rows (82 sts.).

Continue in st.st without shaping until work measures 15 ins. from lower edge, ending with a p. row.

Shape Neck and Shoulders thus:—

Next row.—K. 33 sts., turn.

Work 8 rows in st.st. on these 33 sts., dec. 1 st. at neck edge on each row (25 sts. remain).

Continue without shaping until work measures 16½ ins. from lower edge, ending at armhole edge.

Next row.—Cast off 8 sts., work to end.

Next row.—Work to end.

Rep. last 2 rows once.

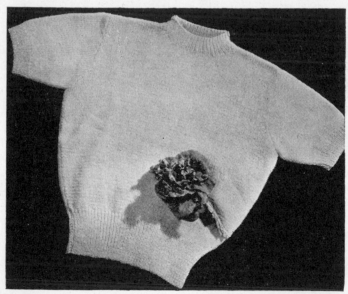

The round-necked classic jersey is still the most popular knitting design. This one is knitted in plain stocking stitch.

"*I say, look!*" *Pam looking at the ducks in the park draws many sympathetic smiles from passers-by. She seems such a jolly little girl in her pink, well-fitting jersey, with its simple round neck and short sleeves.*

Cast off remaining sts.

Slip the centre 16 sts. on to a spare needle and leave for the neck band, rejoin wool to remaining 33 sts. at needle point and work to match the first side.

The Front Neck Band.—With right side of work facing and using No. 12 needles pick up and k. 16 sts. along neck edge, k. 16 sts. from spare needle, pick up and k. 16 sts. along neck edge (48 sts.).

Work 1 in. in k. 1, p. 1 rib.

Cast off loosely in rib.

The Back.—Work as given for the front until armhole shapings are completed and 82 sts. remain.

Continue without shaping until work measures 16½ ins. from lower edge, ending with a p. row.

Shape Neck and Shoulders thus:—

Next row.—Cast off 8 sts., there now being 1 st. on right-hand needle, k. 18 sts., k. 2 tog., turn.

Work on these 20 sts. for first shoulder thus:—

Next row.—P. 2 tog., p. to end.

Next row.—Cast off 8 sts., k. to last 2 sts., k. 2 tog.

Next row.—P. 2 tog., p. to end.

Cast off remaining 9 sts.

Slip the centre 24 sts. on to a spare needle and leave for the neck band, rejoin wool to remaining 29 sts. and k. to end of row.

Work for the second shoulder thus:—

Next row.—Cast off 8 sts., p. to last 2 sts., p. 2 tog.

Next row.—K. 2 tog., k. to end.

Rep. last 2 rows once.

Cast off remaining 9 sts.

The Back Neck Band.—With right side of work facing

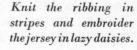

Knit the ribbing in stripes and embroider the jersey in lazy daisies.

and using No. 12 needles, pick up and k. 6 sts. along neck edge, k. across 24 sts. from spare needle, pick up and k. 6 sts. along neck edge (36 sts.).

Work 1 in. in k. 1, p. 1 rib.

Cast off loosely in rib.

The Sleeves.—Using No. 12 needles cast on 68 sts. and work 1 in. in k. 1, p. 1 rib.

Change to No. 9 needles and continue in st.st inc. 1 st. at each end of the 3rd row and every following 4th row until there are 78 sts. on the needle.

Continue without shaping until work measures 3½ ins. from commencement, ending with a p. row.

Shape Top thus: Continuing in st.st. dec. 1 st. at each end of every row until 22 sts. remain.

Cast off remaining sts.

Make-up.—Press work lightly on wrong side using a hot iron over a damp cloth.

Join side and sleeve seams. Join shoulders, leaving about ¾ in. open at neck edge on each side.

Stitch sleeves into armholes, matching seams with side seams.

Make a button loop on each front shoulder and sew on buttons to correspond.

Press the seams.

Make it Fun to Wear

You can turn the classic jersey into the gayest garment any small girl could hope for —make all the ribbing in multicolour stripes and embroider lazy daisies round the neck and sleeves to match, or you can choose one of the simple patterns on page 217.

Tailored Cardigan

JUST LIKE MUMMY'S

TWELVE TO FOURTEEN YEARS OLD

MATERIALS

12 oz. 3-ply wool.
1 pair No. 10 and 1 pair No. 14 knitting needles. 8 buttons.

MEASUREMENTS

Length, 19 ins.
Width all round at underarm, 33 ins.
Sleeve seam, 15 ins. (with cuff turned back 3 ins.).

TENSION

8 sts. to 1 in., using No. 10 needles, measured over the patt.

The Right Front.—Using No. 10 needles cast on 64 sts.

1st row.—* K. 1, p. 1; rep. from * to end.

2nd row.—As 1st row.

3rd row.—* P. 1, k. 1; rep. from * to end.

4th row.—As 3rd row.

These 4 rows form the long double moss st. patt.

Continue in patt. until work measures 13 ins. from the commencement.

Shape Armhole thus: Continuing in patt., cast off 8 sts. at beg. of the next row, then dec. 1 st. at this same edge on every row until 46 sts. remain. Continue without shaping until work measures 17 ins. from lower edge, ending at straight front edge.

Shape Neck and Shoulder thus: Continuing in patt., cast off 3 sts. at beg. of the next row, then dec. 1 st. at this same edge on every row until 32 sts. remain.

Continue without shaping until work measures 19 ins. from lower edge, ending at armhole edge.

Next row.—Cast off 8 sts., patt. to end.

Next row.—Patt. to end.

Rep. last 2 rows once.

Cast off remaining sts.

The Left Front.—Work exactly as given for the right front.

The Back.—Using No. 10 needles cast on 134 sts. and work in patt. as given for the right front until work measures 13 ins. from commencement.

Shape Armholes thus: Continuing in patt., cast off 8 sts. at beg. of the next 2 rows, then dec. 1 st. at each end of every row until 98 sts. remain.

Continue without shaping until work measures 19 ins. from lower edge.

Shape Neck and Shoulders thus:—

Next row.—Cast off 8 sts., patt. 28 sts., counting st. already on the needle after casting off, k. 2 tog., cast off 22 sts., patt. to end.

Work on last set of 38 sts. thus:—

1st row.—Cast off 8 sts., patt. to last 2 sts., k. 2 tog.

2nd row.—K. 2 tog., patt. to end.

Rep. last 2 rows twice.

Cast off remaining sts.

Rejoin wool to second set of sts. at needle point and work thus:—

1st row.—K. 2 tog., patt. to end.

2nd row.—Cast off 8 sts., patt. to last 2 sts., k. 2 tog.

3rd row.—As 1st row.

Rep. last 2 rows once.

Cast off remaining sts.

The Sleeves.—Using No. 10 needles cast on 64 sts. and work in patt. as given for the right front for 2 ins.

Continuing in patt., inc. 1 st. at each end of next row and every following 8th row until there are 96 sts. on the needle.

Continue without shaping until work measures 18 ins. from commencement.

Shape Top thus: Continuing in patt., dec. 1 st. at the beg. of every row until 80 sts. remain, then dec. at both ends of every row until 16 sts. remain.

Cast off remaining sts.

The Pockets.—Using No. 10 needles cast on 32 sts.

for 17 ins. when it is slightly stretched. Cast off.

The Neck Band.—Using No. 14 needles cast on 114 sts. and work in g.st. for $\frac{1}{2}$ in.

Next row.—K. 3, cast off 3 sts. for a buttonhole, k. to end.

Next row.—K. to last 3 sts., cast on 3 sts., k. 3.

Continue in g.st. until the band measures 1 in. from commencement. Cast off.

Make-up.—Press each piece lightly with a hot iron over a damp cloth.

Join side, sleeve and shoulder seams and set sleeves into armholes. Stitch front borders to front edges (buttonhole border to right front edge). Stitch neck band to neck edge stretching it slightly but taking care not to stretch the neck edge. Work a row of d.c. round each pocket and stitch two to each front, the upper ones in line with the lower ones. Sew on buttons to match buttonholes. Press all seams.

The jacket is knitted in a double moss stitch with four pockets. Gilt buttons add a smart finishing touch.

Work in patt. as given for right front for $4\frac{1}{2}$ ins. Cast off.

Work three more pieces in the same way.

The Right Front Band.—Using No. 14 needles cast on 9 sts. and work in g.st. (each row k.) for 1 in.

Next row.—K. 3, cast off 3 sts. for a buttonhole, k. to end.

Next row.—K. 3, cast on 3 sts., k. 3.

Continue in g.st. making 6 further buttonholes at $2\frac{1}{4}$-in. intervals. Continue in g.st. until the band measures 17 ins. from the commencement, when slightly stretched (about a further 2 ins.). Cast off.

The Left Front Band.—Using No. 14 needles cast on 9 sts. and work in g.st.

Schoolgirls' Jacket

This blazer-type jacket is useful to wear over summer frocks, with a classic jersey and plain skirt, or with slacks. Any simple patt. can replace the double moss st. (*see* page 217) or plain st.st. with pockets and cuffs in g.st. to match the front bands would be effective and would use less wool. In st.st. 10 oz. of 3-ply wool should be sufficient, but in this case use No. 11 needles to obtain the correct tension.

Ring the changes of this smart, tailored jacket by making cuffs, pockets and borders in a contrasting colour.

Mummy's out of the picture — but she has the grown-up edition of Pam's cardigan. Do you remember it? Look on page 54. Pam, however, has four pockets and that, of course, makes her feel very superior.

Pick up these Stitches!

Spot Pattern

This stitch requires a number of stitches divisible by 8.

1st row.—K. to end.

2nd row.—P. to end.

3rd and 4th rows.—Rep. 1st and 2nd rows once.

5th row.—K. 3, * p. 2, k. 6; rep. from * to last 5 sts. p. 2, k. 3.

6th row.—P. 3, * k. 2, p. 6; rep. from * to last 5 sts., k. 2, p. 3.

7th to 10th rows.—Rep. 1st and 2nd rows twice.

11th row.—K. 7, * p. 2, k. 6; rep. from * to last 9 sts., p. 2, k. 7.

12th row.—P. 7, * k. 2, p. 6; rep. from * to last 9 sts., k. 2, p. 7.

These 12 rows form the pattern.

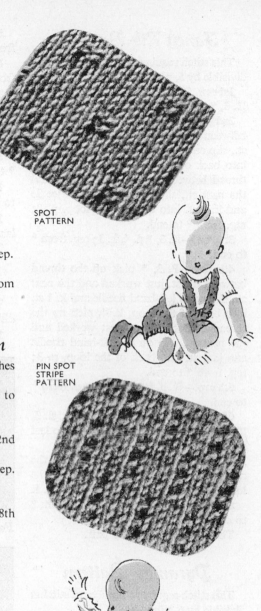

SPOT PATTERN

Pin Spot Stripe Pattern

This stitch requires a number of stitches divisible by 4, plus 3 sts.

1st row.— * K. 3, p. 1, rep. from * to last 3 sts., k. 3.

2nd row.—P. to end.

3rd to 6th rows.—Rep. 1st and 2nd rows twice.

7th row.—K. 1, p. 1, * k. 3, p. 1; rep. from * to last st., k. 1.

8th row.—P. to end.

9th to 12th rows.—Rep. 7th and 8th rows twice.

These 12 rows form the pattern.

PIN SPOT STRIPE PATTERN

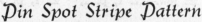

Fancy Rib Pattern

This stitch requires a number of stitches divisible by 5, plus 3 sts.

1st row. (Wrong side of work facing.)—K. 3, * p. 2, k. 3; rep. from * to end.

2nd row.—P. 3, * pick up the thread between the st. just worked and the next st., slip on to left-hand needle and k. 1 st. into back of the loop, k. 2, pick up the thread between the st. just worked and the next st., slip on to left-hand needle and k. 1 st. into back of the loop, p. 3; rep. from * to end.

3rd row.—K. 3, * p. 4, k. 3; rep. from * to end.

4th row.—P. 3, * pick up the thread between the st. just worked and the next st., slip on to left-hand needle and k. 1 st. into back of the loop, k. 4, pick up the thread between the st. just worked and the next st., slip on to left-hand needle and k. 1 st. into back of the loop, p. 3; rep. from * to end.

5th row.—K. 3, * p. 6, k. 3; rep. from * to end.

6th row.—P. 2, * k. 4 tog., w.fd., sl. 3, k. 1, p.s. sts.o., p. 1; rep. from * to last st., p. 1.

7th row.—K. 2, * p. 1, p. 2 into the next st., working into the back of the loop, p. 1, k. 1; rep. from * to last st., k. 1.

8th row.—P. 3, * k. 2, p. 3; rep. from * to end.

These 8 rows form the patt.

Pyramid Pattern

This stitch requires a number of stitches divisible by 6, plus 1 st.

1st row.—* P. 1, k. 5; rep. from * to last st., p. 1.

2nd row.—K. 1, * p. 5, k. 1; rep. from * to end.

3rd row.—P. 2, * k. 3, p. 3; rep. from * to last 5 sts., k. 3, p. 2.

4th row.—K. 2, * p. 3, k. 3; rep. from * to last 5 sts., p. 3, k. 2.

5th row.—P. 3, k. 1, * p. 5, k. 1; rep. from * to last 3 sts., p. 3.

6th row.—K. 3, p. 1, * k. 5, p. 1; rep. from * to last 3 sts., k. 3.

7th row.—As 6th row.

8th row.—As 5th row.

9th row.—K. 2, * p. 3, k. 3; rep. from * to last 5 sts., p. 3, k. 2.

10th row.—P. 2, * k. 3, p. 3; rep. from * to last 5 sts., k. 3, p. 2.

11th row.—* K. 1, p. 5; rep. from * to last st., k. 1.

12th row.—* P. 1, k. 5; rep. from * to last st., p. 1.

These 12 rows form the pattern.

Leaf Stitch

This stitch requires a number of stitches divisible by 4, plus 1 st.

1st row.—K. 1, p. 1, * k. 1, p. 3;

Fancy rib suitable for children's clothes.

Detail of pyramid pattern which is a very good stitch for children's clothes.

rep. from * to last 3 sts., k. 1, p. 2.

2nd row.—K. 2, p. 1, * k. 3, p. 1; rep. from * to last 2 sts., k. 2.

3rd row.—P. 2, k. 1, p. 1, * k. 5 sts. into next st. as follows: (k. 1, m. 1, k. 1, m. 1, k. 1) into previous row of the next st., p. 1, k. 1, p. 1; rep. from * to last st., p. 1.

4th row.—K. 2, p. 1, * k. 1, p. 5, k. 1, p. 1; rep. from * to last 2 sts., k. 2.

5th row.—P. 2, k. 1, p. 1, * sl. 1, k. 1, p.s.s.o., k. 1, k. 2 tog., p. 1, k. 1, p. 1; rep. from * to last st., p. 1.

6th row.—K. 2, p. 1, k. 1, * p. 3, k. 1, p. 1, k. 1; rep. from * to last st., k. 1.

7th row.—P. 2, k. 1, p. 1, * sl. 1, k. 2 tog., p.s.s.o., p. 1, k. 1, p. 1; rep. from * to last st., p. 1.

8th row.—K. 2, p. 1, * k. 3, p. 1; rep. from * to last 2 sts., k. 2.

9th row.—P. 2, * work 5 times into

Leaf stitch suitable for children's clothes.

Detail of two-colour spot pattern which is a good stitch for children's clothes.

next st. (as given in the 3rd row), p. 3; rep. from * to last 3 sts., work 5 times into next st., p. 2.

10th row.—K. 2, * p. 5, k. 3; rep. from * to last 7 sts., p. 5, k. 2.

11th row.—P. 2, * sl. 1, k. 1, p.s.s.o., k. 1, k. 2 tog., p. 3; rep. from * to end, ending the last rep. with p. 2 instead of p. 3.

12th row.—K. 2, p. 3, * k. 3, p. 3; rep. from * to last 2 sts., k. 2.

13th row.—P. 2, * sl. 1, k. 2 tog., p.s.s.o., p. 3; rep. from * to last 5 sts., sl. 1, k. 2 tog., p.s.s.o., p. 2.

14th row.—K. 2, * p. 1, k. 3; rep. from * to last 3 sts., p. 1, k. 2.

The last 12 rows, that is, 3rd to 14th rows inclusive, form the pattern.

Two-colour Spot Pattern

This stitch requires a number of stitches divisible by 4, plus 1 st.

One ball of red and one ball of white wool will be required.

Do not break off the colour not in use but carry this up the side of the work to avoid ends.

Commence with the white wool.

1st row. (Wrong side of work.)—P. Change to red wool.

2nd row.—K.

3rd row.—P.

4th and 5th rows.—Rep. the 2nd and 3rd rows once.

Change to white wool.

6th row.—* K. 3, drop the next st. down 4 rows to the white st. and k. through the white st. and the loops of red; rep. from * to the last st.; k. 1.

7th row.—P.

Change to the red wool.

8th to 11th rows.—Rep. the 2nd and 3rd rows twice. Change to white wool.

12th row.—K. 1, * drop the next st. down 4 rows to the white st. and k. through the white st. and the loops of red, k. 3; rep. from * to the end. Rep. these 12 rows.

"Wonder if the fishing's any good?" John is out for a day's fun in his lumber jacket. It's a handy garment, buttoning close to the neck. The *"other side of the mantelpiece"* garment—a school jersey—is on page 224.

Boy's Lumber Jacket

THIS SAVES IN CLOTHES

TEN TO TWELVE YEARS OLD

MATERIALS

7 oz. 4-ply wool.
2 No. 8 and 2 No. 12 knitting needles.
8 buttons.

MEASUREMENTS

Length, 18 ins. Chest, 29 ins.
Sleeve seam, 16 ins.

TENSION

Using No. 8 needles about 6½ sts. to
1 in., measured over a slightly stretched
patt.

The Back.—Using No. 12 needles cast
on 96 sts. and work 3 ins. in a rib of
k. 2, p. 2. Change to No. 8 needles and
work 1 row in rib, inc. 1 st. at both ends
of the row. There are now 98 sts. on the
needle.

Continue in the following reversible
rib as follows:—

1st row.—P. 4, * k. 2, p. 6; rep. from
* to last 6 sts., k. 2, p. 4.

2nd row.—K. 4, * p. 2, k. 6; rep. from
* to last 6 sts., p. 2, k. 4.

3rd to 6th rows.—Rep. 1st and 2nd
rows twice.

7th row.—* K. 2, p. 2; rep. from * to
last 2 sts., k. 2.

8th row.—* P. 2, k. 2; rep. from * to
last 2 sts., p. 2.

9th to 12th rows.—Rep. 7th and 8th
rows twice.

13th row.—* K. 2, p. 6; rep. from * to
last 2 sts., k. 2.

14th row.—P. 2, * k. 6, p. 2; rep. from
* to end.

15th to 18th rows.—Rep. 13th and 14th
rows twice.

19th row.—* K. 2, p. 2; rep. from * to
last 2 sts., k. 2.

20th row.—* P. 2, k. 2; rep. from * to
last 2 sts., p. 2.

21st to 24th rows.—Rep. 19th and 20th
rows twice.

These 24 rows form the patt. Continue
in patt. until work measures 12 ins. from
the beg.

Shape Armholes thus: Cast off 8 sts. at
the beg. of the next 2 rows. Then dec.
1 st. at both ends of the next 6 rows.
There are now 70 sts. on the needle. Continue without shaping until work measures
18 ins. from the beg.

Shape Neck and Shoulders thus: Cast
off 7 sts. at the beg. of each of the next
4 rows. Then cast off 6 sts. at the beg.
of each of the next 2 rows. Cast off
remaining sts.

The Left Front.—Using No. 12 needles
cast on 44 sts. and work 3 ins. in a rib
of k. 2, p. 2. Change to No. 8 needles and
with the wrong side of the work facing,
work 1 more row in rib, inc. 1 st. in the
last 2 sts. of the row. There are now 46 sts.
on the needle.

Now continue in patt. as follows:—

1st row.—P. 4, * k. 2, p. 6; rep. from *
to last 2 sts., k. 2.

2nd row.—* P. 2, k. 6; rep. from * to
last 4 sts., k. 4.

3rd to 6th row.—Rep. 1st and 2nd
rows twice.

7th row.—* K. 2, p. 2; rep. from * to
last 2 sts., k. 2.

8th row.— * P. 2, k. 2; rep. from * to
last 2 sts., p. 2.

9th to 12th rows.—Rep. 7th and 8th
rows twice.

"*I'll be over in a sec.*" *Peter grins at his friends, but waits patiently while we look at his jersey. A zipp fastens it close to the neck, so that no shirt need be worn. These close-to-the-neck garments are an economy in clothes and laundering.*

Here are the lumber jacket and the school jersey with collar, designed for boys between ten and twelve years of age. Shirts need not be worn with either of them. The stitch is a simple, reversible rib.

13th row.—* K. 2, p. 6; rep. from * to last 4 sts., p. 4.

14th row.—K. 4, * p. 2, k. 6; rep. from * to last 2 sts., p. 2.

15th to 18th rows.—Rep. 13th and 14th rows twice.

19th row.—* K. 2, p. 2; rep. from * to last 2 sts., k. 2.

20th row.—* P. 2, k. 2; rep. from * to last 2 sts., p. 2.

21st to 24th rows.—Rep. 19th and 20th rows twice.

These 24 rows form the patt. Rep. them until work measures 12 ins. from the beg., ending with a row on the wrong side of the work.

Shape Armholes thus: Cast off 8 sts. at the beg. of the next row. Then dec. 1 st.

at this edge on every row until there are 32 sts. on the needle.

Continue in patt. on these 32 sts. until work measures 17 ins. from the beg., ending with a row at the front edge.

Shape Neck and Shoulders thus: Cast off 6 sts. at the beg. of the next row. Then dec. 1 st. at this edge on every row until 20 sts. remain. Continue without shaping until work measures 18 ins. from the beg., ending with a row at the armhole edge.

Next row.—Cast off 7 sts., patt. to the end.

Next row.—Patt. to the end.

Rep. the last 2 rows once. Cast off remaining sts.

The Right Front.—Work exactly as given for the left front until the waist ribbing has been completed and there are 46 sts. on the needle. Then work in patt. as given for the left front, but reversing the inc. and dec. The first row of the patt. will read:—

1st row.—* K. 2, p. 6; rep. from * to last 6 sts., k. 2, p. 4.

Keeping the patt. correct work the rest of the front as above.

The Sleeves.—Using No. 12 needles cast on 48 sts. and work 2½ ins. in a rib of k. 2, p. 2. Change to No. 8 needles and work 1 row in rib, inc. 1 st at both ends of the row. There are now 50 sts.

Continue in patt. as given for the back, inc. 1 st. at both ends of the 5th row and every following 8th row until there are 78 sts. on the needle. Continue without shaping until work measures 16 ins. from the beg.

Shape Top thus: Dec. 1 st. at both ends of every alternate row until there are 58 sts. on the needle. Then dec. 1 st. at both ends of every row until there are 18 sts. on the needle. Cast off.

The Front Bands.—Using No. 12 needles cast on 7 sts. and k. in g.st.

(k. every row) until the band measures 17¾ ins. from the beg. Cast off.

Knit a second band to correspond, but make 8 buttonholes about 1¾ in. apart, the first ½ in. from the bottom and the last ½ in. from the top.

To make a buttonhole.—K. 2, cast off 3, k. to end. In the following row cast on 3 sts. over those cast off.

The Neck Band.—Join the shoulder seams, using No. 12 needles, and with the right side of the work facing, pick up and k. 24 sts. along the right side of the neck, 30 sts. along the back of the neck and 24 along the left side of the neck. There are now 78 sts. Work on these sts. in a rib of k. 2, p. 2 for ¾ in. Cast off loosely in rib.

Make-up.—Press all knitting lightly on the wrong side, using a warm iron over a damp cloth, with the exception of the waist, neck and wrist ribbing. Join the side and sleeve seams, and stitch the sleeves into the armholes. Stitch the plain front band to the right front, and the button-hole band to the left front. Press all seams and sew buttons to the right front to correspond to the buttonholes.

School Jersey with Collar

TEN TO TWELVE YEARS OLD

MATERIALS

7 oz. 4-ply wool.
2 No. 8 and 2 No. 12 knitting needles.
A 4-in. zipp fastener.
A medium-sized crochet hook.

MEASUREMENTS

Length, 18 ins. Chest, 29 ins.
Sleeve seam, 16 ins.

TENSION

Using No. 8 needles about 6½ sts. to 1 in., measured over the slightly stretched pattern.

The Back.—This is worked exactly as the back of the original lumber jacket.

The Front.—This is worked in one piece with a neck opening of about 4 ins. Work exactly as given in the instructions for the back of original lumber jacket until the armhole shapings have been completed and there are 70 sts. on the needle.

Divide for Front Opening:—

Next row.—Patt. 34 sts., cast off next 2 sts., patt. to the end.

Continue in patt. on the last set of 34 sts., without shaping, until work measures 17 ins. from the beg., ending with a row at the centre front edge.

Shape Neck and Shoulders thus: Cast off 9 sts. at beg. of next row. Then dec. 1 st. at this edge on every row until there are 20 sts. on the needle.

Continue without shaping until work measures 18 ins. from the beg., ending with a row at the armhole edge.

Next row.—Cast off 7, patt. to the end.

Next row.—Patt. to the end.

Rep. these last 2 rows once more.

Cast off remaining sts.

Rejoin wool at the needle point and work the other front to correspond.

The Sleeves.—These are worked exactly as given in the instructions for the sleeves of the original lumber jacket.

The Collar.—Using No. 12 needles cast on 134 sts. and work in a rib of k. 2, p .2, dec. 1 st. at both ends of every alternate row until the work measures 2½ ins. from the beg. Cast off 12 sts. at the beg. of each of the next 4 rows. Cast off remaining sts.

Make-up.—Press all the work lightly on

The rib in which the boy's jersey and lumber jacket are knitted.

the wrong side, using a warm iron over a damp cloth, with the exception of the waist and wrist ribbing.

Join the side, shoulder and sleeve seams and stitch the sleeves into the armholes.

Stitch the cast-off edge of the collar to the neck edge, beginning and ending at each front opening edge. Work a row of d.c. along each front opening edge. Stitch the zipp fastener into the front opening. Press all seams.

Polo-necked Pullover

FOR THE YOUNG SPORTSMAN OF FOURTEEN

MATERIALS

9 oz. 4-ply wool.
2 No. 8 knitting needles.
4 No. 10 and 4 No. 12 knitting needles pointed at both ends.

MEASUREMENTS

Length, 20 ins.
Chest, 31 ins.
Sleeve seam, 16 ins.

TENSION

About 7 sts. to 1 in. measured over the slightly stretched rib.

The Front.—Using No. 10 needles cast on 110 sts. and work in k. 6, p. 4 rib as follows:—

1st row.—P. 2, * k. 6, p. 4; rep. from * to last 8 sts., k. 6, p. 2.

2nd row.—K. 2, * p. 6, k. 4; rep. from * to last 8 sts., p. 6, k. 2.

Rep. these 2 rows for 3 ins.

Change to No. 8 needles and continue in the rib until work measures 13½ ins. from lower edge, ending with row on wrong side of work.

Shape Armholes thus: Continue in rib, cast off 5 sts. at beg. of the next 2 rows,

"It's a honey," says Tom, and he's just as pleased with his pullover as he is with his model aeroplane. Boys like the polo neck which does admittedly save a lot of bother about dressing in holiday times.

then dec. 1 st. at each end of the next 5 rows (90 sts.).

Work 1 row without shaping, thus ending with row on wrong side of work.

Commence Yoke thus:—

1st row.—P. 2, * sl. next 3 sts. on to spare needle and leave at front of work, k. next 3 sts., then k. 3 sts. from spare

14th to 16th rows.—Rep. 2nd to 4th rows inclusive once.

17th to 24th rows.—Rep. 13th to 16th rows inclusive twice.

These 24 rows form the pattern.

Continue in patt. until work measures 19 ins. from lower edge, ending with row on wrong side of work.

To slip on after games this polo-neck jersey is ideal.
The body is knitted in a wide rib, the yoke has a simple cable.

needle (this will be referred to as "cable next 6 sts."), p. 4, k. 6, p. 4; rep. from * to last 8 sts., cable next 6 sts., p. 2.

2nd row.—K. 2, * p. 6, k. 4; rep. from * to last 8 sts., p. 6, k. 2.

3rd row.—P. 2, * k. 6, p. 4; rep. from * to last 8 sts., k. 6, p. 2.

4th row.—As 2nd row.

5th to 12th rows.—Rep. 1st to 4th rows inclusive twice.

13th row.—P. 2, * k. 6, p. 4, cable next 6 sts., leaving spare needle at back of work, p. 4; rep. from * to last 8 sts., k. 6, p. 2.

Shape Neck thus:—

Next row.—Patt. 31, turn.

Work 6 rows in patt. on these 31 sts., dec. 1 st. at neck edge on each row. Continue in patt. on 25 sts. until work measures 20 ins. from lower edge, ending at armhole edge.

Shape Shoulder thus:—

Next row.—Cast off 8 sts., patt. to end.

Next row.—Patt. to end.

Rep. last 2 rows once.

Cast off remaining sts.

Now sl. the centre 28 sts. on to a spare needle and leave for the collar, rejoin wool to needle point and continue in patt. on remaining 31 sts. to match the first side.

The Back.—Work exactly as given for the front, continuing in patt. until work measures 20 ins. from lower edge, ending with row on wrong side of work.

Shape Neck and Shoulders thus:—

Next row.—Cast off 8 sts., there now being 1 st. on right-hand needle, patt. 18 sts., k. 2 tog., turn.

Continue in patt. on 20 sts. for one shoulder thus:

Next row.—K. 2 tog., patt. to end.

Next row.—Cast off 8 sts., patt. to last 2 sts., k. 2 tog.

Next row.—K. 2 tog., patt. to end.

Cast off remaining 9 sts.

Now sl. the centre 32 sts. on to a spare needle and leave for the collar, rejoin wool to needle point and work in patt. to end of row. Work for second shoulder thus:—

Next row.—Cast off 8 sts., patt. to last 2 sts., k. 2 tog.

Next row.—P. 2 tog., patt. to end.

Rep. last 2 rows once.

Cast off remaining 9 sts.

The Sleeves.—Using No. 10 needles cast on 50 sts. and work in k. 6, p. 4 rib as given for the front for 2½ ins.

Change to No. 8 needles and continue in rib, inc. 1 st. at each end of the 5th row and every following 6th row until there are 82 sts. on the needle, working the increased sts. into the rib.

Continue without shaping until work measures 16 ins. from lower edge, ending with row on wrong side of work.

Shape Top thus: Continuing in rib, dec. 1 st. at each end of every alternate row

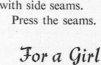

The girl must have her jersey too. The polo is replaced by a neck band and the sleeves are short.

until 70 sts. remain, then dec. 1 st. at each end of every row until 22 sts. remain. Cast off remaining sts.

The Collar.—Join the shoulder seams.

Using the No. 12 needles commence at left shoulder seam with right side of work facing and pick up and k. 16 sts. along neck edge, k. 28 sts. from spare needle, 16 sts. along neck edge to right shoulder seam, 6 sts. along back neck edge, k. 32 sts. from spare needle, 6 sts. along back neck edge to the left shoulder seam (104 sts.).

Arrange these sts. on 3 needles (32, 36, 36) and work in rounds of k. 2, p. 2 rib for 2 ins.

Change to No. 10 needles and continue in rib for a further 3 ins., until the collar measures 5 ins. from commencement, ending at the left shoulder seam.

Cast off loosely in rib.

Make-up.—Press work lightly on wrong side with a hot iron over a damp cloth. Join side and sleeve seams. Stitch sleeves into armholes, matching seams with side seams.

Press the seams.

For a Girl

For a girl's jersey cast off after working 1 in. of ribbing at the neck edge instead of making the polo collar. Make short sleeves by casting on 60 sts. instead of 50, working 1 in. of k. 1, p. 1 rib on No. 12 needles, then in the next row inc. to 82 sts. and continue in the wide rib. After a further inch change to No. 8 needles and continue in the wide rib until sleeve measures 4 ins. (or desired length), then shape the top as given for the long sleeve.

RE-KNITTING, RENOVATIONS

COMBINING FABRIC AND KNITTING

THE most fashionable indoor sport for women these days is cunningly contriving old bits and pieces of this frock and that into a stunning model that hits every one in the eye, and makes the wearer the envy of all beholders.

The only strict rule of the game is that no new materials of any sort should be bought, though it is permissible to bring into play any odds and ends already in hand.

In the section that follows, we offer you some interesting variations of this game as applied to knitting. How to unpick and reknit, how to make new garments out of felted misfits, new ways with old socks, and so on. But the newest and most fascinating idea is the combination of knitting and fabric. Quite a number of suggestions and instructions on these lines are introduced. Use your ingenuity and imagination and you'll get grand results.

Re-knitting Wool

If wool is short, knit yoke and sleeves in stripes.

THE fact that a knitted garment is bedraggled, faded and stretched does not mean that the yarn from which it was knitted is ruined. Unless the garment is absolutely riddled with holes, you should be able to reclaim the yarn, and you should have enough to make up into another very serviceable garment. First, unpick all seams—side, sleeve, front bands, neck bands, etc. Avoid snicking the fabric or you will have short ends. Now, beginning at the cast-off edge, unravel the knitting by pulling the yarn in gentle jerks. Wind the wool round the back of a chair or over and over a largish book until you have an ounce skein—in other words if the unwinding is straightforward and there are no holes or breaks—until you come to an end. Tie this skein in about four places and keep on one side until the whole garment is unravelled. Short ends should be kept for sewing up. This is the stage for redyeing if the yarn is patchy, although unless the colour has become really ugly, knitting up patchy yarn often produces very interesting effects. At any rate, it is best to wash the yarn in the skein stage as washing will rid it of the kinks caused by knitting. Some people prefer to steam the yarn at this stage. To do this, put the skeins in the top part of a large steamer and steam for about ten minutes. Hang them up to dry, shaking occasionally to separate all the threads.

When the yarn is quite dry, wind into balls and weigh it as a guide to reknitting. Unravelled yarn is generally thinner and less resilient than originally, so your tension sample is more than ever important.

If, on weighing the yarn, you think there will not be enough for your garment, remember that yokes in stripes or contrasting colours are fashionable and becoming, so here is an opportunity for using up that odd ounce. Work on the back and front of the garment at the same time—that is, cast-on on two pairs of needles and work alternately on both so that you don't find yourself with the front and two sleeves and only enough wool for half the back. Contrasting sleeves linked up with the neck bands in the same colour are smart and wool saving.

Sleeves and neck band in contrasting wool look smart.

Dealing with felted garment

Now we come to the garment that has felted and won't unpick. This is generally made of soft fleecy yarn which was quite expensive when it was bought, and although great care was taken when washing it, has shrunk. The best thing to do with this is to cut—yes cut—another garment from it as you would from one made of ordinary material. A sleeveless jerkin is good, as the rubbed places under the arm can be cut away. Finish off the edges with bright crochet bands and brush the fabric itself with a wire brush to raise the surface. The small pieces can be soaked in cold water to felt them more, and then you can make them into toys, bonnets or even small coats for the babies.

All the scraps should be cut up for stuffing toys, tea cosys and if you are really industrious, for quilts.

A yoke in contrasting colour helps the wool to go round.

Odds and ends

Short lengths of yarn which have been reconditioned should be wound into balls and used as they come to make "rainbow" gloves, ankle socks and hoods for children. If you can spare an ounce or so of wool in a neutral colour to make stripes between the "rainbow" ones, you can make jerseys and cardigans which will be jolly and economical. If that ounce or so could be grey, you'll find it particularly good for this purpose.

Not one scrap of wool or woollen fabric, however small, should be thrown away now that wool is so precious. It will have a use. It may be just the scrap you need to make a success out of last year's failure.

A jersey can look very effective if knitted in broad stripes of three contrasting colours.

Re-knitting unpicked yarn

WHEN the yarn has been unravelled and reconditioned, there are two important things to be done before choosing a new design. First weigh the yarn to find out how much remains, then experiment with one or two tension samples and compare the results with your average tension in new yarn of the same ply. You may find that after being unpicked a 3-ply yarn will be equivalent to a new 2-ply yarn in tension. If so, choose a design planned for 2-ply. Generally speaking it will be found advisable to use needles one or two sizes finer than those used for new yarn of the same ply. Unless the unpicked wool is in very good condition, avoid stocking stitch, which is inclined to show up the least blemish. A stitch with a raised surface, such as moss stitch, or a fancy rib such as that used for the jumper with contrasting yoke panels, will help to disguise any unevenness in either colour or texture.

It is best to choose a simple design which depends on good "line" rather than on elaborate detail for its effect. You can then introduce a contrasting colour if necessary without fear of complications. Specially helpful is a design which already features a contrasting colour in some form or another, as this will give you a lead for repeating the colour elsewhere if the unpicked yarn seems likely to be exhausted too soon. The ribbed jersey with contrasting yoke panels is an example of this type of design. The original model (for which instructions are given) is a simple ribbed design, the shaping obtained by changing the size of the needles and the only decoration a band of a contrasting colour with medallions of the main colour. The garment to be unpicked was a 4-ply jersey in k. 1, p. 1 rib. This had been washed many times and was considerably stretched. When the wool was unravelled it was found to be as thin as an ordinary 3-ply and was therefore suitable for the new design. Since the original garment had long sleeves there was sufficient wool to make short sleeves in the main colour for the new garment, but had there been much wastage in unpicking, due to wear, or had the original garment been a short-sleeved one, a simple and effective solution could have been found by making the sleeves in the same colour as the yoke panel. The panel could also be repeated across the back.

As has been mentioned previously, don't be in too much of a hurry to dye your wool if it looks patchy in colour. It is very possible that it will, for it is extremely likely that the colour may appear to have faded all over, but that part of the thread which was not exposed has not faded. The result is that the unravelled wool will look very uneven in colour. Nevertheless when you knit your tension sample, knit sufficient to give you an idea of the colour effect. It is more than likely that it will give a charming variegated or shaded effect. Dyeing wool, on the other hand, is not always successful, and may be disappointing—especially after a few washes.

Fashionable Ribbed Jumper

WITH CONTRASTING PANELS

MATERIALS

7 oz. 3-ply wool in dark shade.
A small ball 3-ply wool in light shade.
2 No. 9, 2 No. 10, 2 No. 11 and 2 No. 12 knitting needles.

MEASUREMENTS

Length, 24 ins. Bust size, 34 ins.
Sleeve seam, 5½ ins.

TENSION

7 sts. to 1 in. worked on No. 9 needles.

The Front.—Using No. 9 needles and dark wool cast on 113 sts. and work in rib as follows:—

1st row.—P. 2, * k. twice into next st., p. 3; rep. from * to last 3 sts., k. twice into next st., p. 2.

2nd row.—K. 2, * p. 2 tog., k. 3; rep. from * to last 4 sts., p. 2 tog., k. 2.

These 2 rows form the patt.
Continue in patt. for 2 ins.
Change to No. 10 needles and work 2 ins. in patt. (4 ins. from lower edge).
Change to No. 11 needles and work 2 ins. in patt. (6 ins. from lower edge).
Change to No. 12 needles and work 2 ins. in patt. (8 ins. from lower edge).
Change to No. 11 needles and work 1½ ins. in patt. (9½ ins. from lower edge).
Change to No. 10 needles and work 1½ ins. in patt. (11 ins. from lower edge).
Change to No. 9 needles and continue in patt. until work measures 16½ ins. from lower edge, ending with a second patt. row.

Divide for Neck Opening thus:—

Next row.—Patt. 57 sts., turn, leave remaining sts. on a spare needle.

Continue in patt. on these 57 sts. until work measures 17½ ins. from lower edge, ending at side edge.

Shape Armhole thus: Continuing in patt., cast off 7 sts. at beginning of the next row, then dec. 1 st. at this same edge on each of the next 5 rows (45 sts. at the end of a second patt. row).

Continue without shaping until work measures 19 ins. from lower edge, ending with a second patt. row.

Commence Yoke Border thus:—

Next row.—* P. 7, drop the next st. down 1 row, then place the st. and strand of wool

This ribbed jersey in 4-ply was knitted in a knit one purl one rib. It became worn and shapeless and was unpicked.

Isn't it charming? And who'd guess it was made out of the sad remains photographed opposite? But it's so simple. Medallions of contrasting colour across the yoke are its only elaboration. For the rest—a simple rib.

back on to left-hand needle and work 11 sts. into them as follows: k. 1, (m. 1, k. 1) 5 times. Turn and work on these 11 sts. only as follows:—

1st row.—P. 11.

2nd row.—K. 11.

3rd row.—P. 11.

4th row.—K. 3, m. 1, k. 2, m. 1, k. 1, m. 1, k. 2, m. 1, k. 3.

5th row.—P. 15.

6th row.—K. 2, m. 1, sl. 1, k. 2 tog., p.s.s.o., m. 1, sl. 1, k. 1, p.s.s.o., k. 1, k. 2 tog., m. 1, sl. 1, k. 2 tog., p.s.s.o., m. 1, k. 2.

7th row.—P. 13.

8th row.—Cast off 3 sts., there now being 1 st. on right-hand needle, k. 1, m. 1, sl. 1, k. 2 tog., p.s.s.o., m. 1, k. to end.

9th row.—Cast off 3 sts., p. to end.

10th row.—Sl. 1, k. 1, p.s.s.o., k. 3, k. 2 tog.

11th row.—P. 5.

12th row.—Sl. 1, k. 1, p.s.s.o., k. 1, k. 2 tog.

13th row.—P. 3.

14th row.—Sl. 1, k. 2 tog., p.s.s.o.

Break off the wool, slip the remaining st. on to a safety-pin and leave at front of work. Rejoin wool to main set of sts., p. 7. Rep. from * twice.

Change to the light wool. Work 14 rows in st.st., commencing with a p. row.

Change to the dark wool.

Next row.—* P. 7, p. the st. from the safety pin, p. 7; rep. from * to end (45 sts.). Continue in the rib for 1½ ins., ending with a second patt. row.

Change to No. 12 needles and dec. as follows:—

Next row.—P. 2 tog., * k. twice into next st., p. 2 tog., p. 1; rep. from * to last 3 sts., k. twice into next st., p. 2 tog.

Next row.—K. 1, p. 2 tog., * k. 2, p. 2 tog.; rep. from * to last st., k. 1 (33 sts.).

Next row.—P. 1, * k. twice into next st., p. 2; rep. from * to last 2 sts., k. twice into next st., p. 1.

Next row.—K. 1, * p. 2 tog., k. 2;

rep. from * to last 3 sts., p. 2 tog., k. 1.

Rep. the last 2 rows until work measures 24½ ins. from lower edge, ending at arm-hole edge.

Shape Shoulder thus:—

Next row.—Cast off 8 sts., patt. to end.

Next row.—Patt. to end.

Rep. last 2 rows twice.

Cast off remaining sts.

Rejoin wool to second set of sts. for right side of the front and work thus:—

Next row.—K. twice into first st., patt. to end (57 sts.).

Continue in patt. on these 57 sts. until work measures 17½ ins. from lower edge, ending at the side edge.

Shape armhole and complete the front exactly as given for the left side of the front, reversing all shapings.

N.B.—When casting off sts. or dec. on or after a second patt. row always work the double sts. as 1 st.

The Back.—Work exactly as given for the front, continuing in patt. until work measures 17½ ins. from lower edge, ending with a second patt. row.

Shape Armholes thus: Continuing in patt., cast off 7 sts. at beginning of the next 2 rows, then dec. 1 st. at each end of the next 5 rows (89 sts. remain at the end of a second patt. row).

Continue in patt. without shaping until work measures 24½ ins. from lower edge, ending with a second patt. row.

Shape Shoulders thus: Continuing in patt., cast off 8 sts. at beginning of the next 6 rows, then cast off 9 sts. at beginning of the next 2 rows.

Cast off remaining sts.

The Sleeves.—Using No. 12 needles and dark wool cast on 85 sts.

Work in patt. as given for the front for 1 in.

Change to No. 11 needles and continue in patt. for 1 in. (2 ins. from commencement).

Change to No. 10 needles. Continue in patt. for 1 in. (3 ins. from commencement).

Change to No. 9 needles and continue in patt. until work measures 5½ ins. from commencement, ending with a second patt. row.

Shape Top thus: Continuing in patt., dec. 1 st. at both ends of the next 9 rows (67 sts. at end of a second patt. row).

Continue in patt. (beginning and ending the row with p. 1 instead of p. 2) without shaping for 3½ ins., ending with a second patt. row.

Now dec. 1 st. at each end of the next 14 rows. Cast off remaining 39 sts.

Make-up.—Press work lightly on wrong side using a hot iron over a damp cloth.

Join side, shoulder and sleeve seams.

Stitch sleeves into armholes, matching seams with side seams. Press all seams.

Woman's Sports Jersey

FROM OLD CARDIGAN

A GARMENT made in a heavy sports wool will often go badly out of shape after a good deal of wear, but the yarn is generally of the hard-wearing type which is well worth unpicking and reknitting. A point to be remembered is that comparatively few designs are planned for heavy yarns, and if you do not choose one of these the difference in tension must be taken into consideration, either by using fewer stitches or by finding a design with smaller measurements than those you wish to obtain. The instructions for the boys' polonecked pullover on page 226 were successfully adapted as a woman's sports jersey by using the double-knitting wool from a cardigan which had stretched and become shapeless in wear. This wool had also "fluffed" considerably (a common failing of so-called "sports" yarns), but when the hanks of unpicked yarn had been carefully washed it was found that this surface fluff had entirely disappear-

ed, leaving the wool somewhat thinner but of excellent texture for reknitting. After making one or two experimental tension samples, it was decided that No. 7 needles with the slightly thicker yarn would give an extra 3 ins. in the bust measurement. Nos. 10 and 12 needles were used where stated, to ensure a close fit at waist, neck and wrists. The looser tension made the sleeves slightly wider than in the original garment, so the armholes were made correspondingly deeper by shaping the

This cardigan made in a heavy sports wool went very badly out of shape, but the wool itself was good.

Pretty smart, isn't it? It's our old friend the cardigan of page 235 after a rejuvenating course. The pattern used to knit up the unravelled wool is the boy's pullover (page 226) adapted as explained on page 235

neck at 20 ins. instead of 19 ins. and the shoulders at 21 ins. instead of 20 ins. The sleeves were worked for 18 ins. instead of 16 ins. before shaping the top. To make a deeper welt, the No. 10 needles were used for 4½ ins. instead of 3 ins. at the waist. Owing to the fact that the cardigan sleeves were worn at the elbows, there was not enough wool to make a polo collar, so a ribbed neck border was substituted, by picking up the stitches exactly as stated but working for only ¾ in. before casting off.

Knitting and fabric

THIS method of combining knitting with woven fabric is useful in a great number of different ways. A frock which is worn in parts can be renovated with knitted yoke, sleeves or panels. A short length of material can be eked out in the same way. The best parts of an old frock can be combined with the wool from an unpicked knitted garment. Bands of knitting can be inserted to widen or lengthen a fabric garment which has shrunk in width or become too short, or bands of fabric can be used in the same way to enlarge a too small knitted garment. Generally speaking, unless you are a good dressmaker, it is better to arrange the shaped parts of the garment to be in knitting, so that you can follow the appropriate sections of an existing design, and have the straight parts of the garment in fabric so that there is not very much cutting out to be done. For instance, an excellent frock for a child can be made with a straight strip of material for the skirt and the bodice in knitting, made from any suitable jumper pattern, omitting the welt and substituting bands of fabric for the neck and sleeve borders, or adding a fabric collar to a plain neckline.

The child's frock with knitted yoke and sleeves is a good example of this type of design. The skirt is almost a straight strip of material (shaped only at the armholes as shown in the diagram) pleated into a knitted yoke. The sleeves are also knitted. Instructions are given for making the sleeves and yoke pieces, but any knitter could adapt the appropriate parts of a jumper pattern for a similar design. The result is a delightful frock made, in the case of the original model, from the skirt of a grown-up frock and the wool from an unpicked cardigan which had become far too small for its owner long before it was in any way worn out.

Child's Frock in Fabric

WITH KNITTED SLEEVES AND YOKES

MATERIALS

   2 oz. 3-ply wool in blue.
   A small quantity 3-ply wool in red.
   2 No. 12 and 2 No. 9 knitting needles.
   1¾ yds. material, 27 ins. wide, or the best parts of an old garment.

MEASUREMENTS

   Chest, 30 ins.
   Length, 33 ins.
   Sleeve seam, 4 ins.

TENSION

   Using No. 9 needles, 7 sts. to 1 in.

   Back Yoke.—Using No. 9 needles and red wool, cast on 85 sts.

   1st row.—* K. 1, p. 1; rep. from * to last st., k. 1.

   2nd row.—* P. 1, k. 1; rep. from * to last st., p. 1. Rep. these 2 rows until work measures ½ in. Change to blue wool and p. 1 row, continue in moss st.

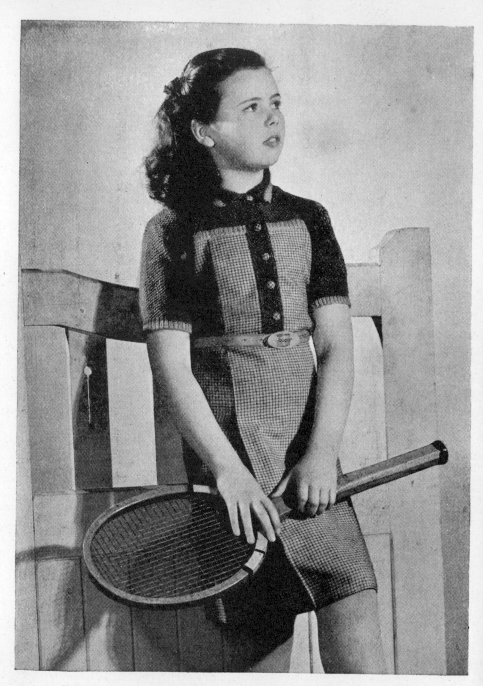

"*Joan grows out of her clothes so quickly. . . :*" *The only remedy is to make the clothes grow with Joan. Fabric skirt, and knitted sleeves and yokes, makes last year's cast off this year's "favourite frock."*

Next row.—* K. 1, p. 1 ; rep. from * to last st., k. 1.

Rep. this row until work measures 4 ins. from beginning.

Shape Shoulders thus: Cast off 7 sts. at beginning of each of next 8 rows. Cast off remaining sts.

Front Yokes. Left Front.—Using red wool and No. 9 needles cast on 39 sts.

1st row.—* K. 1, p. 1 ; rep. from * to last st., k. 1.

2nd row.—* P. 1, k. 1 ; rep. from * to last st., p. 1.

Rep. these 2 rows until work measures ½ in. Change to blue wool and p. 1 row, continue in moss st.

Next row.—* K. 1, p. 1 ; rep. from * to last st., k. 1.

Rep. this row until work measures 3 ins. from beginning, ending with a row on right side of work.

Shape Neck thus: Cast off 7 sts. at beginning of next row. Now continue in moss st. dec. 1 st. at neck edge on every row until 28 sts. remain. Continue without shaping until work measures 4 ins. from beginning, ending with a row on wrong side of work.

Shape Shoulders thus:—

1st row.—Cast off 7, work to end.

2nd row.—Work to end.

Rep. these 2 rows twice more. Cast off remaining sts.

Right Front.—Work as given for left front, reversing the shapings.

The Sleeves.—Using No. 12 needles and red wool cast on 63 sts.

1st row.—* K. 1, p. 1 ; rep. from * to last st., k. 1.

2nd row.—* P. 1, k. 1 ; rep. from * to last st., p. 1.

Rep. these 2 rows until work measures ½ in. Change to blue wool and continue in rib until work measures 1 in. Change to No. 9 needles and moss st.

Next row.—* K. 1, p. 1 ; rep. from * to last st., k. 1.

Rep. this row, inc. 1 st. at both ends of

the next and every following 4th row until there are 79 sts. on needle. Continue without shaping until work measures 4 ins.

Shape Top thus: Dec. 1 st. at both ends of every alternate row until there are 49 sts. on needles. Now dec. 1 st. at both ends

SCALE: 1 SQ.=1 IN.

ALLOW ¾ IN. TURNING ON ALL SEAMS

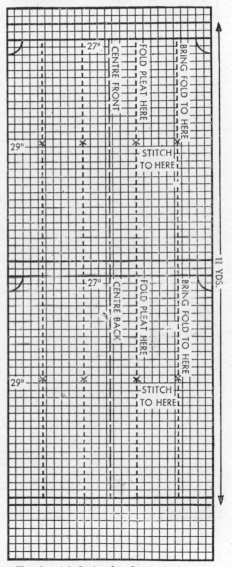

Frock with knitted yoke and sleeves.

Such pretty material, but by itself not enough for a frock—so we found some wool that toned with the predominant colour and knitted a bodice. The result is really charming and something novel too.

of every row until 29 sts. remain. Cast off.

Work a second sleeve in the same way.

The Collar.—Using No. 9 needles and red wool cast on 85 sts.

1st row.—* K. 1, p. 1; rep. from * to last st., k. 1.

2nd row.—* P. 1, k. 1; rep. from * to last st., p. 1.

Rep. these 2 rows until work measures ½ in. Change to No. 9 needles and blue wool and p. 1 row, continue in moss st.

Next row.—* K. 1, p. 1; rep. from * to last st., k. 1.

Rep. this row until work measures 2 ins. from beg. Cast off.

The Right Front Band.—Using No. 9 needles and blue wool cast on 9 sts. and work in moss st. for 1 in. Make a buttonhole in the next 2 rows as follows:—

1st row.—K. 1, p. 1, k. 1, cast off 3 sts., work to end.

2nd row.—K. 1, p. 1, k. 1, cast on 3 sts., work to end. Continue in moss st. making a buttonhole in the same way every 2 ins., measured from the cast-off edge of the previous buttonhole until the fifth buttonhole has been worked and band measures 10 ins. Cast off.

The Left Front Band.—Work as given for right front band, omitting the buttonholes.

Make-up.—Press all knitting lightly on the wrong side, using a warm iron over a damp cloth.

Cut the skirt pieces back and front as shown in the diagram, and make the box pleats, stitching on the edge for 13½ ins. from top.

Stitch the back yoke to the skirt back and the front yoke to the skirt front, leaving a gap of 1 in. at centre front for front bands. Stitch front bands to yoke and skirt front, ½ in. from centre front of skirt, lapping right band over left and stitching across the bottom.

Cut the material away from the back of the bands and neaten.

Join side, shoulder and sleeve seams, and set sleeves into armholes, making 4 small pleats at top of sleeve. Sew collar to neck, finishing at centre front. Press all seams.

Make a small hem and finish with 2 rows of machine stitching

Attach buttons to left front to correspond with buttonholes.

Child's Frock with Knitted Bodice

AND FABRIC SKIRT AND SLEEVES

THE child's frock with knitted bodice and fabric skirt and sleeves was made from the skirt of a grown-up frock and the best parts of a child's jumper which had been unpicked. Since the child had grown out of the jumper it was necessary to use some of the wool from the sleeves to make the bodice big enough, so fabric sleeves were substituted. To link up with these, a fabric neck border and fabric-covered buttons were added. This is the kind of finishing touch which helps to avoid any suggestion of renovation in the finished garment. Instructions are given for the knitted bodice, but this could equally well be adapted from a suitable jumper pattern. The sleeves could also be knitted if sufficient wool were available, but in this case fabric strips should be used at the sleeve edges to match the neck border and link up with the skirt. A diagram is given for the fabric sleeves, but these could, of course, be cut from a paper pattern or by using a favourite frock as a guide.

MATERIALS

3 oz. 3-ply wool.
2 No. 10 and 2 No. 14 knitting needles.
1½ yds. material 27 ins. wide (or the best parts of an old frock material).

MEASUREMENTS

Length, 30 ins. Chest, 28 ins.
Sleeve seam, 3 ins.

TENSION

8 sts. to 1 in.

The Back.—Using No. 14 needles cast on 98 sts. and work in rib of k. 1, p. 1 for

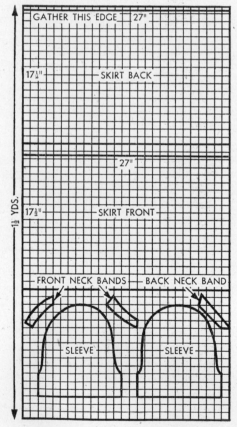

SCALE: 1 SQ.=1 IN.
ALLOW ¾ IN. TURNING ON ALL SEAMS

GATHER THIS EDGE   27"

17½" —SKIRT BACK—

27"

1½ YDS.

17½" —SKIRT FRONT—

—FRONT NECK BANDS— —BACK NECK BAND—

—SLEEVE— —SLEEVE—

Fabric frock with knitted bodice.

1½ ins. Change to No. 10 needles and proceed in patt.

1st row.—K.
2nd row.—P.
3rd row.—K. 1, * sl. 2, k. 2; rep. from * to last st., k. 1.
4th row.—K. 1, * p. 2, sl. 2; rep. from * to last st., k. 1.
5th row.—K.
6th row.—P.
7th row.—K. 1, * k. 2, sl. 2; rep. from * to last st., k. 1.
8th row.—K. 1, * sl. 2, p. 2; rep. from * to last st., k. 1.

These 8 rows form patt. Rep. them, inc. 1 st. at both ends of the next and every following 6th row until there are 114 sts. on the needle. Continue in patt. without shaping until work measures 7½ ins. from the beg., ending with a p. row.

Shape Armholes thus.—Cast off 8 sts. at beg. of each of next 2 rows. Dec. 1 st. at both ends of every row until 90 sts. remain. Continue without shaping until work measures 12½ ins. from beg., ending with a p. row.

Shape Shoulders thus.—Cast off 7 sts. at beg. of each of next 8 rows. Cast off remaining sts.

The Front.—Using No. 14 needles cast on 98 sts. and work in rib of k. 1, p. 1 for 1½ ins., ending with a row on wrong side of work. Now divide front as follows, working in patt. as given for back.

The Left Front.

Next row.—Using No. 10 needles k. 45 sts., turn, and place remaining sts. on a spare needle and leave for the present.

Continue working in patt. on these 45 sts., inc. 1 st. at the side edge on 9th and every following 6th row until there are 54 sts. on needle. Continue without shaping until work measures 7½ ins. from beg., ending with a row at side edge.

Shape Armholes thus: Cast off 8 sts. at beg. of next row. Now dec. 1 st. at side edge of every row until 42 sts. remain. Continue without shaping until work measures 11 ins. from beg., ending with a row at centre front.

Shape Neck thus:—

Next row.—Cast off 4 sts., work to end.

Now dec. 1 st. at the neck edge on every row until 28 sts. remain.

Continue without shaping until the work measures 12½ ins. from beg., ending with a row at armhole edge.

Shape Shoulders thus:—

1st row.—Cast off 7 sts., work to end.

2nd row.—Work to end.

Rep. these 2 rows twice more. Cast off remaining sts.

Rejoin wool at needle point and using No. 14 needles pick up and k. 8 sts. at centre front.

The Front Band.—Work on these 8 sts. in g.st. (k. every row) for 1½ ins. Make a buttonhole as follows:—

Next row.—K. 3, cast off 2, k. to end.

Next row.—K. 3, cast on 2, k. to end.

Continue in g.st., making 4 more buttonholes in the same way, 1¾ ins. apart, measured from the cast-off edge of the previous buttonhole, until the band measures 9½ ins. from beg. Cast off.

Rejoin wool at needle point and, using No. 10 needles, pick up and k. remaining sts. for right front, as given for left front.

The Underwrap.—Using No. 14 needles cast on 8 sts. and work in g.st. for 9½ ins. Cast off.

Make-up.—Press all knitting lightly on the wrong side, using a warm iron over a damp cloth. Join left front band to left front, and right band to right front, securing neatly at bottom.

Cut the pieces of fabric as shown in the diagram, allowing ¾ in. on all seams for turnings. Gather the skirt back and front at waist, ¾ in. from edge and 2 rows below ⅛ in. apart, and pull up to fit the knitted welt, when stretched to its widest limit. Stitch knitted welt to skirt. Join side seams, leaving a placket of about 6 ins. on the left-hand side. Join the shoulder and sleeve seams and set sleeves into armholes, easing any fullness into the top of the sleeve. Join the pieces of neck band at the shoulders, and turn in top and bottom. Stitch to neck of frock. Press all seams carefully.

Turn up a narrow hem at bottom of skirt and of sleeves and finish with a double row of machine stitching. Stitch fasteners to placket and buttons to left front to correspond with buttonholes.

Woman's Frock

WITH KNITTED BACK, FRONT YOKE AND SLEEVES.

THIS is an example of the type of renovation which can be applied to a worn frock, with the help of a few ounces of new wool or the wool from an unpicked garment.

In this particular case the original frock had an unbecoming neckline, and was worn under the arms and at the elbows. Most of the wear under the arms was on the sleeve itself so it was decided to discard the sleeves and substitute knitted ones. It would have been possible to leave the fabric back, but in this case the garment was rather tight between the armholes, so that a knitted back and knitted front yoke provided a good solution. The diamond-patterned sleeves and yoke for which instructions are given would be effective with any plain fabric, but with a patterned fabric a plainer stitch for the knitting would be a better choice. A bright-coloured yoke and sleeves will give a new lease of life to the dowdiest and most hopeless of dark or neutral-coloured frocks.

She's risen to great heights, don't you agree? "That old thing" was due for the rag bag—a neckline she hated, and worn under the arms; but 4 oz. of wool and courage, made it into a new creation.

MATERIALS

4 oz. 4-ply wool.
2 No. 12 and 2 No. 9
knitting needles.
10 buttons.

MEASUREMENTS

Length of back, 16 ins.
Width across back when
buttoned, 17 ins.
Sleeve seam, 5 ins.

TENSION

A complete pattern equals
$1\frac{1}{4}$ ins.

Front Yoke.—Using No.
9 needles cast on 63 sts. and
work in the following patt.:
1st row.—* K. 5, p. 3, k.
2; rep. from * to last 3 sts.,
k. 3.
2nd row.—* P. 5, k. 3, p.
2; rep. from * to last 3 sts.,
p. 3.
3rd row.—* K. 5, w.fd.,
sl. 1, p. 1, sl 1, w.b., k. 2;
rep. from * to last 3 sts., k. 3.
4th row.—* P. 4, (k. the
second st. on the left-hand
needle, then p. the first st.
and sl. both sts. off the
needle tog.), this will be referred to as 1st cross, p. 1,
(sl. the next st. off the left-
hand needle and keep at the
front of the work, p. 1, then
k. the slipped st.), this will
be referred to as 2nd cross, p. 1; rep.
from * to last 3 sts., k. 3.
5th row.—* K. 4, w.fd., sl. 1, w.b., k. 3,
w.fd., sl. 1, w.b., k. 1; rep. from * to last
3 sts., k. 3.
6th row.—* P. 3, 1st cross next 2 sts.,
p. 3, 2nd cross next 2 sts.; rep. from * to
last 3 sts., p. 3.
7th row.—* K. 3, w.fd., sl. 1, w.b., k. 5,
w.fd., sl. 1, w.b.; rep. from * to last 3
sts., k. 3.

*The skirt was left untouched, but bodice and sleeves
were cut into, and knitted sleeves and yoke added.*

8th row.—K. 1, * k. 1, 1st cross next 2
sts., p. 5, 2nd cross next 2 sts. rep. from *
to last 2 sts., k. 2.
9th row.—* P. 3, k. 7; rep. from * to
last 3 sts., p. 3.
10th row.—* K. 3, p. 7; rep. from * to
last 3 sts., k. 3.
11th row.—Rep. 9th row.
12th row.—K. 1, * p. 1, 2nd cross next
2 sts., p. 5, 1st cross next 2 sts.; rep. from
* to last 2 sts., p. 2.

13th row.—* K. 3, w.fd., sl. 1, w.b., k. 5, w.fd., sl. 1, w.b.; rep. from * to last 3 sts., k. 3.

14th row.—* P. 3, 2nd cross next 2 sts., p. 3, 1st cross next 2 sts.; rep. from * to last 3 sts., p. 3.

15th row.—* K. 4, w.fd., sl. 1, w.b., k. 3, w.fd., sl. 1, w.b., k. 1; rep. from * to last 3 sts., k. 3.

16th row.—* P. 4, 2nd cross next 2 sts., k. 1, 1st cross next 2 sts., p. 1; rep. from * to last 3 sts., p. 3.

Cast off. Rejoin wool at the needle point and work on the other set of 22 sts. in the same way, dec. 1 st. at the beg. of the 1st row instead of the end.

The Back:—

The Left Side.—Using No. 9 needles cast on 58 sts. and work in the patt. as given for the front yoke, but keeping the 5 extra sts. in g.st. at the end of the 1st row for the underwrap, thus:—

1st row.—* K. 5, p. 3, k. 2; rep. from * to last 8 sts., k. 8.

Here you can see how the back of the knitted yoke is arranged. It reaches to the waist line and is fastened with buttons.

These 16 rows form the patt., beg. again at the 1st row rep. them until the work measures 7 ins.

Shape the Neck thus:—

Next row.—Patt. 22 sts., cast off next 19 sts., patt. to the end.

Work on this second set of 22 sts. as follows:—

1st row.—Patt. to the last 2 sts., k. 2 tog.

2nd row.—K. 2 tog., patt. to the end.

Rep. these last 2 rows until 8 sts. remain.

2nd row.—K. 5, * p. 5, k. 3, p. 2; rep. from * to last 3 sts., p. 3.

Continue in this way until the work measures 2 ins. from the beg., ending with a row on the right side of the work. Now begin the side shaping by inc. 1 st. at the beg. of the next and every following 10th row until there are 68 sts. on the needle, working the extra sts. into the patt. Continue without shaping until the work measures 9½ ins. from the beg., ending with a row on the right side of the work.

Shape the Armholes thus: Cast off 8 sts. at the beg. of the next row. Then dec. 1 st. at this edge on every row until 52 sts. remain. Continue in patt., keeping the g.st. border intact until the work measures 16 ins. from the lower edge, ending with a row on the wrong side of the work.

Shape the Shoulders thus:—

1st row.—Cast off 16 sts., patt. to the end.

2nd row.—Cast off 8 sts., patt. to the last 2 sts., k. 2 tog.

3rd row.—K. 2 tog., patt. to the end.

Rep. the last 2 rows once more, then rep. the 2nd row once. Cast off remaining sts.

The Right Side.—Work as given for the left side, reversing the shapings and the g.st. border and working 10 buttonholes in the border, the first ¾ in. from the bottom and the rest 1¼ ins. apart.

Make a buttonhole as follows:—

1st row.—K. 2, cast off 2, patt. to the end.

2nd row.—Patt. to the last 3 sts., k. 1, cast on 2 sts., k. 2.

The Sleeves.—Using No. 12 needles cast on 68 sts. and work the cuff as follows:—

1st row.—K.

2nd row.—P.

3rd row.—K.

Rep. these 3 rows 3 times more, then rep. the 1st and 2nd rows again.

Next row.—K. 6, * inc. in next st., k. 3; rep. from * to last 2 sts., k. 2. There are now 83 sts. on the needle.

Change to No. 9 needles and work in patt. as given for the front yoke, inc. 1 st. at both ends of the 1st and every following 3rd row until there are 103 sts. on the needle. Continue without shaping until the work measures 5 ins. from the beg.

Shape the Top thus: Keeping the patt. correct, dec. 1 st. at both ends of every row until there are 30 sts. on the needle. Cast off.

Make-up.—Press all the knitted pieces carefully on the wrong side using a warm iron over a damp cloth, and keeping them exactly in shape.

Unpick the frock and press out the marks of the seams wherever possible.

Place the front of the bodice of the frock flat on the table with the wrong side towards you and pin the knitted yoke to it, placing the narrow shoulder of the yoke level with the original shoulder seam; the yoke should, of course, also have the wrong side facing you. Tack very carefully round the yoke, being careful not to stretch either the knitting or the fabric. Now cut the material away from the yoke, leaving enough to turn in neatly. Turn in the edge of this square and tack back on to the yoke, and stitch carefully, slashing the corners of the frock where necessary to make it lie flat.

Join the knitted back to the front at the side and shoulder seams, leaving the left side open for about 4 ins. above the waist for the placket and being very careful not to stretch the back in the process. Join the sleeve seams and stitch the sleeves into the armholes, easing in any fullness towards the top. Join the bodice of the frock to the skirt, and finish the placket with a zipp fastener or hooks and eyes.

The Neck Band.—With the wrong side of the work facing and using No. 12 needles, pick up and k. 102 sts. evenly round the neck. Work on these sts. as follows:—

1st row.—P.

2nd row.—K.

3rd row.—P.

Rep. these 3 rows 3 times more. Cast off using No. 9 needles to give a more elastic edge.

Turn this band out on to the right side and catch it down to the frock by means of a slip stitch.

Press all the seams carefully and attach buttons to the left back to correspond with the buttonholes.

Man's Shirt of Terry Towelling

THE combination of terry towelling and knitted ribbing is a particularly effective one. New towelling was used for the original model, but a child's shirt on similar lines could easily be made from the best parts of an old towel. Again, the merest scraps from an old towel would make a child's jumper and knickers or a romper, using an ounce of new wool or oddments left over from another garment to knit welts, sleeve borders and neck bands or collars. Discoloured white towel-

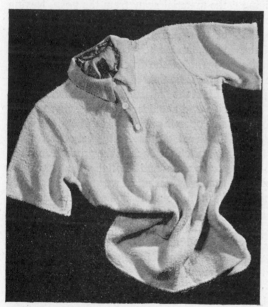

Towelling shirts are popular. This one needing renovation was given knitted collar and bands.

ling should be dyed before being cut out, but if the fabric is still a good white or can be effectively bleached in the sun it will look most attractive with bright-coloured knitted borders.

MATERIALS

- 1 oz. 3-ply wool.
- 2 No. 12 knitting needles.
- 3 buttons.

$1\frac{1}{4}$ yds. of terry towelling or other material at least 44 ins. wide, or $2\frac{1}{2}$ yds. of narrower material.

MEASUREMENTS

Length from shoulder to hem, 28 ins.
Chest size, 40 ins.
Sleeve seam, 6 ins.

TENSION (of knitted collar, etc.)

10 sts. to 1 in. measured over the slightly stretched rib.

The Collar.—Using No. 12 needles cast on 180 sts. and work in a rib of k. 1, p. 1, dec. 1 st. at both ends of every 3rd row until there are 160 sts. on the needle. Continue without shaping until work measures $2\frac{1}{2}$ ins.

Shape the Neck Edge thus: Cast off 17 sts. at the beg. of each of next 6 rows. Cast off remaining sts.

The Left Front Band.—Using No. 12 needles cast on 10 sts. and work in a rib of k. 1, p. 1 for $\frac{1}{2}$ in. Make a buttonhole in the next 2 rows as follows:—

Next row.—Rib 3, cast off 4, rib 3.

Next row.—Rib 3, cast on 4, rib 3.

Continue in rib making 2 more buttonholes $2\frac{1}{2}$ ins. apart, measured from the cast-off edge of the previous buttonhole, until 3 buttonholes have been worked. Work a further $\frac{1}{2}$ in. in rib and cast off.

The Right Front Band.—Work as given for left front band omitting buttonholes.

Make-up.—The back and front of the shirt are cut from the same pattern, with the exception of the neck; the back neckline being indicated in the diagram by a dotted line. Cut out 2 pieces for the back

This man is in holiday mood—and signifies it by wearing his favourite sports shirt. This particular towelling shirt was somewhat worn at the neck and was renovated by a knitted collar and bands. The idea can be carried further.

A small boy's suit can very easily be made from an old towel with the addition of knitted welts, bands and collar.

used on an existing sports shirt, which had become rather worn round the neck and collar.

In the case of a partly worn shirt it might be necessary to alter the length of the front bands and add more buttonholes to fit the opening in the shirt.

If the cuffs of the shirt you are renovating had become worn the sleeves could be cut off about $6\frac{3}{4}$ ins. below the armhole and just turned in and hemmed neatly.

and front and 2 pieces for the sleeves as shown, marking the position of the front bands by a tacking thread.

All the seams should be run and felled for extra strength. Join the shoulder seams in this way and the side seams of the shirt, as far as the shaped ends. Join the sleeve seams and set the sleeves into the armholes, again using a run and fell seam.

Stitch the front bands to the front of the shirt along the lines marked by the dotted line in the diagram, lapping the left band over the right and stitching securely at the bottom. Now cut the material away behind the bands and neaten the edges by herring-boning them to the bands, being careful that the stitches do not show on the outside.

Stitch the shaped edge of the collar to the neck edge, placing the ends of the collar to the middle of the knitted bands. Neaten the neck either by turning in the edges or with a bias binding. Press the shirt carefully and attach buttons to the right front band to correspond with the buttonholes.

The knitted collar and bands used for this shirt could equally well be

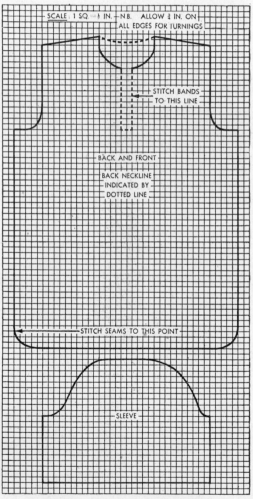

SCALE : 1 SQ = ½ IN. —N.B. ALLOW ½ IN. ON ALL EDGES FOR TURNINGS

STITCH BANDS TO THIS LINE

BACK AND FRONT

BACK NECKLINE INDICATED BY DOTTED LINE

STITCH SEAMS TO THIS POINT

SLEEVE

Man's shirt of terry towelling.

Woman's Frock with Knitted Bodice

AND TARTAN SKIRT, YOKE AND SLEEVES

I N this case, the materials in hand were 3 oz. of black bouclé yarn and a pair of wide-legged gaudy beach slacks. The lower part of the legs made the skirt (cut from a frock pattern) while the narrow part of the legs and the body of the slacks provided sufficient material for yoke and sleeves. The bodice was knitted from a classic jersey pattern, beginning above the welt and casting off about 2 ins. after the completion of the armhole shaping. An opening was arranged at the front by dividing the work in two just above the armholes and knitting on each half separately. To link up with the knitted bodice, narrow strips of garter stitch were used for sleeve borders and a garter stitch collar to match was made by casting on enough stitches to give a length of about 13 ins., working straight for 2 ins. then casting off in groups of about 10 stitches to give a little extra depth at the back of the collar. This casting off in groups is an invaluable hint for making a collar "set" really neatly. The fabric sleeves were cut from a favourite blouse pattern and the yokes from the body part of the same pattern, but most home dressmakers could manage this quite well without a pattern.

This type of renovation is useful in many ways. The bottom of a skirt which is too long to be fashionable will often provide enough material for short sleeves and a narrow shoulder yoke, while 2 oz. of 3-ply or 3 oz. of 4-ply yarn will make the rest of the bodice and strips for cuffs and neckline. If the fabric available is too narrow for sleeves, these can be made in two pieces, joined down the centre with a strip of knitting. If the skirt is only *just* too long, so that only a narrow strip of fabric is available, make both bodice and sleeves in knitting, using the fabric for a narrow shoulder yoke, cuffs and collar. A

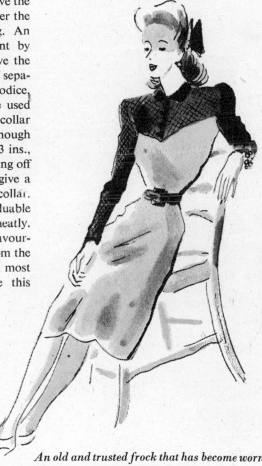

An old and trusted frock that has become worn in the bodice or under the arms can be given a new lease of life by knitting in a new bodice and sleeves.

classic jersey design (or a classic cardigan if you like a front opening) can be used for the bodice. The only alterations you will need to make are to omit the ribbed welt, and to cast off below the shoulder line to allow for the depth of your yoke. This cast-off edge should be straight as the necessary shoulder and neck shaping will be in the fabric yoke.

If you have a frock which is worn or too tight in the bodice, a knitted bodice will make it wearable again. Leave the skirt

Shrank in the wash, did it? How about inserting bands of knitting from shoulder to hem? Add knitted sleeves and collar too.

and sleeves as they are and cut away the lower part of the bodice, except for the shoulder yoke which may be left attached to the sleeves. Then knit your bodice to replace the fabric cut away. The extra elasticity of a knitted fabric will in itself provide extra room, but if the original garment was much too small, either knit a bigger bodice and ease it into the yoke, or dispense with the fabric yoke and make your bodice entirely in knitting.

A careful choice of colour will make your new garment look as if it had been specially planned to combine knitting and fabric. For instance, if you are knitting a new bodice and sleeves, it is a good idea to bind the sleeves with a band of the fabric, or make fabric cuffs, if you knit long sleeves. Make a little collar in fabric too, and carry on the motif by binding the front opening with the material. In fact you should always take care to link up any big expanse of knitting with neck borders, cuffs or front bands to match. If both fabric and wool are plain in colour you can indulge in striking contrasts. In fact it is much better to do so, if you are dealing with a frock. A harmonizing tone is just a little apt to give a heavy appearance whereas a contrast in colour relieves the eye and breaks up the whole very pleasantly. If your fabric is patterned or checked choose wool to match one of the colours or in a dark or neutral shade which tones with them all. A flecked or "mixture" tweed can be matched up with wool in any of its main colours, and a perfectly plain fabric will look well with a flecked or bouclé yarn.

Finally, be very careful if you feel that your figure is "difficult." Work your colour contrast so that it does not accentuate where it should not. For instance, if you are short, and inclined to be stocky, don't cut yourself in half at the waist. You need a long, unbroken slimming line, and any contrast in colour should run from shoulder to hem, not across the body.

That Bond Street Look—and this radiance is achieved from an old pair of wide-legged tartan beach pyjamas and 3 oz. of bouclé yarn. Bodice and sleeve bands are knitted, the rest is fabric (see page 251).

Enlarging a Fabric Garment

BY THE ADDITION OF KNITTED BANDS

IF the original garment is simple in shape, this is a job which can be successfully tackled by any amateur knitter-dressmaker. For instance, a perfectly plain frock which is too tight can have bands of knitting inserted down its whole length from shoulder to hem, one on each side (*see* page 252).

If the sleeves are too tight, cut them down the centre back and insert a narrow band of knitting. In this case the armhole of the garment should be cut a little deeper to correspond, or the bands inserted in the main part could be extended to form a shoulder yoke (by casting on extra stitches and knitting right across), thus giving extra depth to the armhole without cutting it.

A jacket can be enlarged in the same way. For example, the method was tried on one that was very much too tight in both body and sleeves and quite useless to its owner. The fabric was a "bouclé" one, and by a stroke of luck a bouclé yarn in a slightly darker shade was discovered. This was used to make bands which were inserted in the front and back and in the sleeves. To make the armholes deeper the front bands were continued into shoulder yokes.

It is important, also, to match up the thickness of the woven and knitted fabrics as far as possible. A light woollen fabric will match up well with 3-ply yarn finely knitted. A heavier fabric needs a 4-ply yarn, while a thick tweed or bouclé material will go best with a bouclé yarn, very firmly knitted, or a 3-ply yarn used double. Unpicked yarn is particularly good for this purpose, since it will have lost some of its elasticity, and it is the "stretchiness" of new yarn which makes it difficult for the amateur to handle in combination with the firmness of a woven fabric. If the knitted pieces are well pressed before being made up they will have no tendency either to stretch or to shrink.

The jacket was originally made too small and it was decided to enlarge it by the addition of bands knitted in bouclé. Here you can see the "before and after" effect.

Enlarging children's garments

THIS method of combining fabric with knitting is invaluable for enlarging children's garments, since two out-grown garments, one knitted and one fabric may often be combined to produce a new garment of the required size. A fabric frock, for instance, could be lengthened by inserting a band of knitting (using wool from an unpicked jersey) just above the hem, or, if it was much too short the hem could be unpicked and the knitted border sewn to the lower edge. Introducing a front opening with knitted front borders will often give sufficient extra width to the bodice, while the waist gathers can easily be rearranged to spread out across the new front borders. A knitted collar and knitted sleeve borders to match, complete the new frock. If the bodice is much too small, a knitted one

Knit a new bodice to a "too small" frock or knit collar and bands. Lengthen a skirt with a knitted band inserted into fabric.

A child's cardigan can be enlarged by knitted front bands, collar and cuffs.

is the solution, and in this case the old bodice will provide material for enlarging the sleeves if necessary. An outgrown jersey will supply all the wool required for the larger knitted bodice since the extra wool from welt and sleeves will be available, and sufficient of this should remain for knitted sleeve and neck borders.

A knitted jersey which is a little too tight in the body and a little too short in the sleeves can easily be made into a cardigan one size larger. First machine stitch twice down the centre front, leaving about $\frac{1}{4}$ in. between the two rows, then cut along this $\frac{1}{4}$-in. space. The machine stitching will prevent the stitches from unravelling. Now add front borders of any suitable fabric—spots or checks will look specially attractive. One border should be plain and one should have evenly spaced buttonholes—or if you shy at buttonholes fall back on press studs and stitch the buttons over them. Bind the neck to match or add a shaped facing, and lengthen the knitted sleeves with matching fabric cuffs.

Re-footing and re-heeling socks and stockings

HAND-KNITTED and some machine-knitted socks and stockings can be repaired far more satisfactorily by re-knitting the heels and toes than by darning, which, however neatly done, is unsightly and often uncomfortable.

Four-needle Method.—New toes are simple. Cut off the worn parts, pick up the stitches and knit new ones, using a silk thread with the yarn for reinforcement.

Heels should be cut away well above the worn part so that a row of stitches above the thin part is obtained. Pick up the heel flap stitches on one needle and the side stitches on two others. Knit the heel flap as before (reinforcing it as for the toe) knitting in the side stitches as follows:—

* Knit to end of row putting the first stitch from the side needle on to the centre needle and knitting it together with the last stitch. Turn and purl back, transferring a stitch as before and knitting it with the last stitch on the centre needle. Repeat from * until the heel flap is completed. The stitches left on the side needles are for the sole; count these and leave on a spare needle. Turn the heel as for the original heel leaving the same number of stitches as are on the sole needle. Graft the two sets of stitches together and fasten off.

Two-needle Method.—This is a more economical method than using four needles as no new instep is knitted. Unpick the foot seams, then unravel the bottom of the foot to above the worn part. Reknit, using the good wool for the part that shows if you have no new wool of the same colour.

What to do with worn knitted gloves

FINGERTIPS of hand-knitted gloves generally "go" first. The simplest renovation of all is to turn them into mittens by unravelling fingers and thumb until they are only about ½ in. long and using some of the unravelled yarn to finish off the edges with two or three rows of k. 1, p. 1 rib. If the gloves were knitted on two needles it will be easier to unpick the finger seams and work the ribbing on two needles, but if the gloves were made on four needles so that the fingers have no seams, you must use four needles for the ribbing.

If you want your old gloves to finish their life as gloves rather than mittens, unravel the worn fingertips just as far as necessary and knit them up in a gaily contrasting colour, taking care that all the "tips" are the same length. Repeat the contrasting colour at the wrist edge by picking up the stitches and adding a row or two of knitting, or, if the gloves are made on two needles, undo the side seam of the wrist and work two or three rows of double crochet all round the top and side edges, to match the finger tips. Plain gloves could be decorated with a little simple embroidery.

If the idea of contrasting fingertips does not appeal to you, it may be possible to take enough wool from the wrist of the glove to reknit the ends of the fingers. A 3-in. ribbed wrist can easily be shortened to 1½ ins. or 2 ins. without spoiling the gloves. To do this, draw up a thread about 1 in. or 1½ ins. from the wrist edge, and cut this thread so that the stitches are separated. Now pick up and cast off loosely the line of loops left at the edge of the glove and unravel the piece of ribbing cut off, using the wool thus obtained to reknit the fingertips.

This renovation is useful for either two-needle or four-needle gloves, but for two-needle gloves it is necessary to unpick the side seam of the gloves for a short distance before drawing up the thread.

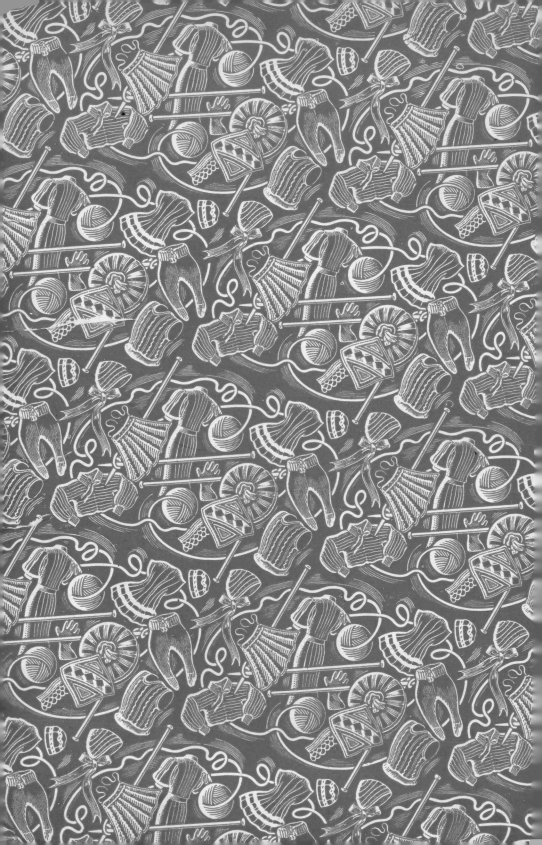